HIKING FROM HOME
A LONG-DISTANCE HIKING GUIDE FOR FAMILY AND FRIENDS

BY JULIANA CHAUNCEY

Happy trails!

DEDICATED TO MY PARENTS, SARAH AND STEPHEN, FOR ALWAYS
SUPPORTING ME ON ANY TRAIL I TAKE

TABLE OF CONTENTS

TABLE OF CONTENTS

INTRODUCTION

"I'm going to hike a long-distance trail."
Whether it's the Appalachian Trail, the Pacific Crest Trail, or any other long-trail, these can be jarring words to hear from a loved one. Hikers spend months, even years, preparing for a long-distance hike, and by the time they announce their intentions, it's not uncommon for those at home to feel like they have some catching up to do.

If you are the parents, children, spouse, family, friends, or significant others of the long-distance hiker, this book is for you. It is for anyone who will wonder and worry while their hiker is away. The upcoming pages will cover terms and phrases that will become a part of your hiker's vocabulary, brief you on the basics of long-distance hiking, and calm your nerves as you watch your loved one set off on a journey that will change their life and maybe yours too. From questions about how your hiker will eat and where they will sleep, to concerns about hiking alone and safety on the trail, this book will address the many forms of the one question we all ask:

Will they be okay?
Buckle your hip belts and tighten the straps, because this educational guide to long-distance hiking will put you at ease as you send your loved one off to the trail.

SECTION ONE
THE BASICS

THE BASICS

By 2050, 75 % of the population is predicted to live in cities. The U.S. Environmental Protection Agency indicates that the average American spends 93 % of their time indoors, with Europeans close behind at 90 %. This equates to one half of one day outside in an entire week.[1] What we are doing in the other 6.5 days is startling. Americans spend as much as ten hours and thirty-nine minutes a day consuming media, which is longer than the average person is asleep.[2] This equates to 44 % of every day in front of a screen.

In the early 1980s, the term *technostress* was introduced for the negative side effects associated with technology. Today, technostress can result from checking your phone constantly, compulsively sharing updates and feeling that you always need to be connected. "Symptoms run from anxiety, headaches, depression, mental fatigue, eye and neck strain, to insomnia, frustration, irritability, and loss of temper."[3] Interestingly, the term was coined before WiFi was introduced into homes, and before cell phones, text messaging, or social media existed. If we were experiencing those side effects with the technology of the early 1980s, imagine how symptoms have grown with the technologies overwhelming us over 35 years later.

The scary part is that people don't seem to mind. We might notice that being glued to a screen makes us less engaged and more distracted, but we ignore it because we seem to be addicted to our devices. Researchers from the University of Maryland School of Business found that mobile phones satisfy our sense of connectivity with others, "saturating the natural sense of belonging needed by human beings. This explains the decreased desire to personally interact with neighbors or engage in empathetic or prosocial behavior. Along with the physical exclusion of others comes less empathy toward nature and our peers, self-centeredness, and loss of emotional intelligence."[4]

The truth is, we seek the dopamine that flows with the never-ending buzzing of notifications. While these dopamine bursts may temporarily relieve stress, they have also caused our attention spans

to dwindle to a mere eight seconds,[5] empathy to decrease, and minds
to fatigue. Additionally, our genes have not yet caught up with our
new sedentary nature. Historically, our ancestors needed to walk
five to ten miles each day to find food. Today, we now burn over 60
% less energy per unit body mass as our bodies store calories while
we sit on our couch or at our desk.[6] While humans have spent 99.5
% of their evolutionary time in completely natural environments,
we've since transitioned into an urban species and the neglect
of our need for the outdoors has impacted both our physical and
mental health.[7] According to *Spark: The Revolutionary New Science
Between Exercise and the Brain*, "65 % of our nation's adults are
overweight or obese, and 10 % of the population has type 2 diabetes,
a preventable and ruinous disease that stems from inactivity and poor
nutrition... It's now becoming an epidemic among children. We're
literally killing ourselves... What's even more disturbing, and what
virtually no one recognizes, is that inactivity is killing our brains
too—physically shriveling them."[8]

"THE 24/7 STREAMING TORRENT OF TRAGEDY AND DEMANDS
FLASHING AT US FROM AN ARRAY OF DIGITAL DISPLAYS KEEPS
THE AMYGDALA FLYING. THE NEGATIVE AND THE HECTIC AND
THE HOPELESS HEAP ON THE STRESS, BUT WE FIGURE WE CAN
HANDLE IT BECAUSE WE ALWAYS HAVE. UP TO A POINT. THEN,
WE JUST WANT TO RELAX AND TAKE A BREAK, SO WE GRAB A
DRINK AND PLOP DOWN IN FRONT OF THE TV OR GO SIT ON A
BEACH SOMEWHERE. IT'S NO WONDER THAT OBESITY HAS DOUBLED
IN THE PAST TWENTY YEARS - OUR LIFESTYLE TODAY IS BOTH
MORE STRESSFUL AND MORE SEDENTARY."[II]
    SPARK: THE REVOLUTIONARY NEW SCIENCE OF EXERCISE AND THE BRAIN
    BY JOHN RATEY

The problem is that we're ignoring the science because the
solution relies on making changes that go against the comforts we're
accustomed to. It's easier for people to remain oblivious than to
acknowledge that our lifestyles are flawed. "When environmental
neglect is the most common sight around us, it's easy to get used
to the mind-set that there is no viable alternative, and thus the only
solution is to adapt. But reducing our sensitivity to a situation that
implicitly creates chronic stress is not the solution."[9]

Long-distance trails have been around for centuries, serving as pilgrimages of religious practice, avenues of meditation, and paths to better understand the self. Fast-forward to today, and long-distance hiking has boomed into a recreational community of outdoor enthusiasts who choose to give up the luxuries of modern life, and take to the hills with only what they can carry on their backs. Bill Bryson's, *A Walk in the Woods*, and Cheryl Strayed's, *Wild*, have motivated a spike in the number of hikers on national trail systems like the Appalachian Trail and the Pacific Crest Trail, while other trails, like the Continental Divide Trail, still maintain a feeling of untouched remoteness.

Let's pause here.

The Appalachian Trail
The Pacific Crest Trail
The Continental Divide Trail

These are often referred to as the Triple Crown of long-distance hiking trails in America. The Appalachian Trail (A.T.) spans roughly 2,200 mi (3540.5 km) from Georgia to Maine, the Pacific Crest Trail (PCT) runs 2,650 mi (4264.8 km) from Mexico to Canada via California, Oregon, and Washington, and the Continental Divide Trail (CDT) covers 3,100 mi (4989 km) of less-structured routes and alternatives from Mexico to Canada through the center of the U.S. including the Rockies. These are the big guys. The massive multi-month undertakings that cause people to quit their jobs, pack their belongings, kiss their loved ones goodbye, and say, *"I'll see you in half a year."*

As the lure of long-distance hiking grows, smaller trails have also gained traction. A popular example is the John Muir Trail in the Sierra Nevada mountains of California. The 211-mile trail has drawn so many hikers that permits need to be obtained half a year in advance, a commonality shared with its bigger sibling, the Pacific Crest Trail. Which trail is being hiked is less important in these pages, as many of the concerns and anxieties one feels about watching a loved one embark on such a journey are similar regardless of the trail. We'll work through the basics and note examples which may only apply to certain hikes.

OTHER POPULAR TRAILS

THE COLORADO TRAIL   485 MILES
DENVER TO DURANGO, COLORADO

THE LONG TRAIL   272 MILES
MASSACHUSETTS-VERMONT STATE LINE TO CANADA BORDER

THE ARIZONA TRAIL   800 MILES
MEXICO BORDER TO ARIZONA-UTAH STATE LINE

THE PACIFIC NORTHWEST TRAIL   1,200 MILES
CONTINENTAL DIVIDE IN MONTANA TO WASHINGTON'S OLYMPIC COAST

THE SUPERIOR HIKING TRAIL   310 MILES
LAKE SUPERIOR'S NORTH SHORE, MINNESOTA

THE OREGON COAST TRAIL   382 MILES
MOUTH OF COLUMBIA RIVER TO CALIFORNIA BORDER

THE TAHOE RIM TRAIL   165 MILES
LOOP TRAIL AROUND CALIFORNIA'S LAKE TAHOE

One topic that applies to any long trail is the question of *why? Why do people embark on a long-distance hike?*

What is the allure of stripping down to life's basic necessities and living austerely? Why walk from town to town when we've built roads to connect them? Or give up a warm bed to sleep on the cold, hard ground? Why would grown adults dig 6-inch holes and imitate cats in a litter box when flushing toilets exist? It seems crazy, and that's because to an extent, it is. However, the purpose behind a long-distance hike isn't comfort or convenience, and many who hike are doing so for deeper reasons than getting from point A to point B.

I asked over 100 aspiring hikers the question, "Why?"

The responses were more meaningful than expected. People are seeking simplicity, a break from the pressures and demands of society, and a way to re-find their core values.

A study revealed that since 2000, over three out of four books on Amazon had the word happiness in the title.[10] Between this significant demand for lessons on happiness, and my own conversations with hikers, it's clear that people are desperate for a solution, and many turn to long-distance trails as a way to push the reset button on life. Hikers want to flip the page and dig deeper into who they are, who they want to be, and how to cope with parts of their lives that have caused pain, fear, or stress.

Many hikers are at transition points and need time to ease into a new era of themselves. I spoke to students who were unsure of what their future would hold, what career path they should take, where they would live, and uncertain about their readiness for adulthood. I talked to retirees who spent a majority of their lives at desks, dreaming of the day they could step outside and ease back into the slow lane as they prepared for a less demanding phase of life. I also heard from people in between, tired of trudging through high-pressure jobs, bustling cities, and an inability to find time to disconnect and focus on themselves. In fact, the responses that had to do with walking paled in comparison, reinforcing that as reckless as it may seem to pack a bag and take off to the woods, a long-distance hike isn't usually decided on a whim. When asking what would make a person crazy enough to spend six months walking from one end of the country to the other, the answer becomes simple. They need to.

As someone who is important in your hiker's life, they need you too. They need those closest to them to understand that what they are doing is on a level beyond what may seem like a vacation in nature. They need you to understand that there will be times they need to kick and scream about how they hate the trail, while not wanting to give up or quit. Regardless of which long trail, no one gets through it alone. The questions you ask and the support you provide may help them to have a more positive sense of self and improve their relationship with you.

WHY DO YOU WANT TO TAKE ON A LONG-DISTANCE HIKE?

"I SUFFER FROM PTSD AND DEPRESSION. I HATE TAKING MEDICATION AND I'VE FOUND THAT BEING IN NATURE IS MY WAY OF HEALING." - ANNJOLIE, 33, INDIANA

"I'VE ALWAYS FOLLOWED THE SUGGESTED PATH THAT MY PARENTS AND FRIENDS TOLD ME TO TAKE. LAST YEAR I ASKED MYSELF A LOT OF QUESTIONS CONCERNING MY FUTURE. I DIDN'T FEEL SUPER GREAT AND NEEDED TO DO SOMETHING TO REGAIN MOTIVATION AND TO REFLECT ON MY TRUE SELF." - ANTOINE, 20, QUÉBEC

"BECAUSE I CAN, AND THAT WON'T ALWAYS BE THE CASE. BEING IN MY MID-FORTIES HAS REALLY MADE ME APPRECIATE WHAT I CAN DO AND NOT TAKE HEALTH AND MOBILITY FOR GRANTED THE WAY I DID WHEN I WAS YOUNGER." - KRISTAN, 43, WASHINGTON

"I LOVE MY FAMILY, BUT I NEED TO RESET. I HAVEN'T DONE ANYTHING FOR MYSELF SINCE I'VE HAD MY FOUR KIDS, AND I'M STIR CRAZY. THE OUTDOORS HAS ALWAYS BEEN A PART OF MY LIFE, BUT EVER SINCE MY FIRST KID WAS BORN I'VE PUT IT ON THE BACK BURNER. I NEED THAT RECONNECTION TO THE OUTDOORS." - ANDY, 44, MASSACHUSETTS

"I PUSH MY KIDS TO EXPERIENCE THEIR LIVES AND TRY TO TEACH THEM THE IMPORTANCE OF DOING SOMETHING LIKE THIS. PEOPLE DON'T GET OUT AND HAVE A LOT OF EXPERIENCES. A SMALL NUMBER OF PEOPLE HAVE A LOT OF EXPERIENCES AND PEOPLE LIVE VICARIOUSLY THROUGH THEM WITH TECHNOLOGY, BUT NOT A LOT OF PEOPLE ARE GETTING OUT AND DOING IT THEMSELVES. SOMEONE TOLD ME A LONG TIME AGO THAT LIFE IS AN EXPERIENCE AND YOU HAVE TO HAVE EXPERIENCES IN ORDER TO EXPERIENCE LIFE, BUT YOU CAN'T DO THAT FROM BEHIND A DESK. THAT'S THE WHOLE THING. I THINK A LOT MORE ATTENTION WOULD BE PAID TOWARDS GLOBAL WARMING AND CLIMATE CHANGE IF PEOPLE GOT OUT, EXPERIENCED IT, AND SAW IT DISAPPEARING." - CHRIS, 44, CALIFORNIA

BENEFITS OF THE OUTDOORS

Positive effects of time in nature are popping up as studies continue to prove that time outdoors is crucial for a healthy body and mind. The benefits are so profound that "forest bathing," the practice of improving health through time in nature, has become a popular therapy method in countries like Japan. Psychologists are encouraging schools to get children outside more and healthcare professionals are using exposure to nature as preventive medication. A 2018 study by the University of East Anglia extracted information from over 140 studies and 290 million people finding that time spent in undeveloped land with natural vegetation reduces the risk of type II diabetes, cardiovascular disease, premature death, pre-term birth, stress, and high blood pressure.[12] But it goes deeper.

I. SHORT-TERM MEMORY IMPROVES

The University of Michigan found that time in nature improves short-term memory and information retention in students.[13] In *Spark: The Revolutionary New Science Between Exercise and the Brain,* Ratey says, "It's about growth versus decay, activity versus inactivity. The body was designed to be pushed, and in pushing our bodies we push our brains too. Learning and memory evolved in concert with the motor functions that allowed our ancestors to track down food, so as far as our brains are concerned, if we're not moving, there's no real need to learn anything."[14] When nerve cells bind to one another we are able to log new information in our brains. Exercise not only encourages this, but promotes the growth of new nerve cells. A study comparing inactive mice to ones that run several miles a night even found that active mice were able to find safety more quickly and had twice as many new stem cells in the hippocampus.[15] Adding complex activities to exercise, such as balance, coordination, and motor skills required for long-distance hiking (rock hopping across a stream, pulling oneself up rebar or ladders, climbing over downed trees, etc.) has been proven to strengthen and expand networks in the brain.[16]

2. STRESS DECREASES

Time in nature significantly reduces cortisol levels in the body; cortisol being a hormone indicative of stress. In fact, parasympathetic nerve activity (a relaxed state) increased by 55 % in people who spent time in nature.[17] Why is decreasing stress important? Stress that becomes chronic can sever synaptic connections in the brain and cause cells to die, shriveling the hippocampus.[18] "Chronic stress is linked to some of our most deadly diseases... An unchecked stress response can stockpile fat around the midsection, which studies have shown to be more dangerous than fat stored elsewhere."[19] The overload of cortisol from chronic stress leaves the body open to diseases and the results can be deadly.

3. BETTER SLEEP

Our bodies are better able to release the right levels of melatonin and properly regulate sleep patterns when we are around natural light. Studies on forest bathing found that even a two-hour walk in a forest could increase sleep time by nearly an hour.[20] Just ask any current or former long-distance hiker about hiker midnight.[1] Night owls are some of the least common creatures on the trail.

4. STRONGER IMMUNE SYSTEM

Getting enough sunlight not only increases our levels of Vitamin D, but also strengthens our immune systems, helping us fight disease and stay healthy. A study at the Chiba University in Japan showed that natural killer (NK) cells, an indicator of immune function, remained at a 23 % increase for an entire month after subjects returned from the forest to an urban environment.[21]

---

1 Hiker Midnight usually refers to when the sun goes down, which is the unwritten start of quiet hours on the trail.

5. REDUCED BLOOD PRESSURE AND HEART RATE

That same study at the Chiba University showed a 5.8 %
decrease in heart rate after time in forests, as well as an
increase in cardiovascular and metabolic health. "Forest-
bathing lowers the stress hormones cortisol and adrenaline,
suppresses the sympathetic or 'fight or flight' system,
enhances the parasympathetic or 'rest and recover' system,
lowers blood pressure, and increases heart-rate variability."[22]

6. LOWER LEVELS OF INFLAMMATION

A study at Zhejiang Hospital in China proved that time in
forests has therapeutic effects on human hypertension and
reduces inflammation, showing a preventive advantage
against cardiovascular disorders.[23]

7. PROTECTIVE EFFECT ON EYES AND REDUCED RISK OF DEVELOPING NEARSIGHTEDNESS

A study at the University of Sydney showed that higher levels
of time spent outdoors were associated with less myopia
(nearsightedness).[24]

8. HELPS PREVENT CANCER

Preliminary studies from Nippon Medical School in Tokyo
found that time spent in nature showed an increase in the
production of anti-cancer proteins,[25] as well as a lower
mortality rate from a variety of cancers in areas with larger
forest coverage.[26] Twenty-three out of thirty-five studies
linked an increased risk of breast cancer to inactive women.
Other research found that active people are 50 % less likely to
develop colon cancer, and active men over the age of 65 are
70 % less likely to develop prostate cancer.[27]

9. INCREASES HAPPINESS

I would argue that there are very few people who have
ever looked back on a long-distance hike without noting
that it was a time where they felt truly happy. Researchers

found excursions to forests significantly decreased anxiety, depression, anger, confusion, and fatigue.[28] A study at the University of Essex also showed improvements in both self-esteem and mood, with the greatest improvements among the mentally-ill.[29] Forests aside, exercise reduces the symptoms of anxiety by more than 50 %, boosts confidence, and helps us establish and maintain social connections.[30] The more physically active we are, the more socially active we become.[31] If your hiker is introverted or has trouble socializing, heading to a long-distance trail is a great way to connect with others face to face.

"A CULTURE VERSED IN THE WORKINGS OF EMOTIONAL LIFE WOULD ENCOURAGE AND PROMOTE THE ACTIVITIES THAT SUSTAIN HEALTH... THE CONTRAST BETWEEN THAT CULTURE AND OUR OWN COULD NOT BE MORE EVIDENT. LIMBIC PURSUITS SINK SLOWLY AND STEADILY LOWER ON AMERICA'S LIST OF COLLECTIVE PRIORITIES. TOP-RANKING ITEMS REMAIN THE PURSUIT OF WEALTH, PHYSICAL BEAUTY, YOUTHFUL APPEARANCE, AND THE SHIFTING, ELUSIVE MARKERS OF STATUS. THERE ARE BRIEF SPASMS OF PLEASURE TO BE HAD AT THE END OF THOSE PURSUITS—THE RAZOR-THIN DELIGHT OF THE LATEST PURCHASE, THE MOMENTARY GLEE OF FLAUNTING THIS PROMOTION OR THAT UNNECESSARY TRINKET—PLEASURE HERE, BUT NO CONTENTMENT. HAPPINESS IS WITHIN RANGE ONLY FOR ADROIT PEOPLE WHO GIVE THE SLIP TO AMERICA'S VALUES. THESE REBELS WILL NECESSARILY FORGO EXALTED TITLES, GLAMOROUS FRIENDS, EXOTIC VACATIONS, WASHBOARD ABS, DESIGNER EVERYTHING - ALL THE PROUD INDICATORS OF UPWARD MOBILITY - AND IN EXCHANGE, THEY MAY JUST GET A CHANCE AT A DECENT LIFE."[32]
A GENERAL THEORY OF LOVE,
BY THOMAS LEWIS, FARI AMINI, AND RICHARD LANNON

WHAT ARE THE BENEFITS OF A LONG-DISTANCE HIKE?

"MY BOYFRIEND HAS BECOME A LOT MORE CONFIDENT IN HIMSELF. HE'S NEVER BEEN A PERSON TO FLAUNT ANYTHING, BUT NOW HE CARRIES HIMSELF WITH A CONFIDENCE THAT I DON'T THINK HE HAD BEFORE - WITHOUT BEING A JERK OR ACTING LIKE HE'S BETTER THAN ANYBODY. THE MAIN THING IS THE CONFIDENCE, FEELING GOOD ABOUT HIMSELF, AND FEELING LIKE HE'S WORTHY."
- EMILY, 21, KENTUCKY

"MOST OF THE BENEFITS ARE MENTAL. IT'S JUST NICE TO GET OUT AND NOT WORRY ABOUT ANYTHING AND JUST TAKE THE TIME. IT'S A VERY SIMPLE LIFE. YOU GO AT YOUR PACE, YOU DON'T HAVE ANYONE OR ANYTHING PRESSURING YOU. YOU DON'T HAVE TO WORRY ABOUT YOUR PHONE, YOUR WORK, ANYTHING LIKE THAT. IT'S JUST TIME FOR YOU. FOR ME, THATS A VERY PRECIOUS THING." - BRAD, 28, OHIO

"MY BROTHER USED TO BE VERY PARTICULAR AND PRIVATE. EVERYTHING HAD TO ALWAYS BE IN ITS OWN PLACE AND THINGS ALWAYS HAD TO GO A CERTAIN WAY, BUT IT'S VERY OBVIOUS THAT'S CHANGED NOW. HIS WHOLE PERSONALITY CHANGED A LITTLE BIT. JUST TALKING TO HIM, HE SEEMS A LOT MORE RELAXED." - VICTORIA, 29, GEORGIA

"MY NIECE SEEMS MORE EXPRESSIVE AND OPEN. I DON'T KNOW HOW TO PUT IT, BUT JUST MORE EXPRESSIVE AND OPEN TO THE WORLD. NOT THAT HER HORIZONS WEREN'T BROADENED BEFORE, BUT NOW IT SEEMS LIKE SHE'S MORE EXPRESSIVE OF WHAT'S GOING ON AND WANTING TO SHARE HER EXPERIENCES WITH PEOPLE." - CHRIS, 44, CALIFORNIA

"THRU-HIKING HELPED MY SON TO LET GO OF SOME THINGS, POSSIBLY EVEN CHILL OUT MORE, AND DEAL WITH THINGS AS THEY COME. I THINK THAT'S WHAT A LOT OF PEOPLE SAY WHEN THEY DO THE TRAIL, ESPECIALLY IF THEY'RE PRETTY WOUND TIGHT. THEY LEARN TO BE FLEXIBLE." - DEBBIE, 64, KENTUCKY

UNDERSTANDING THIS ISN'T A VACATION

It's undeniable that one of the many draws of a long-distance trail is the scenery. From the jagged mountains of the Pacific Northwest, to the sweeping vistas of New England, our trail systems are direct paths to some of the best views the world has to offer. These landscapes are magnificent enough to leave anyone awe-struck, but as incredible as a long-distance trail can be portrayed online and in writing, the feelings you can't obtain through media come from the physical and mental challenges behind successfully seeing a long hike through to fruition.

So why isn't a long-distance hike a vacation? Hikers are taking months off work to spend every day in the sun with a cool breeze blowing through their hair and fresh air filling their lungs. They send photos that are incomparable to anything we see at our desks; they make friends from all over the world; they wear goofy shirts and short-shorts; and are out there living their dreams. They are not spending 40 hours a week in an office. They are not dealing with issues that crop up at home. They are not watching the kids, or walking the dogs, or mowing the lawn, or fixing the faucet.

Sounds like a vacation to me.

The problem, however, is the vacation feeling wears off fast. It dissolves when hikers spend the first night in their tent waking up every half hour because they started in early March during a cold snap. It dissolves when they realize that what they thought was their lowest possible base weight[1] still hurts to carry all day. It dissolves when they're so sick of mashed potatoes and ramen that they would rather skip dinner than force down another spoonful of the same bland foods that they've been eating week after week.

It's true that there is a honeymoon phase, but as with any other honeymoon phase, it wears off. A part of them will begin to hate the trail as much as they love it, to loathe waking up because it means having to walk again, to put tape over tape as the blisters monopolize every vacant area of their feet, to feel like embarking on such a

---

1 A hiker's base weight refers to their total pack weight without food and water. See pg. 31.

quest was possibly the stupidest thing they could have done, and that they've been irresponsible for putting their real-world life on hold. When the physical pain numbs, the mental pain takes its place. I'd like to challenge you to step on a treadmill and leave your phone in the other room. Turn off the TV, turn off the music, put down this book, and just walk. How much time passes before you check your watch? How long before you're bored enough to get off? How long can your mind handle nothingness?

In Michael Finkel's, *The Stranger in the Woods*, he explores the effects of prolonged solitude, saying, "unwanted loneliness makes you sick—social isolation is as damaging as high blood pressure, obesity, or smoking as a risk factor for illness and early death." Finkel cites a study at the University of Virginia that found a majority of men and 25 % of women, "would rather subject themselves to mild electric shocks than do nothing but sit quietly with their thoughts for fifteen minutes."[33]

But you said going outside was good for our health? And it is. However, the constant hustle and bustle of society paired with the multitude of media platforms that will scroll for hours without ever running out of content has left our minds unable to handle stillness. We, as a society, have depleted our attention spans by spending so much time staring at screens that we can handle our own thoughts for only short periods at a time. So, what happens on a long-distance hike? We get bored. We get so bored that we make it a challenge to see how far into the morning we can hike before we need to put on headphones and listen to music. Then it gets worse. We listen to music to the point that we can't stand it anymore. So, we switch to podcasts, and believe it or not, we run out of episodes that interest us. Then we switch to audiobooks, but we can't listen to more than a few chapters without checking our map to see how much further is left. We talk to those around us until we no longer have anything new to talk about and then opt to hike at our own pace because hiking with others turns to hiking in silence anyway. It's a mental struggle that everyone is warned about, but few can prepare for. Spending hours a day in silence allows hikers to analyze every problem or situation they have ever been in. This can cause mental stress, especially for those carrying extra emotional baggage. Being alone with your own thoughts can be scary. It's an obstacle that forces as many, if not more, people off-trail than injury and physical limitations combined.

Remember this when your hiker is away because the hardest thing to hear when they call home is that their support system chalks up their hard work and struggles to a vacation. It creates a rift from feeling like no one understands what they are really doing. It causes them to fear returning to a community that never fully grasped the challenges they had to overcome to get there, and consequently puts you in a box of people who will never understand, so why bother trying.

It can be tough to remember when your boss spent the day nit-picking your work or the kids won't stop screaming, but don't refer to your loved one's hike as a vacation. Don't tell them that this is what they signed up for when they complain about the pain. Don't make them feel guilty for taking time to pursue an endeavor that they aren't even appreciating. *Do listen.* Do tell them that you understand it's hard. Encourage them to tell you the things they're looking forward to that week. Help them see the good in what they are accomplishing. When asking hikers what people at home could do to show support, many responses were simply to show interest and reinforce that you are proud of them.

"EXPLAINING THAT IT WASN'T A VACATION IS THE SOUNDTRACK OF MY LIFE. THIS WAS NOT A VACATION, THIS WAS WORK. I DON'T THINK A LOT OF PEOPLE CAN GRASP THE AMOUNT OF DISTANCE WE COVER IN A DAY OR THAT LONG-DISTANCE HIKING IS A JOB. THAT WAS SOMETHING I DIDN'T EXPECT IT TO FEEL LIKE. I DIDN'T UNDERSTAND THAT WAS HOW IT WOULD BE."
- KATIE, 25, COLORADO

Long-distance hiking is hard work. It's long hours of walking through pain. It's late nights and early mornings. It's pushing yourself through each day while counting down the steps until you reach a town to rest again. In any situation where a person says that they've been working hard for long hours and extended lengths of time, we usually tell them they should take a vacation. We don't say, "Wow, that vacation you've been on really sounds like fun!" By comparing a long-distance hike to a vacation we are unintentionally suggesting that it isn't challenging, that the hiker does not struggle, and that it does not require hard work to complete. Anyone can go on a vacation if they have the money to do so, but a majority of hikers will quit a long-distance hike before money runs out because few people can work their body and mind for that long.

HIKING TERMS: TYPES OF LONG DISTANCE HIKES

THRU-HIKE - A THRU-HIKE IS AN END-TO-END HIKE OF AN ESTABLISHED LONG-DISTANCE TRAIL THAT IS COMPLETED WITHIN ONE CALENDAR YEAR. A THRU-HIKE IS USUALLY DONE IN ONE LARGE PUSH RATHER THAN BITS AT A TIME.

SECTION HIKE - A HIKE OF A SECTION OF A LONG-TRAIL RATHER THAN THE ENTIRE TRAIL. MANY HIKERS WILL COMPLETE LONG-DISTANCE TRAILS ONE SECTION AT A TIME. SECTION HIKES DO NOT NEED TO BE IN SEQUENCE OR COMPLETED WITHIN ONE HIKING SEASON.

NORTHBOUND / NOBO - HIKING A TRAIL FROM SOUTH TO NORTH. HIKERS ARE REFERRED TO AS NORTHBOUNDERS OR NOBOS.

SOUTHBOUND / SOBO - HIKING A TRAIL FROM NORTH TO SOUTH. HIKERS ARE REFERRED TO AS SOUTHBOUNDERS OR SOBOS.

FLIP-FLOP - A FLIP-FLOP IS A THRU-HIKE THAT IS NOT COMPLETED CONSECUTIVELY. MANY HIKERS WILL CHOOSE A FLIP-FLOP HIKE TO ELONGATE WEATHER WINDOWS AND LESSEN THE IMPACT OF LARGE NUMBERS OF HIKERS THAT TAKE THE TRADITIONAL THRU-HIKING ROUTES. THEY ARE REFERRED TO AS FLIP-FLOPPERS RATHER THAN NORTHBOUNDERS OR SOUTHBOUNDERS.

LEAVE NO TRACE

Leave No Trace is a set of seven principles that provide information on leaving a minimal impact on the outdoors.[34] They will be referenced throughout this book and are important to follow to ensure our trails stay preserved for generations to come.

1. PLAN AHEAD AND PREPARE
PLAN AHEAD BY CONSIDERING YOUR GOALS AND THOSE OF YOUR GROUP. KNOW BEFORE YOU GO. GET LOCAL INFORMATION. MAKE SURE YOU HAVE THE SKILLS NECESSARY AND THE RIGHT GEAR TO MAKE YOUR TRIP A SUCCESS.

2. TRAVEL AND CAMP ON DURABLE SURFACES
CHOOSE TO CAMP AND TRAVEL ON THE MOST DURABLE SURFACE YOU CAN. IMPACTS ON FRAGILE NATURAL FEATURES CAN TAKE MANY YEARS TO HEAL.

3. DISPOSE OF WASTE PROPERLY
PACK IT IN, PACK IT OUT. WE HAVE A RESPONSIBILITY TO CLEAN UP AFTER OURSELVES. TRASH AND WASTE CAN INTRODUCE UNWANTED ORGANISMS INTO THE ENVIRONMENT AND ATTRACT UNWANTED WILDLIFE. LEAD BY EXAMPLE AND PICK UP ANY TRASH YOU SEE ALONG THE WAY.

4. LEAVE WHAT YOU FIND
ALLOW OTHERS TO ENJOY THE ENVIRONMENT AND NATURAL RESOURCES BY LEAVING PLACES AS YOU FIND THEM. DON'T TAKE ROCKS OR OTHER PIECES OF NATURE WITH YOU.

5. MINIMIZE CAMPFIRE IMPACTS
BUILD CAMPFIRES ONLY IN PERMITTED AREAS AND MAKE SURE TO FULLY EXTINGUISH FIRES. FOLLOW LOCAL RULES AND REGULATIONS WHEN CONSIDERING HAVING A FIRE.

6. RESPECT WILDLIFE
KEEP YOUR DISTANCE, DON'T FEED THE ANIMALS, AND RESPECT THE NATURAL ENVIRONMENT. DON'T REMOVE ANY PLANTS FROM THEIR HABITATS.

7. BE CONSIDERATE OF OTHER VISITORS
BE THOUGHTFUL OF OTHER VISITORS WHO ALSO WANT TO ENJOY NATURE AND THE OUTDOORS. KEEP PETS ON A LEASH AND BE RESPECTFUL WITH THE USE OF ELECTRONICS AND THEIR IMPACT ON THOSE AROUND YOU.

SECTION TWO
LOGISTICS

WHAT GEAR DO THEY CARRY?

The gear a person carries can make or break a long-distance hike. The frustrating thing is that there's no right or wrong answer to what the *best* gear is. What works for one person may be the wrong choice for another. It's important to research each piece of gear before deciding to purchase as well as to get out and test gear before the big day. There is no way to know if a piece of gear is right for your hiker until they try it, which is why many will go on shakedown hikes in preparation. Swapping out gear mid-trail won't be the end of the world, as most trails intersect roads to bail out and seek replacements, but it is more cost-efficient to avoid replacing items due to a lack of research and testing.

Talking about gear means using lingo, like *shakedown*, that may confuse non-hikers. Therefore, I'd like to share some terms before diving into the nitty-gritty.

BASE WEIGHT - BASE WEIGHT REFERS TO THE BACKPACK'S TOTAL WEIGHT WITH EVERYTHING EXCEPT CONSUMABLES (FOOD, WATER, FUEL).

TRADITIONAL - A BASE WEIGHT UNDER 30 LB (13.6 KG)

LIGHTWEIGHT - A BASE WEIGHT UNDER 15LBS (6.8 KG)

ULTRALIGHT - A BASE WEIGHT UNDER 10LBS (4.5 KG)

BIG 3 - A HIKER'S BACKPACK, SHELTER, AND SLEEP SYSTEM

SHAKEDOWN HIKE - A HIKE THAT IS TAKEN TO TEST GEAR IN ORDER TO FIND OUT IF THERE ARE ITEMS THAT COULD BE IMPROVED, REPLACED, OR ELIMINATED.

Why does a hiker's base weight matter? Well, having a pack that is too heavy can cause injury. According to REI, a pack loaded for backpacking shouldn't weigh more than 20 % of the hiker's body weight.[35] A 180 lb (81.6 kg) man carrying a 36 lb (16.3 kg) pack falls right in the sweet spot, though petite backpackers may have more trouble sticking to the 20 % rule. It may also be difficult to adhere to in conditions where cold-weather gear, like extra layers, need to be added. As a 115 lb (52.2 kg), petite female, keeping my total pack weight below 23 lb (10.4 kg), or 20 %, is sometimes impossible. For example, when I entered the 100 Mile Wilderness on the Appalachian Trail, my total pack weighed 27 lb (12.2 kg) due to the extra food I needed to carry for a longer-than-usual stretch between towns. While not a deal-breaker, I can personally say that at my size I definitely notice the difference when my pack weighs closer to 30 lb (13.6 kg) than 20 lb (9.1 kg). I hike at a slower pace, I take breaks more frequently, and I take my pack off more often during the day. These adjustments aren't always convenient, but they keep me from injuring myself when my pack is heavier than I'd prefer.

Many people find fault with terms like *lightweight* and *ultralight* due to the competitive nature of lowering one's pack weight as an ego-boost or to brag about how light a person can travel. The problem is that eliminating too much gear can be dangerous when the hiker is no longer carrying the necessities for survival. I've included these terms because for myself, at 5 ft 1 in (1.55m) and 115 lb (52.2 kg), I feel most comfortable hiking with what is technically considered an ultralight setup, as might others with similar heights and weights. Also, some items, like frameless backpacks, have a maximum-weight that the pack can comfortably carry, and neglecting these numbers can lead to the wrong gear choices.

Although the topic of pack weight can be common conversation at the start of a long-distance hike when everyone is getting used to their gear, the truth is that hikers stop paying attention to their exact pack weight as long as it is not hurting them. A hiker might decide to buy a notebook in town, or to carry a deck of cards to deal with monotony on the trail. Base weights often fluctuate due to additions and subtractions in gear based on weather conditions, comfort, and pleasure. A hiker may have a different base weight in winter due to added gear.

Starting off with a smart pack weight is like researching a company before showing up to an interview; it allows hikers to put their best foot forward and provides a greater chance of success. Again, a smart pack weight does not mean having the lightest pack on the trail, nor does it mean having the heaviest.

The figure below is commonly referred to as The Gear Triangle. It is what every decision on gear will ultimately boil down to based on three important factors; comfort, weight, and price. Unfortunately, you can usually only pick two.

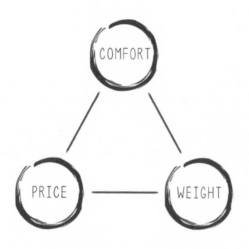

COMFORT + PRICE = PROBABLY HEAVY

PRICE + WEIGHT = OFTEN UNCOMFORTABLE

COMFORT + WEIGHT = YOU WILL NOT LIKE THE PRICE TAG

THE BIG 3

The Big 3 are usually where most people will opt for comfort and weight. A backpack, shelter, and sleep system are the most important pieces of gear a hiker will carry, so spending a little more on these items often makes sense.

BACKPACK

A backpack is one of the last pieces of gear a hiker should purchase. It's hard to know if your gear is overloading a pack's maximum load-bearing weight before knowing how much all the gear weighs. It's also hard to know what size pack to purchase without know how much space the gear takes up. Keep in mind that people have successfully hiked long-distance trails using huge packs with external frames, and frameless packs so small that they could be rolled up and stuffed into a Nalgene bottle. Having an old, heavy pack won't ruin your hiker's chances of success; it just may end up being less comfortable and they may choose to purchase a better option along the way.

SHELTER

I use the term shelter instead of tent because tents are no longer the only option for long-distance hiking. Some hikers will choose a tarp or a hammock as their shelter instead. This mainly comes down to the hiker's preferences and comfort level. While trails like the Appalachian Trail are known for three-walled shelters that exist nearly every ten miles, one should not go on a long-distance hike without a personal shelter. It's common for established shelters on trail to fill up early, which makes relying on them risky, especially if there's a possibility of rain. If your hiker doesn't want to pack a personal shelter I would encourage them to research why this is not a sound decision. Don't sweat which type your hiker chooses so long as he or she has done research and is willing to test it before leaving.

SLEEP SYSTEM

Similar to the variety of shelters on the market, a sleeping bag is no longer the only option for a sleep system; there are now quilt options, too. Although the name is the same, these are not the quilts that grandma patched together and sewed for the guest room, but a relative to the sleeping bag that saves weight by only being sewn or zippered together to the thighs. Quilts often have straps that attach to a sleeping pad to keep in warmth, and there are also options that can unzip fully into a blanket. I enjoy using a quilt on my long-distance hikes because I'm weight-conscious and find them to be less constraining than a sleeping bag. This is my personal preference. Others enjoy sleeping bags because they zip all the way up and warm air is less likely to escape in the night.

If you are worried about your hiker being too cold, ask them which sleep system they are leaning towards and why, as well as what temperature rating they are considering. Is the hiker a cold sleeper or do they sleep hot? What are the lowest temperatures expected during the trip? What are the highest? As someone who cares for the hiker, it may be easy to conclude that a bag rated for very cold temperatures would be best, but since a long-distance hike can last several months and see seasonal transitions from frigid cold snaps to searing summer heat, a bag that is too warm in the cold could be uncomfortable in months like July and August. A sleep system can always be supplemented with extra clothing layers if needed.

Some hikers choose to use a separate sleep system in warm months and cold months. If your hiker has a summer bag and a winter bag, offer to ship them the spare when they're ready to make the switch. That being said, separate sleep systems are often more of a luxury than a necessity.

I personally use a lower temperature rating than recommended because I know that I'm a colder sleeper than the average hiker. I didn't learn this on the Internet, I learned this from on-trail experience. When I realized I was too cold on the Pacific Crest Trail, I added clothing layers until the weather warmed up, then reinvested in a better quilt before heading to the Appalachian Trail. The main downside from the wrong initial purchase was the money spent reinvesting in gear. On my first hike, I was uncomfortable for a few nights until I made it to town and bought another clothing layer (again, spending more money), but because my first sleep system was nearly right, I was not in danger of suffering from hypothermia. Discomfort and danger are two different things, and when examining concerns it's important to differentiate what might cause a period of discomfort versus what could invite danger. Bringing a 50 °F (10 °C) sleeping bag to the Arctic Circle is dangerous. Bringing a 20 °F (-6.7 °C) bag on a hike where a 15 °F (-9.4 °C) bag makes more sense will only result in temporary discomfort. When in doubt, try using a 20 °F (-6.7 °C) buffer for comfort. If the anticipated temperatures go down to 40 °F (4.4 °C) and the hiker doesn't plan on using extra layers, they may choose to bring a 20 °F (-6.7 °C) quilt.

THE PLUTO OF THE BIG 3: SLEEPING PAD

Depending on who you ask, some will talk about the *Big 4*, including a sleeping pad in the core items of a hiker's gear. This is an item where hikers may lean on comfort more than weight or price. If they can't sleep on the hard ground, then a thin, foam pad won't be a good choice over an inflatable pad that offers cushion. I can fall asleep anywhere, so I use the cheapest, lightest option that will still give a layer between me and the ground, adds a bit of warmth,[1] and helps to protect my quilt. I've talked to hikers who use an inflatable sleeping pad and think I'm nuts for using foam. It's okay. The important thing is that the hiker sleeps comfortably through the night so that they can perform well during the day. The specifics of what each person considers comfortable is up to them.

---

1 Sleeping pads measure warmth using a rating called R-Value. The higher the R-Value, the warmer a sleeping pad will keep your hiker through the night.

EVERYTHING BUT THE KITCHEN SINK

We've talked about the most important pieces of gear, but four items won't get a hiker through a long-trail. Here are other pieces of equipment you might find in someone's pack:

TREKKING POLES

Okay, so these don't go *in* the pack, but trekking poles are extremely useful. They help with balance, assist on uphill climbs, and alleviate the pressure on knees on down hills.

STOVE AND POT (AND SPORK/UTENSIL)

Options range from individual backpacking stoves and pots to products that combine both in one. There are also hikers who go stoveless[1] or cold-soak[2]. Sometimes in the summer when it's too hot I'll send my stove home and pack out peanut butter, jelly, and a loaf of bread. If your hiker is having trouble deciding if they should bring a stove, suggest that they bring it and send it home if they decide they don't want it. Remind them that you can mail it back if they change their mind.

WATER FILTER/TREATMENT

Having a method of water filtration or treatment is a necessity. There are numerous ways to filter or treat water[3] and as long as a hiker is using their chosen method properly, they are doing their part to protect themselves from contracting illnesses like Giardia or Norovirus.

PACK LINER

Because my backpack isn't water proof, I choose to use a pack liner as an added barrier against weather. Gear

---

1 Stoveless means exactly what it says; the hiker is not carrying a stove.
2 Cold-soaking is a method of soaking food in water rather than cooking it. Noodles and oatmeal are easy to cold-soak, though finding variety can take time and practice.
3 Explained in-depth later on.

companies manufacture these, but some hikers just use a trash compactor bag because they are cheap.[4] In a pinch, I've doubled two heavy-duty garbage bags and replaced them when they wore down.

FOOD BAG

Options are endless for how to store food. Some trails require bear cannisters in sections where habituated bears are a problem. Some trails have trouble with rodents that make an odor-proof bag the smart choice. Other times an extra large Ziplock bag is sufficient. Your hiker can research what the best option or requirement for their trail will be.

RAIN GEAR

This depends on the trail. On the Appalachian Trail where rain is common, I carried a rain jacket and rain pants for the duration of my hike. In the desert section of the Pacific Crest Trail, I left my rain pants at home. Options like ponchos and rain skirts work well in wet environments too.

GROUND CLOTH

A sheet that goes below the tent to give a layer of protection between the tent and the ground. Also referred to as a *footprint*, ground cloths help prevent the bottom of the tent from soaking through when it's wet, and can protect against tears, especially in fragile light-weight shelters. This can be as simple as a small piece of waterproof plastic sheeting used in construction and purchased at a hardware store. Sometimes if a tent has a strong enough floor, a hiker may choose to forgo a ground cloth.

BATTERY PACK

Many hikers carry a battery pack to keep devices like cell phones charged. Those who need minimal charges or will be in town frequently may choose a smaller battery pack than someone charging multiple devices or going longer durations

4 If using a trash compactor bag, make sure to choose an unscented option.

between towns. Hikers recharge their battery pack in town and fuel their devices from it while on the trail. A 20,100 mAh battery can recharge a smart phone roughly 7 times, while a 10,000 mAh battery can recharge a smart phone roughly 3.5 times. Some battery packs come with a *fast charge* input. This can be useful to recharge quickly when on stopping in town for only a few hours. Battery packs can be heavy, so it's helpful for a hiker to know how many charges they'll want in order to pick the correct size.

HEADLAMP

Headlamps are useful for early mornings before the sun rises and on nights where a hiker might get to camp late. Additionally, they are useful for when the hiker needs to leave their shelter at night to use the bathroom. A headlamp with a red light option helps a hiker be considerate of others at camp.

CLOTHING

The clothing a hiker carries depends on their comfort levels and willingness to re-wear dirty clothes. Some hikers carry only two pairs of socks, re-wearing them until they reach the next town to do laundry. Others carry 5 to 7 pairs. The exact clothing a hiker brings is based on personal preference. I carried one set of clothes that I'd also sleep in, as well as a long sleeved base shirt and leggings for if it was cold or my hiking outfit got wet. Others can't go to bed without a designated sleep outfit. There is no right answer so long as the hiker is prepared for the correct temperatures and weather conditions.

SHOES

There are endless options for shoes. Should a person use hiking boots? Should they use trail runners? What about shoes with a zero-drop?[5] I have hiked trails where I needed the ankle support of boots. I have also hiked trails where hiking boots

---

5 Zero-drop is a term describing when the heel of the foot sits at the same height as the ball of the foot in the shoe. A zero-drop better imitates natural, barefoot walking, but can take some adjusting to when first switching to from standard footwear.

seemed like overkill and trail runners felt more comfortable. The hiker will go through more than one pair of shoes, as they are usually worn-through and replaced every 300 mi (482.8 km) to 500 mi (804.7 km). If a shoe isn't perfect, the hiker can try a different pair when they replace them.

QUESTION FROM A MOM:

"MY DAUGHTER SAID SHE'D BUY SHOES AS SHE GOES, BUT I HEARD IT TAKES TIME TO BREAK IN A NEW PAIR. WOULDN'T IT BE BETTER TO GET ALL HER PAIRS AND BREAK THEM IN BEFORE SHE LEAVES THAT WAY SHE WON'T NEED TO GO THROUGH THE BREAK-IN PHASE ON THE TRAIL?"

WHILE THIS MIGHT SEEM LIKE A GOOD STRATEGY, THERE'S A REASON HIKERS DON'T BUY MULTIPLE PAIRS IN ADVANCE, OUR FEET GROW ON THE TRAIL. IT'S COMMON FOR HIKERS TO REPORT AN INCREASE IN FOOT-SIZE AFTER WEEKS ON TRAIL AND MANY HAVE HAD TO BUY A LARGER SIZE WHEN THEY REPLACE THEIR FIRST PAIR. FOOT GROWTH DOESN'T HAPPEN TO EVERYONE, AND HOW MUCH IT GROWS WILL VARY, WHICH MAKES IT HARD TO PREDICT BEFOREHAND. I WENT FROM A 6 TO A 6.5 ON THE PCT AND STAYED A 6.5 FOR THE DURATION OF THE A.T. I ALSO HAVE A FRIEND WHO WENT FROM A SIZE 7 TO A SIZE 9 ON HER TRAIL. FOR THIS REASON, IT'S WISER TO WAIT UNTIL YOUR HIKER NEEDS NEW SHOES TO PURCHASE THEM RATHER THAN TO BUY THEM ALL IN ADVANCE.

SMALLER ITEMS

Smaller items, like a lighter, fuel, gloves, first aid supplies, tent stakes, and extra batteries, get into the fine details of everything you might find in a hiker's pack. For the sake of simplicity we can skip past these; whether or not a person is carrying nail clippers won't make much difference.

LUXURY ITEMS

The number of luxury items hikers choose to carry varies from person to person. Some swear they could never hike without a lightweight pillow. Others want a camera or a book. All you need to know is that luxury items are not essential and are usually carried to help the hiker maintain their sanity. If someone is willing to carry the added weight, that's their choice. If they end up not needing an item they'll likely send it home at the closest town.

SAFETY TIP

MANY HIKERS TAKE A PHOTO OF THEMSELVES WITH THEIR TRAIL CLOTHES AND BACKPACKS ON AS WELL AS A PHOTO OF THEIR GEAR LAID OUT ARTISTICALLY BEFORE THEY DEPART ON A LONG-DISTANCE HIKE. ENCOURAGE YOUR HIKER TO TAKE PHOTOS LIKE THIS, EVEN IF YOUR HIKER HAS NO INTENTION OF POSTING THEM TO SOCIAL MEDIA. HAVING A LIST OF YOUR HIKER'S GEAR, ALONG WITH PHOTOS THAT INCLUDE COLOR, CHOICES OF CLOTHING, AND OTHER ITEMS, IS IMPORTANT IN THE EVENT OF AN EMERGENCY. PHOTOS CAN ALSO BE USEFUL SHOULD AN AIRLINE MISPLACE YOUR HIKER'S BACKPACK, OR IF YOUR HIKER FORGETS AN ITEM SOMEWHERE ON-TRAIL AND WANTS TO POST ABOUT IT SO THAT OTHER HIKERS CAN KEEP AN EYE OUT.

HOW DO THEY GET FOOD?

Your friend or loved one's trek to the mountains might invoke images of hunting deer and trapping squirrels in order to add protein to a diet of foraged berries and plants. Shows like *Naked and Afraid* give the impression that spending prolonged periods outdoors is a foodless battle for survival, but that couldn't be further from the truth when it comes to long-distance trails.

When I returned from the Appalachian Trail, no fewer than six of my friends asked the same question within our first conversation.

"So, what was the grossest thing you had to eat?"

I'd explain that I never really had to eat anything gross. Everything I ate was food I chose to carry, and that if I thought something was gross I simply wouldn't buy it. They never seemed satisfied with this answer.

"But if you had to pick just one thing; one gross thing. What would it be? Anything?"

I'd try again to stress that what's in a hiker's food bag is entirely up to them and that we usually have a supermarket full of options to choose from when we arrive to towns.

"But what about Spam? Did you ever have to eat Spam?"

When people expect you to be out there hunting and gathering, the idea that you didn't need to eat the occasional cricket to make it through the summer seems to disappoint. While some people like Spam, I don't. Therefore, there would never be a town that I'd walk into where I'd purchase a can of Spam to bring on the next stretch of trail. Why would I do that to myself when I have other options? That being said, here's an example of what the logistics of a food carrying plan typically looks like. The type and amount of foods carried will depend on a hiker's weight, hunger levels, and preferences.

APPALACHIAN TRAIL: SPRINGER TO HIAWASSEE - MILE 0-69

LET'S ASSUME THIS STRETCH MIGHT TAKE 5 DAYS, WITH AN
AVERAGE OF 13.8 MILES HIKED PER DAY.

DAY 1: HIKE 14 MILES WITH 3 DAYS OF FOOD.

DAY 2: HIKE 14 MILES.

DAY 3: HIKE 3.3 MILES INTO NEEL GAP. THERE'S AN
OUTFITTER ON THE TRAIL FOR RESUPPLYING FOOD AND
REPLACING GEAR IF NECESSARY. TOP UP ANOTHER 2 DAYS
OF FOOD TO YOUR PACK. TAKE A LONG BREAK, THEN HIKE
ANOTHER 7.7 MILES.

DAY 4: HIKE 14 MILES.

DAY 5: HIKE 16 MILES INTO HIAWASSEE. GET A BUNK AT A
HOSTEL AND ENJOY A NIGHT IN TOWN.

DAY 6: CHECK YOUR MAP TO SEE HOW MANY DAYS TO PLAN
FOR YOUR NEXT STRETCH OF HIKING. HEAD TO THE GROCERY
STORE IN TOWN TO ADD THE APPROPRIATE AMOUNT OF FOOD
TO YOUR PACK. IF YOU'RE FEELING GOOD, HIKE A FEW MILES
OUT OF TOWN IN THE EVENING AND SLEEP ON THE TRAIL. IF
NOT, BOOK YOUR BUNK FOR ANOTHER NIGHT AND SPEND THE
DAY RESTING.

This 5-day section shows an option to add more food and
rest halfway through, so if the hiker is eating more or less than
anticipated, they have the ability to adjust accordingly on the third
day. What this example does not show is that the hiker doesn't *need*
to make it three days before they can resupply, or to replace faulty
gear. If I look at my map, I'll also see the roads that intersect the trail
throughout this stretch.

DAY 1 ROAD CROSSINGS:
MILE 1.0 - USFS 42 PARKING AREA
MILE 4.4 - THREE FORKS PARKING AREA
MILE 8.6 - HIGHTOWER GAP PARKING AREA
MILE 10.5 - HORSE GAP PARKING AREA
MILE 12.3 - COOPER GAP PARKING AREA

DAY 2 ROAD CROSSINGS:
MILE 16.9 - GOOCH GAP PARKING AREA
MILE 20.5 - WOODY GAP PARKING AREA

DAY 3 ROAD CROSSINGS:
MILE 31.3 - NEEL GAP, MOUNTAIN CROSSINGS OUTFITTER
MILE 37.3 - TESNATEE GAP PARKING AREA
MILE 38.2 - HOGPEN GAP PARKING AREA

DAY 4 ROAD CROSSINGS:
MILE 52.5 - UNICOI GAP PARKING AREA

DAY 5 ROAD CROSSINGS:
MILE 55.1 - INDIAN GRAVE GAP PARKING AREA
MILE 56.9 - TRAY GAP PARKING AREA
MILE 69.2 - DICK'S CREEK GAP PARKING AREA

While some roads are more heavily trafficked than others, there are options to bail out of the 5-day stretch early if necessary. Woody Gap is a popular spot for hikers to get off-trail. When I hiked through, the temperature at night was predicted to drop to single-digits, and many of the hikers around me chose to get a ride from Woody Gap to Neel Gap to spend the night indoors. Additionally, Unicoi Gap happens to be another popular spot to go into Hiawassee. I chose to add the 5th day to my example itinerary since there is a store on Day 3, but it would have been just as easy to head into town after 13.5 mi (19.3 km) to Unicoi Gap on Day 4.

My point is that many trails that people choose for their first long-distance hike are not as remote as it may seem. While it can be frustrating if poor planning causes someone to have to go into town early or take a road that wasn't part of their original plan, at least the option is there. Furthermore, the longer hikers are on the trail, the better they are able to check the distance between towns, estimate how many days it will take to get there, and determine how much food they will need each day. It's a good idea for hikers to keep an extra day of food in their packs to account for unexpected hurdles that may slow them down. Something as simple as a $1.00 packet of powdered mashed potatoes can count as an emergency meal. The anticlimactic thing about long-distance hiking is that the food situation is never as intense as the people at home expect.

FOOD WEIGHT - IT'S COMMON FOR HIKERS TO ASSUME THAT EACH DAY OF FOOD CARRIED WILL WEIGH ROUGHLY 2 LB (0.9 KG).

WATER WEIGHT - EACH LITER OF WATER WEIGHS 2.2 LB (1 KG).

IF I LOOK AT MY SAMPLE FOOD-CARRY AND ASSUME I AM ALWAYS CARRYING 2 L OF WATER, I CAN SEE THAT MY PACK WILL HAVE 6 LB OF FOOD (3 DAYS) AND 4.4 LB (2 KG) OF WATER AT ITS HEAVIEST. I CAN ADD THIS 10.4 LB (4.7 KG) TO MY BASE WEIGHT TO FIND OUT MY TOTAL PACK WEIGHT. IF IT SEEMS TOO HEAVY, I CAN ADJUST WHICH ROAD I TAKE TO TOWN IN ORDER TO LOWER MY FOOD WEIGHT.

RESUPPLY BOXES

A resupply box is a package of food or supplies that a hiker will mail, or have mailed, to themselves while they are on the trail. There is debate on each trail as to whether resupply boxes are necessary and how many are appropriate to send. The more remote a trail, the more likely a hiker will send resupply boxes. This is usually because remote areas of trail often go through towns that don't have supermarkets or only stock a limited selection of foods that carry well on the trail. It is also because with a smaller selection of food comes a higher price tag, so buying food at a Walmart and boxing it up to send to a remote town may end up being cheaper than buying the same foods at the local convenience store. Unless a hiker has strict dietary concerns, it is usually possible to resupply in towns; it just might end up being expensive and limited in variety at times.

BENEFITS OF A RESUPPLY BOX
- Purchasing food in bulk and splitting it up between several boxes can increase the variety of foods carried
- Potentially saves money when sent to remote towns
- Potentially allows more variety than food options in town
- Saves time in town by not having to shop for food

DISADVANTAGES OF A RESUPPLY BOX
- Food preferences can change over time and options your hiker once liked can become ones they hate
- Pre-packing food takes away your hiker's ability to choose foods that they are in the mood for at that moment
- For shorter resupply stretches or towns with well-stocked stores, the cost of postage to ship a box might end up being more expensive than buying food in town
- Reliant on post office or hotel/hostel hours to pick up food

Whether or not the benefits outweigh the disadvantages depends on the hiker. Someone who enjoys dehydrating their own meals or has specific dietary needs might want to send more boxes. Others may find the work involved in creating resupply boxes to be too much of a hassle and choose not to send any. There are also hikers who send a few boxes to remote towns and resupply at local grocery stores in others.

I knew the Pacific Crest Trail would have limited resupply options when I got to Washington, but didn't want to worry about putting together those boxes before the trail in case my taste preferences changed. Instead, when I got to Bend, Oregon, I went to Walmart and bought enough food for four to five boxes. I spent my zero day[1] sorting and packaging food and mailed the boxes to upcoming remote towns. Post offices will usually hold general delivery boxes for up to two months before returning them to the sender.

The most popular way to send a resupply box is using a flat-rate priority box from USPS. The flat-rate usually gives your hiker the best price given that each day of food weighs roughly 2 lb. It's also more common for places along the trail to accept USPS than FedEx or other shippers. Another benefit is that if the hiker ends up not needing the box, the post office will bounce it to another post office up to two times before the hiker must claim it. I've used the bounce option when mailing myself gear, like warmer clothing layers, that I did not need as soon as I expected. Your hiker can even purchase postage for their boxes in advance so that they are ready to send when needed.

Some hikers will put together a *bounce box* to send from town to town, containing things like a clean outfit to wear in town, shampoo or other toiletries that don't make sense to carry on the trail, and other items that might be swapped, like spare batteries or a book. I never used a dedicated bounce box because I found working around post office hours to be inconvenient and I prefer to keep a loose schedule that doesn't require getting to town by a certain time of day. It's frustrating to arrive to town on a Saturday afternoon and needing to wait until Monday morning to claim a box. For me, taking days off when my body doesn't need them isn't worth the benefits of a bounce box, but other hikers might see the extra town time as positive.

1 A Zero Day is a day where a hiker does not hike any miles - a zero-mile day. A day where a hiker does nearly zero miles (usually under 10 miles) is referred to as a Near-o day - for *nearly zero* miles.

HOW TO ADDRESS A RESUPPLY BOX

SENDING A BOX VIA GENERAL DELIVERY FOR THE FIRST
TIME MIGHT SEEM CONFUSING. IF YOU FOLLOW THIS STYLE
OF ADDRESSING YOUR BOXES, THE POST OFFICE WILL KNOW
WHERE TO SEND THEM AND THEY WILL ARRIVE AT THE RIGHT
LOCATION:

> PLEASE HOLD FOR [NAME OF TRAIL] HIKER
> HIKER'S LEGAL NAME
> C/O GENERAL DELIVERY
> POST OFFICE ADDRESS
> CITY, STATE, ZIP CODE

IF I WANTED MY BOX SENT TO THE POST OFFICE IN LONE PINE
ON THE PACIFIC CREST TRAIL, I COULD SEARCH, "LONE PINE
POST OFFICE, CALIFORNIA," AND FIND THAT THE ADDRESS
IS 121 E BUSH STREET, LONE PINE, CA, 93545 (AT TIME OF
PUBLISHING). THUS, MY BOX WOULD BE ADDRESSED AS FOLLOWS:

> PLEASE HOLD FOR PACIFIC CREST TRAIL HIKER
> JULIANA CHAUNCEY
> C/O GENERAL DELIVERY
> 121 E BUSH STREET
> LONE PINE, CA 93545

THE POST OFFICE WILL CHECK YOUR HIKER'S ID WHEN HE OR SHE
PICKS UP A BOX, SO IT'S IMPORTANT TO WRITE YOUR HIKER'S
REAL NAME AND NOT A TRAIL NICKNAME. PUTTING AN ETA ON
THE BOX IS NOT USUALLY REQUIRED, BUT IT DOES HELP THE
POST OFFICE SORT THE BOXES. WRITING THE HIKER'S LAST NAME
ON THE SIDES OF THE BOX OR USING COLORFUL TAPE TO MAKE
THE BOX MORE RECOGNIZABLE WILL HELP YOUR HIKER GET IN
AND OUT OF THE POST OFFICE FASTER. IF YOU'RE SENDING THE
BOX TO A HOSTEL OR OUTFITTER, REPLACE "GENERAL DELIVERY"
WITH THE HOSTEL/OUTFITTER NAME AND REPLACE THE POST
OFFICE ADDRESS WITH THE HOSTEL/OUTFITTER ADDRESS.

TIPS FOR PACKING A RESUPPLY BOX

TRY NOT TO PACK FOODS THAT ARE HEAVIER THAN NECESSARY
OR UNREASONABLY BULKY. CANNED FOOD OR FOOD WITH HEAVY
PACKAGING IS NOT GREAT TO CARRY, NOR IS FOOD THAT TAKES
UP A LOT OF ROOM IN THE BACKPACK, SUCH AS A BIG BAG
OF POPCORN. ASK YOUR HIKER TO SEND YOU A FEW OF THEIR
PREFERENCES. IF YOU ARE UNSURE, HERE ARE SOME OPTIONS FOR
FOOD THAT HIKERS MIGHT ENJOY HAVING IN A RESUPPLY BOX:

- GRANOLA BARS
- OATMEAL PACKETS
- POPTARTS
- HONEY BUNS
- PEANUT M&M'S
- SNICKERS
- PRETZELS
- COOKIES
- DRIED FRUIT
- NUTS
- BEEF JERKY
- SUMMER SAUSAGE

- KNORR PASTA SIDES
- KNORR RICE SIDES
- POWDERED MASHED POTATOES
- RAMEN NOODLES
- TUNA PACKETS
- QUINOA
- DEHYDRATED BACKPACKING
  MEALS
- PEANUT BUTTER PACKETS
- ENERGY CHEWS
- OLIVE OIL PACKETS
- INSTANT COFFEE PACKETS

HOW DO THEY GET WATER?

Water carries are different on every trail. On the Appalachian Trail I never carried more than two liters at a time due to the availability of water sources. On the Pacific Crest Trail, the desert section had less reliable sources with longer distances between each, that left me carrying four to six liters of water at a time and sometimes planning days around water caches[1]. Just as hikers are able to learn how much food they'll eat over a certain number of miles, they're also able to learn how much water they'll drink and can adjust the amount they carry based on the distance between sources, how hot it is, and how exposed the trail is to direct sunlight. I always try to carry a half-liter more than I think I'll need even if I'm confident that the next source is flowing. If I have reason to suspect the next source won't be flowing, I'll see how far away the source after it is and make sure that I have enough water to get there. I personally got my information on water sources from the Guthook app[2], and if the source is flowing from comments left on the app. This is just one resource.

"I RARELY HAD AN ISSUE GETTING WATER. BE AWARE OF HOW MUCH TO CARRY FOR YOUR BODY AND PACE, AS WELL AS HOW FAR IT IS TO THE NEXT WATER SOURCE. I THINK WE HAD GREAT LUCK WITH STREAMS. I'D SUGGEST BRINGING A LITTLE MORE WATER IN THE BEGINNING UNTIL YOU LEARN HOW MUCH YOU PREFER TO CARRY." - KEITH, 29, NEW JERSEY

I choose to filter my water regardless of how clear or clean it looks to avoid contracting illnesses like Giardia or Norovirus. Using a water filtration or treatment option is a simple process. If you are curious, ask your hiker to demonstrate how the filter or treatment

---

1 People will bring jugs of water to the trail for hikers to resupply. Caches often exist in dry stretches of trail, but are considered unreliable since it's not guaranteed that the jugs will be full. Hikers should never rely on water caches, and caches are discouraged because they violate Leave No Trace principles.
2 Guthook is a popular map app for long-distance trails.

works so you can see for yourself.

  While most hikers won't be thrilled to give up some of their
water because another hiker planned poorly, hikers do look out for
one another, and if a hiker sees that another hiker is struggling, it is
usually the first instinct to help.

POPULAR METHODS OF WATER TREATMENT AND FILTRATION[36]

SAWYER SQUEEZE/MICRO: HOLLOW FIBER MEMBRANE FILTER
CERTIFIED FOR 0.1 MICRON FILTRATION
PROTECTS FROM PROTOZOA AND BACTERIA, BUT NOT VIRUSES

KATADYN BEFREE: HOLLOW FIBER MEMBRANE FILTER CERTIFIED
FOR 0.1 MICRON FILTRATION
PROTECTS FROM PROTOZOA AND BACTERIA, BUT NOT VIRUSES

AQUA MIRA: LIGHTWEIGHT CHLORINE DIOXIDE WITH TWO PARTS
THAT ARE MIXED TOGETHER THEN ADDED TO WATER
PROTECTS FROM BACTERIA, VIRUSES, AND CYSTS

STERIPEN: BATTERY-POWERED STERILIZER USING UV LIGHT
PROTECTS FROM PROTOZOA, BACTERIA, AND VIRUSES, BUT ONLY EFFECTIVE
WITH LOW TURBIDITY (CLOUDINESS) IN THE WATER

POTABLE AQUA IODINE: IODINE TABLETS CAN BE USED TO
TREAT WATER, BUT CAN TASTE UNPLEASANT WITHOUT TASTE-
NEUTRALIZING TABLETS
PROTECTS FROM GIARDIA, BACTERIA, AND VIRUSES, BUT NOT
CRYPTOSPORIDIUM

BLEACH: 2 TO 4 DROPS OF UNSCENTED BLEACH (WITH THE
FEWEST ADDITIVES) CAN BE ADDED TO EACH LITER OF WATER
PROTECTS FROM GIARDIA, BACTERIA, AND VIRUSES, BUT NOT
CRYPTOSPORIDIUM

BOILING WATER: BOILING WATER CAN BE A BACKUP OPTION
IF A FILTER BREAKS OR THE HIKER RUNS OUT OF TREATMENT
DROPS
PROTECTS FROM PROTOZOA, BACTERIA, AND VIRUSES

HOW DO THEY KNOW WHERE TO SLEEP?

Popular map options, like the Guthook app, will identify camping areas along the trail. On the Appalachian Trail Guthook map, it's possible to see where the established three-walled shelters and campsites are, if there's water or a privy[1], and how much space is available for tenting. The comments are useful for checking ahead to see if anyone had trouble with rodents or wildlife, if the water is flowing, and any other important details.

Hikers frequently come across campsites that aren't on their map. Leave No Trace principles suggest choosing campsites on durable, flat surfaces, at least 200 ft away from water sources and the trail itself. It's also important not to disturb fragile environments, like alpine zones, when choosing a site. Selecting a non-established campsite is referred to as *stealth camping*, though hikers should sleep at established campsites whenever possible.

Hikers often form a habit of looking at the next day's maps before going to bed and forming an idea of how far they'd like to hike based on the elevation gain, availability of water, and anticipated weather. On a day with mild elevation gain and fair weather, it may make sense to push further, while a day that has excessive elevation gain or is expecting poor weather might result in a closer site and re-evaluating as the day goes on. It's not uncommon for hikers to re-evaluate their goal at lunch to decide if their intended mileage still makes sense, or if they would like to camp closer or further based on the time and how many miles they already covered.

Other hikers might ask your hiker where they are thinking of camping as a way of making conversation. If a hiker feels uncomfortable telling someone where they will be camping, the answer, "I'm not sure yet," is always acceptable.

---

1 A privy is another name for an outhouse or non-flushing toilet.

HYGIENE + USING THE BATHROOM

Despite how we look and smell, hikers aren't as unhygienic as might be expected. Men grow long, bushy beards by choice rather than necessity, women choose not to shave because they don't feel like it, not because they lack access to a razor, and hikers choose not to carry soap because using it responsibly in the backcountry in accordance with Leave No Trace principles is often more of a hassle than it's worth.

Most hikers don't use soap or shampoo outside of towns because even biodegradable camp soaps, which are marketed for the outdoors, aren't meant to be used in water sources. The Leave No Trace Center for Outdoor Ethics reaffirms that using biodegradable camp soap or shampoo in water sources can cause significant harm to the ecosystem. To use soap in the backcountry responsibly, it should be done at least 200 ft from the water source, and buried in a cathole to reduce the attraction of wildlife.[37] The idea of transporting water 200 ft away from a source just to use soap is too much effort for a full-body shower, and would only makes sense for small tasks, like cleaning out a pot. Even then, a small sponge or rag is usually more than enough to get the job done.

When I go on a long-distance hike, my hygiene kit is usually comprised of a pack of wet wipes, hand sanitizer, a toothbrush, toothpaste, nail clippers, and a small hair brush that I broke the handle off to make it easier to pack. Wet wipes and toilet paper are interchangeable depending on preference, but I like having wipes because I can also use them if I need to clean a cut or blister, or if I want to wipe my face off before bed. While some hikers might carry deodorant, most don't due to the fact that we smell bad regardless. Our clothes get covered in sweat, our gear gets dirty, and the "hiker funk" usually hangs around until we return home. If you are meeting up with your hiker along the trail, you might want to leave the windows open to air out the car!

Hikers will often jump into lakes or ponds to rinse off. They also might clean their feet and socks in rivers or streams. This is always done downstream from the trail in order to keep water at the trail itself clean for drinking. No hiker wants to show up to a water source and see someone rinsing out their pee rag[1] right where they plan to collect water to drink.

A majority of the time, hikers will get to town every four to five days, if not more frequently. On the Appalachian Trail, there are stretches where a hiker could go into town every day if they wanted to. In town, a hiker can take a shower and do a load of laundry. This means that hikers usually have the opportunity to shower and wash their clothes at least one to two times a week. Whether or not they feel like they need to is a personal choice.

As someone with long, thick hair, carrying a brush is a must-have to keep my hair from knotting up. At home, I only wash my hair once or twice a week, which keeps it from over-producing natural oils that can cause greasy hair. Since my hair is already used to limited washes, it doesn't overproduce natural oils on long-distance hikes. Hikers prone to greasy hair might try shampooing less in the months leading up to their hike if that is a concern.

As for the bathroom, unless using a privy or in a fragile alpine zone that recommends otherwise, hikers bury their poop in catholes. A cathole is a 6-inch deep hole that a hiker digs in the ground using a trowel. Catholes need to be dug at least 200 ft away from water sources to avoid contamination, and toilet paper or wipes are always packed out and disposed of in town. If left in the cathole, animals can, and will, dig it up. The only thing worse than showing up to a campsite that looks like it's been toilet papered for Halloween, is having to pack out someone else's used toilet paper because they were too lazy to do it themselves.

---

1 A pee rag is a piece of gear that female hikers may choose to carry in order to wipe after peeing. It can be as simple as a bandana.

MAPS AND NAVIGATION

Map and navigation options vary from trail to trail. There are both traditional paper maps as well as phone apps that provide information on what the trail will look and feel like. Some trails require varying levels of route-finding, while others are simple enough to navigate without ever looking at a compass. That being said, accidents do happen, and planning for worst-case scenarios is important. If a hiker is relying on their phone for a map app like Guthook, what is their plan if their phone dies? If they are traveling over snow, does their map show topography that can be followed when the trail itself is buried? Does their map show side-trails and roads to towns in the event they need to get off early? How difficult is the trail to navigate? A trail that is harder to follow and less trafficked might require more detailed maps than a trail that's clear and well-marked.

The Appalachian Trail, as an example, is well-marked by blazes that are painted on trees and rocks roughly every 70 ft.

BLAZES ON THE APPALACHIAN TRAIL

WHITE BLAZE: SINGLE WHITE BLAZES MARK THE TRAIL. TWO WHITE BLAZES STACKED VERTICALLY USUALLY MEAN THE TRAIL IS APPROACHING AN INTERSECTION. IF THE TOP BLAZE IS SLIGHTLY TO THE LEFT OR RIGHT, THE TRAIL WILL TURN IN THAT DIRECTION.

BLUE BLAZE: BLUE BLAZES MARK SIDE-TRAILS SUCH AS ALTERNATE ROUTES, TRAILS TO VIEWPOINTS, AND TRAILS TO WATER SOURCES.

"GUTHOOK WORKS AMAZING, ESPECIALLY SINCE YOU CAN
DOWNLOAD THE TOPOGRAPHIC MAPS. IT WORKED REALLY WELL.
WE DID A LOT OF NAVIGATING IN THE SIERRA. THERE WAS
NO TRAIL FOR A VERY LONG TIME, SO WE CONSTANTLY HAD
TO CHECK OUR GUTHOOK APP. I WOULDN'T SAY IT'S EASY TO
NAVIGATE. IT'S DEFINITELY A CHALLENGE. BUT ONCE YOU LET
GO OF HAVING TO BE 100 % 'ON THE TRAIL' THE WHOLE TIME,
YOU CAN READ THE TERRAIN AND LOOK AT THE MAP AND FEEL
COMFORTABLE THAT YOU'RE ROUTE-FINDING IN THE RIGHT
DIRECTION." - JUSTIN, 40, TEXAS

Hikers often try to help each other through parts of trail that are
confusing to navigate. When an unmarked side-trail or abandoned
dirt road branched off the Appalachian Trail that could have been
mistaken for the trail itself, there were likely downed branches
tossed over the path to prevent hikers from accidentally wandering
the wrong way. I have also seen arrows drawn into dirt, laid out in
rocks, and created with sticks to help hikers easily see which way to
go at confusing intersections. That being said, it's easier for a hiker to
check their maps regularly than to find their way back to the trail due
to inattentiveness.

"IF YOU EVER STEP OVER DOWNED TREES OR DEAD WOOD, LOOK
UP, BECAUSE THE TRAIL PROBABLY TURNS THERE. FOR MOST OF
THE AT, PEOPLE WOULD PUT DOWNED BRANCHES OVER CONFUSING
SPUR TRAILS. THERE WERE TWO TIMES I ACCIDENTALLY TOOK A
BLUE BLAZE, AND WHEN I TURNED AROUND THERE WAS ANOTHER
PERSON WALKING TOWARDS ME THAT HAD DONE THE SAME THING.
BUT I NEVER GOT TRULY LOST OR WONDERED WHERE I WAS. THE
CLOSEST I WAS TO BEING LOST WOULD BE STEPPING OFF THE
TRAIL FOR A MOMENT AND REALIZING, 'WOAH, THIS DOESN'T
FEEL RIGHT.' YOU LOOK AT YOUR MAP AND SEE YOU'RE ONLY A
FEW FEET TO THE LEFT OR RIGHT OF THE TRAIL. I THOUGHT
HAVING GUTHOOK WAS GREAT FOR THAT BECAUSE IT KEEPS AN
ARROW ON MY LOCATION THAT I COULD TRACK. YOU COULD USE
ONLY THE AT GUIDEBOOK PAPER MAPS AND BE COMPLETELY FINE.'
- KEITH, 29, NEW JERSEY

"I DID A LOT OF RESEARCH FOR THE CDT. WE'RE USING THE GUTHOOK APP AND THE JONATHAN LEY MAPS... I'VE ALSO BEEN USING GAIA... YOU PAY FOR THE PREMIUM PACKAGE, BUT YOU GET ALL THE NATIONAL GEOGRAPHIC MAPS WHEN YOU DO, SO IT'S A GREAT DEAL. YOU CAN'T PRINT THEM, SO YOU'RE STILL RELIANT ON YOUR PHONE, BUT IT SHOWS YOUR GPS COORDINATES AND EXACTLY WHERE YOU ARE ON THE MAP. GAIA WILL BE GREAT WHEN WE GET TO HIGHER ELEVATION, BECAUSE IF THERE'S A STORM WE'LL KNOW WHERE THE TRAILS TO GET OFF THE RIDGE ARE. I'M NOT USING ONLY GUTHOOK BECAUSE IT DOESN'T SHOW ENOUGH OF THE SIDE-TRAILS FOR ME... IT SHOWS ALL OF THE WATER SOURCES AND THE COMMENTS ARE SUPER HELPFUL, BUT PAIRING IT WITH ANOTHER OPTION LIKE GAIA OR THE JONATHAN LEY MAPS ON THE CDT WILL MAKE YOU GOOD-TO-GO. TOWNS ARE SO MUCH FURTHER AWAY FROM THE TRAIL THAN THEY WERE ON THE AT, SO YOU'LL NEED A WIDER SENSE OF WHERE YOU ARE. THERE ARE ALSO ALTERNATES THAT YOU CAN TAKE WHICH MAKE IT A 'CHOOSE YOUR OWN ADVENTURE' TYPE OF TRAIL. THE JONATHAN LEY MAPS SHOW THE ALTERNATES IN DETAIL." - KATRINA, 37, ILLINOIS

Apps that use hiker's GPS location often have an arrow or marker that shows which direction they're facing. Any time I ended up off-trail, I was able to notice quickly based on the lack of maintenance on the new path I was treading, and was able to find my way back by pointing myself in the correct direction on my map and following the most sensible path to the trail.

The Pacific Crest Trail doesn't use blazes, nor does the Continental Divide Trail. Both are marked by either a PCT symbol or a CDT symbol, but the markings are more infrequent than the Appalachian Trail, as wilderness trails intentionally keep markings to road crossings, trail junctions, and the occasional marker for reassurance. On the PCT, it's possible to travel several miles without seeing a marker, and the CDT markers depend on what route or alternative route the hiker is on. Hikers are recommended to carry a paper map option as well as a compass and should spend time familiarizing themselves with how to use them before starting.

WEATHER WINDOWS

Unlike the day-to-day weather that fluctuates on the trail, weather windows refer to the length of time available to safely hike a long-distance trail after snow has melted enough to allow high-elevation segments to become passable at the start of a year, and before winter storms return to bury those same sections again in the fall. A hiker should know the weather window of the trail they will be hiking to ensure that they're starting at a safe time and maintaining a pace that will allow them to complete their journey before conditions become dangerous. Some trails have different weather windows depending on the direction the hiker will be traveling. Weather windows can also be elongated by choosing a flip-flop hike. This may be a good option for hikers looking to go at a slower pace.

WEATHER WINDOWS BY TRAIL

THE APPALACHIAN TRAIL (NOBO): MARCH - SEPTEMBER

THE APPALACHIAN TRAIL (SOBO): JUNE - OCTOBER

THE PACIFIC CREST TRAIL (NOBO): APRIL* - SEPTEMBER
*IT IS NOT RECOMMENDED TO ENTER THE SIERRA BEFORE JUNE, THOUGH HIKERS OFTEN BEGIN THE DESERT AS EARLY AS MARCH

THE PACIFIC CREST TRAIL (SOBO): JUNE - SEPTEMBER*
*IT IS RECOMMENDED TO EXIT THE SIERRA BY THE END OF SEPTEMBER

THE CONTINENTAL DIVIDE TRAIL (NOBO): APRIL - SEPTEMBER

THE CONTINENTAL DIVIDE TRAIL (SOBO): JUNE - SEPTEMBER*
*IT IS RECOMMENDED TO BE SOUTH OF MT. TAYLOR BY SEPTEMBER

"TO GIVE A PARENT SOME DETAILS, EVEN TO SIT DOWN WITH
A MAP AND SHOW THEM HOW TO FOLLOW ALONG AND SEE WHERE
YOU ARE, WHERE THE TOWNS ARE, HOW YOU'LL GET TO THE
TOWNS... I THINK JUST GETTING SPECIFIC WITH THEM HELPS.
ANYTIME I GO OUT, I ALWAYS GIVE MY WIFE AN IDEA OF
WHERE I WILL BE. I'M IN THIS SECTION, IT'S 40 MILES, AND
I'M GOING TO BE DOING IT IN THREE DAYS." - ROB, 34, OHIO

How will your hiker know if they are on-target with their weather window? They can take the number of days left in the hiking season, subtract the number of zero days they anticipate taking, and divide the number of days remaining by the amount of miles they have left to see how many miles a day they will need to hike to stay within the window.

Before I hiked the Appalachian Trail, I created the spreadsheet on the next page that shows the distances between popular resupply towns, and three options for how long it might take me to get to each one. For reference, I was starting my hike on March 4th. The first column of dates was my "fast" itinerary. It had me projected to finish in just under 5 months at the end of July. The next column was my "average" itinerary. It had me finishing in 5.5 months at the middle of August. The final column was my "slow" column. It had me finishing at the start of September in 6 months. These numbers are not fast, average, and slow for everyone, rather what I consider fast, average, and slow for myself. The good thing about making this type of itinerary based on your own pace is that you can look at it on any given day of your hike and see which town stretch you are between and compare it to the current date. I was able to accurately predict when I would finish my hike by periodically checking to see where I was on the trail compared to my three estimated finish dates. I would also know that if I was further behind than the slowest date, I would be risking finishing my hike in September and pushing the weather window. This type of guideline can be adapted for any trail.

CHAUNCE'S APPALACHIAN TRAIL ITINERARY

STRETCH	MILES	TOTAL	FAST	AVG	SLOW
Springer - Neel Gap	0 - 31.1	31.1	3/6	3/6	3/7
Neel Gap - Hiawassee	31.1 - 69	37.9	3/8	3/10	3/11
Hiawassee - Franklin	69 - 109.2	40.2	3/12	3/13	3/14
Franklin - NOC	109.2 - 136.5	27.3	3/14	3/16	3/17
NOC - Fontana Village	136.5 - 163.9	27.4	3/17	3/18	3/20
Fontana Village - Gatlinburg	163.9 - 207.3	43.4	3/20	3/22	3/24
Gatlinburg - Standing Bear	207.3 - 241.1	33.8	3/22	3/25	3/28
Standing Bear - Hot Springs	241.1 - 274.5	33.4	3/24	3/28	3/30
Hot Springs - Erwin	274.5 - 343.9	69.4	3/29	4/3	4/5
Erwin - Hampton	343.9 - 419.6	75.7	4/2	4/8	4/10
Hampton - Damascus	419.6 - 470.1	50.5	4/6	4/11	4/13
Damascus - Troutdale	470.1 - 519.6	49.5	4/9	4/15	4/17
Troutdale - Bland	519.6 - 591.2	71.6	4/13	4/19	4/22
Bland - Pearisburg	591.2 - 636.4	45.2	4/16	4/22	4/25
Pearisburg - Catawba	636.4 - 709.4	73	4/20	4/28	5/1
Catawba - Daleville	709.4 - 729.2	19.8	4/21	4/29	5/4
Daleville - Glasgow	729.2 - 786	56.8	4/24	5/4	5/9
Glasgow - Waynesboro	786 - 863	77	4/28	5/9	5/14
Waynesboro - Front Royal	863 - 967	104	5/4	5/15	5/26
Front Royal - Harpers Ferry	967 - 1024.6	57.6	5/7	5/24	5/31
Harpers Ferry - Waynesboro	1024.6 - 1068.3	43.7	5/10	5/27	6/3
Waynesboro - Pine Grove	1068.3 - 1103.9	35.6	5/12	5/29	6/5
Pine Grove - Boiling Springs	1103.9 - 1122.7	18.8	5/13	5/31	6/7
Boiling Springs - Duncannon	1122.7 - 1147.9	25.2	5/15	6/2	6/9
Duncannon - Hamburg	1147.9 - 1219.2	71.3	5/23	6/6	6/13
Hamburg - Delaware Water Gap	1219.2 - 1294.7	75.5	5/27	6/10	6/19
Delaware Water Gap - Unionville	1294.7 - 1346.2	51.5	5/30	6/14	6/23
Unionville - Warwick	1346.2 - 1373.1	26.9	6/1	6/16	6/25
Warwick - Fort Montgomery	1373.1 - 1404.3	31.2	6/4	6/18	6/27
Fort Montgomery - Pawling	1404.3 - 1447.5	43.2	6/6	6/22	7/1
Pawling - Kent	1447.5 - 1468.4	20.9	6/7	6/23	7/2
Kent - Falls Village	1468.4 - 1493.5	25.1	6/9	6/25	7/4

Falls Village - Great Barrington	1493.5 - 1521.7	28.2	6/10	6/27	7/7
STRETCH	MILES	TOTAL	FAST	AVG	SLOW
Great Barrington - Dalton	1521.7 - 1569.8	48.1	6/13	6/30	7/11
Dalton - Bennington	1569.8 - 1611.7	41.9	6/16	7/3	7/15
Bennington - Manchester Center	1611.7 - 1651.8	40.1	6/18	7/5	7/18
Manchester Center - Killington	1651.8 - 1705.2	53.4	6/22	7/8	7/21
Killington - Hanover	1705.2 - 1748.7	43.5	6/26	7/11	7/24
Hanover - Lincoln	1748.7 - 1818.9	70.2	7/1	7/17	8/1
Lincoln - Gorham	1818.9 - 1871.5	52.6	7/6	7/21	8/6
Gorham - Andover	1871.5 - 1944.1	72.6	7/11	7/27	8/11
Andover - Rangeley	1944.1 - 1970.5	26.4	7/13	7/29	8/14
Rangeley - Stratton	1970.5 - 2002.7	32.2	7/16	7/31	8/17
Stratton - Caratunk	2002.7 - 2039.7	37	7/20	8/4	8/21
Caratunk - Monson	2039.7 - 2076.4	36.7	7/23	8/7	8/24
Monson - Birch's Campsite	2076.4 - 2185.6	109.2	7/30	8/14	8/31
Birch's Campsite - Katahdin	2185.6 - 2192	6.4	7/31	8/15	9/1

Hikers who do not cover enough daily mileage or spend too much time in towns are at risk of a mid-trail wake up call that causes many to have to flip to the section of trail that is most-affected by winter weather and hike through while conditions are still amiable, returning to less risky stretches of trail later on. Poor planning can cause a strategic nightmare, add unexpected travel costs, and can necessitate veering from a continuous foot path in order to hike safely. This is avoidable with good planning.

For a majority of the trail, I stayed mostly in-line with the fast column, slowing down to the average column as we made our way toward New England and the terrain became more challenging. My trail family and I spent the 4th of July in Hanover, and I was able to match that to my chart to see that the fast column would have had me arriving in Hanover on June 26th, while the average column had me arriving in Hanover on July 11th. We were right in between the two dates, so I was able to predict with a glance that I'd finish the trail between July 31st and August 15th. This ended up being true, as we finished on August 7th.

I was never concerned with sticking too closely to my itinerary. Planning for the long-term on the trail is difficult. It's hard to know when hikers will go through a mental slump, when their bodies won't feel like making the miles they had hoped for, or if they'll get to town and see trail friends that they haven't seen in weeks and want to catch up. Hikers may also alter schedules to avoid being on the trail during bad weather. That being said, a chart like this will still help you keep track of your hiker. It will help you see when they might finish and how well he or she is keeping on pace by only needing to ask for a location. This is great for when your hiker is too busy to have a conversation on the phone. It also helps to see a trail broken down in manageable chunks, which is a lot less daunting than thinking of it in its 2,000+ mile entirety.

Look at the first two rows of the chart: Springer to Neel Gap and Neel Gap to Hiawassee. This is the same five-day stretch that we broke down day-by-day in the *Food* chapter. The easiest way to manage a long-trail is to tackle it one piece at a time, planning in detail only for the upcoming stretch. After reaching Hiawassee, I'd look at my chart again and see that I had another 40.2 mi (64.7 km) from Hiawassee to Franklin. I'd then check that with my maps to see if the elevation gain would be more or less than I was used to, and estimate how many miles I could manage a day. Thus, when I'd go to the grocery store in Hiawassee, I'd know exactly how many days of food to buy and what day I'd most likely arrive in the next town. I'd have it broken down the same way I broke down Springer to Hiawassee, and I wouldn't think any further than Franklin until I got there. Then, I'd repeat the process.

"I'M GIVING EVERYBODY A COPY OF WHERE I'M GOING TO BE AND I'LL UPDATE THEM IF I'M MOVING SLOWER OR FASTER THAN I THOUGHT. I REALLY FEEL THAT I OWE THAT TO THEM TO HELP THEM SLEEP BETTER AT NIGHT." - MICHAEL, 65, OHIO

CHAUNCE'S TYPICAL HIKING DAY

WHILE IT MAY SEEM LIKE A LONG-DISTANCE HIKER WILL HAVE
AN ABUNDANCE OF FREE TIME, A TYPICAL HIKING DAY OFTEN
LEAVES LITTLE ROOM FOR DOWN-TIME. KEEP IN MIND THAT
MY AVERAGE HIKING DAY IS BASED ON A 2.8 MPH PACE WITH
MODERATE ELEVATION GAIN AND MAY VARY FROM OTHER HIKERS'
DAYS. SOME WAKE UP HOURS EARLIER THAN I DO AND SOME
HIKE HOURS LONGER. OTHER HIKERS MAY TAKE MORE OR LESS
BREAKS OR TACKLE DIFFERENT DISTANCES.

7:00 A.M. - WAKE UP, PACK UP BELONGINGS

7:30 A.M. - START HIKING, EAT GRANOLA BAR

9:30 A.M. - 5.6 MILES DOWN, TAKE A 10 TO 15 MINUTE BREAK,
            EAT A SNACK

11:30 A.M. - 11.2 MILES DOWN, TAKE A 5 MINUTE BREAK, EAT A
             SNACK

1:00 P.M. - 15.4 MILES DOWN, STOP FOR LUNCH, PREPARE FOOD,
            EAT LUNCH

2:00 P.M. - PACK UP FROM LUNCH, START HIKING

3:30 P.M. - 19.6 MILES DOWN, TAKE A 10 MINUTE BREAK, EAT A
            SNACK

5:30 P.M. - 25.2 MILES DOWN, START LOOKING FOR A CAMPSITE

6:00 P.M. - SET UP TENT, COOK DINNER, EAT, AND RELAX

7:30 P.M. - TIDY UP AREA, PUT AWAY FOOD, CLEAN UP FOR BED

8:00 P.M. - LAY DOWN FOR BED, GO TO SLEEP

COST OF A LONG-DISTANCE HIKE

The cost of a long-distance hike will depend on several factors. How long is the trail? How much time does the hiker anticipate needing to complete their hike? Are they the type of hiker that will pitch their tent at a campground in town, or do they need to sleep in a motel bed every now and then to feel sane? When they resupply, are they buying the $7.99 bag of pistachios or the $1.99 box of honey buns? Are they cooking ramen for dinner at their hostel or heading to the local brewery with other hikers?

There are so many choices that affect the total cost of a long-distance hike that it's hard for anyone to give an exact number, but there are estimates available. The Appalachian Trail Conservancy suggests that most hikers will spend around $1,000 per month, with a new set of gear costing an additional $1,200 to $2,000.[38] The Pacific Crest Trail Association says that the typical hiker will spend $4,000 to $8,000 or more on a thru-hike, which breaks down similarly to the ATC numbers. Common advice would be to budget at least $2 per mile, however that puts your hiker at the lower end of both the ATC and PCTA recommendations.

Budgeting during a hike is just as important as saving before it. Saving for a hike as early as possible will put a hiker in the most financially advantageous position when they start, but poor budgeting will have them back in your arms sooner than anticipated. Looking at the different costs a hiker will encounter and estimating the frequency of those costs based on the amount of time the hiker expects to spend on the trail will help visualize what a hiker's expenses might look like over the course of a long-distance trail.

If I base my budget on my Appalachian Trail spreadsheet average speed column, I can assume I will be on the trail for 5.5 months, or 165 days. I'll estimate $17 for every day of food, which starts my expenses at $2,805. I can also look at my anticipated resupply stretches and see that I will be going through about 45 towns. Even this is an estimate, since there are more towns along the trail than the ones I included on my spreadsheet. I assumed I wouldn't stop in every single one, as they appear more frequently than needed at my pace. I don't usually spend the night in every town, as some days, like Neel Gap on the 5-day resupply example, I will resupply and immediately head back to the trail.

In estimating costs, I will assume that I'll spend the night in town for 30 of the 45 resupply stops. I will also add an extra 5 nights to account for zero days where I might spend two nights in one town. $25 feels like the most accurate cost of accommodations [hostels and shared motel rooms] based on what I've experienced, which adds $875 to my budget. I also know that I can't resist having a meal at a restaurant when I get to town, so I'll add $20 for each of the 45 towns, giving me another $900. I don't always have a beer in town, but the times I do are more likely to consist of two instead of one. 20 towns with two beers in each adds another $280.

I rarely pay for a shower since I tend to split motel rooms, so I'll only add $15 for showers. I also know that I usually do my laundry three times a month on a long-hike, which is about $50. I very rarely take a shuttle over hitch-hiking, so I'll only add $20 for those.

When it comes to mail, sending three to four boxes of gear swaps seems accurate, but I also like to send postcards and will spend $5 purchasing them every several towns. $80 covers four large flat-rate boxes and $50 on ten towns of postcards adds another $130. If my trail is 2,000 miles, I can estimate needing four to five pairs of shoes. Four replacement pairs cost $520. I'll add a final $200 for miscellaneous entertainment since I know if I'm with a group and everyone is doing something fun, I'll want to do it too. Lastly, I think $500 to $1,000 is a good amount of money for an emergency fund. Replacing a piece of gear could cost $100 to $300. Extra days in town for injury or illness could add roughly $100 per day, maybe more if there are no hostels and you can't find someone to split the cost of a motel room. Unexpected flipping to other sections of trail due to weather windows closing, fire closure work-arounds, or skipping around heavy snow could cost a flight ticket in addition to the extra time in town. There are too many ways that expenses could pop up that make me convinced that the more money hikers can add to their emergency fund, the better. There is nothing more frustrating than knowing you can physically and mentally continue to hike, but are forced off-trail due to money running out sooner than expected.

COMMON TRAIL EXPENSES

FOOD RESUPPLY: ESTIMATE $15 TO $20 PER DAY (3 DAYS OF FOOD WILL COST ROUGHLY $45 TO $60).

ACCOMMODATIONS: HOSTELS CAN COST ANYWHERE BETWEEN $15 TO $35 FOR A BUNK AND $30 TO $60 FOR A PRIVATE ROOM. SPLITTING A MOTEL WITH FOUR PEOPLE CAN SAVE MONEY, TOO.

RESTAURANTS: GETTING IN AND OUT OF TOWN WITHOUT HAVING A MEAL AT A RESTAURANT TAKES INCREDIBLE WILL-POWER. ESTIMATE $20 TO $25 PER MEAL AFTER TIP AND TAX.

BEER: ROUGHLY $7 PER BEER AFTER TIP AND TAX.

SHOWER: BUNK PRICES MAY COST LESS IF THEY DON'T INCLUDE A SHOWER OR LAUNDRY. ASSUME $3 EACH OR $5 FOR BOTH.

LAUNDRY: $3 TO $5 DEPENDING ON IF LAUNDRY IS BEING DONE THROUGH A HOSTEL OR AT A LAUNDROMAT.

SHOES: MOST HIKERS GO THROUGH A PAIR OF SHOES EVERY 300 TO 500 MILES. ESTIMATE $130 PER PAIR.

MAIL: SENDING ANYTHING HOME? BOUNCING THINGS AHEAD? MAILING A RESUPPLY BOX? $10 TO $20 FOR A FLAT-RATE BOX.

SHUTTLES: SOME BUSINESSES OFFER SHUTTLES TO AND FROM THE TRAIL WHERE HITCHING IS DIFFICULT FOR $5 TO $10.

ENTERTAINMENT: DOES YOUR HIKER WANT TO GO SEE A MOVIE IN TOWN? IS THERE MINI-GOLF NEAR THE HOSTEL?

EMERGENCY: EVERY HIKER SHOULD HAVE MONEY SET ASIDE FOR EMERGENCIES, LIKE HAVING TO ADD A CLOTHING LAYER, NEEDING TO FLIP TO A DIFFERENT STRETCH OF TRAIL DUE TO FIRE CLOSURES OR WEATHER WINDOWS, OR HAVING TO VISIT THE DOCTOR.

If we add it all together, $2,805 for food, $875 for accommodations, $900 for restaurants, $280 for beer, $15 for showers, $50 for laundry, $20 for shuttles, $130 for mail, $520 for extra shoes, $200 for miscellaneous entertainment, and $1,000 for emergencies, my total budget becomes $6,275. Whether or not that matches the amount of money I need to save for my trip depends on the expenses I have off-trail as well as if I will still have an income during my hike. Before the Appalachian Trail, I ended my lease on my apartment and moved all of my belongings into a storage unit for $55 per month. That's another $330. I also have a car payment and car insurance which add another $300 per month, or $1,800. These, along with mortgages, student loans, health insurance, cellular plans, subscriptions, and any other expenses, all need to be considered, because they are not factored into the $6,795.

If we go back to the 165-day estimate and divide it into weeks, we can plan our budget around 24 weeks. I'll divide $5,795 amongst the 24 weeks rather than $6,795, because $1,000 is meant only for emergencies. This gives me $241 per week. If a hiker is doing 120 miles per week, the $2 per mile method of estimating puts them at $240, which tells me that my number is close to the average recommendation and should be manageable.

"PEOPLE FROM HOME ASKED IF THERE WAS ANYTHING THEY COULD HELP WITH. I TOLD THEM THAT I DIDN'T NEED ANYTHING, BUT IF THEY WANTED TO, THEY COULD CONSIDER GETTING ME A BUNK AT A HOSTEL." - KATIE, 25, COLORADO

SECTION THREE
SAFETY

YOU'RE GOING ALONE?

I've heard this question through text, phone call, and email, all from the same person. Leading up to the Appalachian Trail, this was the one question my mom couldn't keep herself from asking. It was like she believed the answer would change if she tried enough avenues of communication. The only thing missing was a postcard saying, *"Are you still going alone?"*

On the Pacific Crest Trail I talked a friend into doing the first 700 mi (1,126.5 km) with me which kept my mom from worrying. On the Appalachian Trail, I hadn't bothered asking friends to join because I knew from the PCT how easy it would be to meet people on the trail. I also knew how frustrating it could be to hike with someone who might not be on the same page with things like pace or expected daily mileage. I wanted to start at a pace that was comfortable for me. I didn't want to worry about another person or have expectations to hike with the same person for the entire trip. For me, meeting people to hike with on the trail made more sense because I'd naturally fall in line with hikers that were averaging the same mileage. We'd be choosing between the same campsites, getting to town on the same day, and if at some point I wanted to speed up or slow down, there wouldn't be any negotiating.

"I DIDN'T KNOW ANYONE. I HIKED ALONE FOR THE FIRST FEW DAYS BY CHOICE. I'M SHY AND IT TAKES ME A WHILE TO WARM UP TO NEW PEOPLE, BUT EVERYONE WAS SO WARM AND WELCOMING. I ENDED UP WITH AN AMAZING TRAIL FAMILY THAT I STAYED WITH FOR MOST OF THE HIKE. IT WAS REALLY EASY TO MEET OTHER HIKERS. THEY SAY YOU'RE ONLY AS ALONE AS YOU WANT TO BE OUT THERE. IF YOU WANT TO BE ALONE, YOU DEFINITELY CAN BE, BUT IF YOU DON'T WANT TO BE ALONE YOU CAN FIND SOMEBODY TO HIKE WITH." - EMILIO, 29, TEXAS

Of the 5,000 mi (8,046.7 km) I've hiked in the past three years, I have only spent one night alone. While I did start the Appalachian Trail by myself, the first few nights consisted of crowded shelters that I intentionally chose to camp near in order to set my tent up around other hikers. I could have found a stealth site away from everyone, but I enjoy camping around others because I sleep better at night. Call me a sissy, but a twig snapping at 3 A.M. doesn't make you cringe as much when you're surrounded by other tents and can blame it on a hiker finding their way to the privy. Had I been on a more remote trail, like the Continental Divide Trail, my one-night-alone record might not stand, but between the Appalachian Trail, the Pacific Crest Trail, and the Colorado Trail, I've either had a friend with me, was able to make friends that I spent multiple nights with, or made one-night friends who I camped with and never saw again due to pace. The point is, being alone wasn't something that I had to incur. I had the choice every day to stick with the people around me or to go off by myself.

"GUY OR GIRL, PARENTS WORRY, BECAUSE THEY DON'T HIKE THEMSELVES. THEY WORRY ABOUT THE 'ALONE' FACTOR. I JUST TELL THEM, 'LOOK, HE'S NOT ALONE. HE'S WITH SOMEONE EVERY NIGHT, HE'LL DEVELOP A GROUP OF FRIENDS AND HE'LL HIKE TOGETHER WITH OTHERS EVENTUALLY.' EVEN IF THAT DOESN'T HAPPEN, HE'S STILL SURROUNDED BY PEOPLE. THERE WERE ONLY MAYBE FIVE NIGHTS THAT HE CAMPED BY HIMSELF.'
- ROB, 34, OHIO

It takes more effort to remain alone on a trail like the Appalachian Trail than the effort it would take to be around hikers. By being comfortable with your loved one *going alone*, what you're really agreeing to is being comfortable with your loved one going at a pace they feel good about and making friends with hikers they consistently see at breaks, meals, and campsites.

On the Pacific Crest Trail I had a very tough time in the desert because the friend I started with was in much better shape. She wanted to do bigger miles and was constantly stuck waiting for me to catch up at breaks throughout the day. She tried to hike at my pace for a while, but she's half a foot taller than I am and eventually admitted that walking at my speed hurt her knees. On the other hand, I was risking injury trying to keep up with the mileage goals we were setting. My legs were doing so poorly that at one point I was wearing two knee braces and an ankle brace just to keep the pain bearable. Even then, I couldn't walk without limping and any time I'd start to hike I'd have to push through the pain until it numbed enough to get me another few miles. I remember so many mornings where my group would propose a 20 mi (32.2 km) day and I'd start to cry because I personally wasn't ready for 20's. On top of it all, as the stressors of the trail began to wear us down, we became more honest about things that bothered us. We argued a lot over how I needed her to slow down and she needed me to speed up, and it took a lot of the fun out of hiking.

"MY MOTHER HAS NO CLUE WHAT'S GOING ON. HER FIRST RESPONSE WAS THAT OF A PROTECTIVE MOTHER. KEEP IN MIND SHE'S ALMOST 90. HER RESPONSE WAS, 'WHO ARE YOU GOING WITH?' AND I WAS LIKE, 'UH, NOBODY.' AND SHE GOES, 'OOOOH, YOU NEED TO FIND SOMEBODY. FIND SOMEBODY AND GET BACK TO ME.' HERE'S THE THING. I'M A MATURE, OLD GUY WHO USED TO BE A COP. REALLY, YOU DON'T HAVE TO WORRY ABOUT AN OLD GUY WHO USED TO BE A COP. THE ODDS ARE PRETTY GOOD THAT I'M GOING TO BE ABLE TO TAKE CARE OF MYSELF. WITH THAT BEING SAID, MY MOTHER'S STILL MY MOTHER, AND THAT'S WHAT HER CONCERN WAS." - BRUCE, 60, ONTARIO

Had my group been people I met on the trail, it wouldn't have felt weird for me to lower my mileage and stick with other friends that were going slower too. Unfortunately, because I talked a friend into doing the hike with me, we both felt obligated to stay with each other even though neither of us was satisfied with our circumstances. Looking at it that way, I'd say I was less safe starting with a friend than I was on my own. I was hurting my body by forcing it to do mileage it wasn't ready for, and risked injury by pushing through warning pains that kept growing worse.

I was relieved during the first week of the Appalachian Trail when I could decide how hard to hike based on how my body was reacting. If I was tired I could sit without guilt, because there was no one tapping their foot. I never wore a brace because my body was able to rest when I felt pains creeping up. I hadn't felt the pain I had at the start of the Pacific Crest Trail on any other hike, and I attribute that to being more in control of my pace. Long-distance hiking is an adjustment for our bodies. Your hiker should listen to what their body needs, especially in the beginning.

If your loved one has decided starting alone is the best decision for them, know that it isn't in an effort to ruin your chances of getting a decent night's sleep. Many parents I spoke to mentioned that they felt significantly better after taking their child to the trailhead and seeing the other hikers who were also starting. If going alone is your biggest concern and you have the ability to take your loved one to the trailhead, try offering a ride.

"KATIE STARTING ALONE WAS DEFINITELY A CONCERN, BUT SHE CAN MAKE FRIENDS WITH ANYONE SO I KNEW IF THERE WERE PEOPLE AROUND SHE'D FIND FRIENDS. WHEN WE DROPPED HER OFF THERE WERE SO MANY OTHER HIKERS STARTING. WE WENT INSIDE WHERE YOU HAVE YOUR BACKPACK WEIGHED AND GET YOUR NUMBER. KATIE KNEW EVERYTHING SHE NEEDED TO KNOW AND WAS SO WELL PREPARED THAT JUST WATCHING THEM TALK WAS SUCH A RELIEF TO ME. I FELT SO MUCH BETTER AFTER THAT THAN I HAD BEFORE." - CYNTHI, 55, INDIANA

"SHE HIKES ALONE ALL THE TIME. USUALLY I FIND OUT FROM A FACEBOOK POST. A LOT OF PEOPLE ARE WORRIED ABOUT A CRAZY PERSON ATTACKING HER, BUT I THINK MORE ABOUT ACCIDENTS AND INJURIES. THAT'S SOMETHING YOU LEARN IN GIRL SCOUTS OR BOY SCOUTS, YOU DON'T HIKE ALONE. BUT MY DAUGHTER KEEPS SAYING THERE'S SO MANY PEOPLE, THAT SHE'LL FIND HER FAMILY ON THE TRAIL, AND THAT SHE REALLY WON'T BE ALONE. YOU NEED TO TELL ME THAT'S TRUE." - CAROLYN, 60, VIRGINIA

"HE FOUND A TRAMILY AND WAS HIKING WITH THEM A LOT INSTEAD OF BY HIMSELF, SO THAT HELPED. THERE WERE FIVE OR SIX OF THEM HIKING TOGETHER. HE STARTED ALONE, BUT AFTER MY MOM DROPPED HIM OFF AT THE TRAILHEAD AND SAW SEVERAL PEOPLE GOING THROUGH, SHE WASN'T AS WORRIED ABOUT IT. EVERY TIME SHE TALKED TO HIM HE WAS ALWAYS AROUND SEVERAL PEOPLE." - VICTORIA, 29, GEORGIA

"STARTING ALONE WASN'T A CONCERN FOR ME. I WAS ACTUALLY SURPRISED BY THE NUMBER OF PEOPLE I WAS SEEING ON THE TRAIL. SINCE THIS WAS MY FIRST LONG-DISTANCE HIKE, I HAD COMPLETELY DIFFERENT EXPECTATIONS IN REGARDS TO EXACTLY HOW MANY PEOPLE WERE ON THE TRAIL, ESPECIALLY IN THE BEGINNING." - KATIE, 25, COLORADO

"THEY'RE PROBABLY NOT GOING TO BE ALONE FOR A LONG TIME. IF THEY START WHEN ALL THE OTHER HIKERS ARE STARTING THEY'RE GOING TO BE SURROUNDED BY HIKERS AT THE DIFFERENT STOPS ALONG THE WAY." - NIKKI, 40, WISCONSIN

"HE'S BEEN STUBBORN ABOUT STAYING WITH A TRAMILY. HE HAD A GROUP THAT HE'D BEEN WITH FOR A WHILE, BUT ONE GUY WANTED TO GO FASTER AND HE HAD WANTED TO TAKE A DAY OFF, SO THEY SEPARATED. HE'S HAD PEOPLE THAT HE HIKES WITH THAT HE KEEPS SEEING AND RUNNING INTO, BUT HE'S REALLY STUBBORN ABOUT NEEDING TO DO HIS OWN THING. I KNOW HE'S FINE AND THAT HE SEES PEOPLE IN CAMP AT NIGHT, BUT I JUST WISH HE WOULD STAY WITH A TRAIL FAMILY. I GUESS IT'S HARD BECAUSE OF THE PACING."
- JANET, 58, NEW JERSEY

TRAIL CULTURE + COMMUNITY

"I HIKED WITH A TRAIL FAMILY AND I'M STILL REALLY CLOSE
WITH THREE OF THEM. YOU MEET THEM RIGHT AWAY. I MET
MINE AT A HOSTEL AT HARPER'S FERRY. WE STAYED THERE TWO
NIGHTS AND DID THE FLIP-FLOP FESTIVAL. I GOT TO KNOW
THIS WOMAN WHO WAS 66. SHE TOOK OFF AND I THOUGHT I
WOULD NEVER SEE HER AGAIN, BUT WE ENDED UP CONTINUING
TO PASS EACH OTHER AND HIKING WITH EACH OTHER FOR TWO
MONTHS. I MET ANOTHER LADY IN SHENANDOAH WHO WAS IN
HER LATE 40'S. SHE WAS REALLY COOL. SHE WAS LIKE MY TECH
ANGEL. SHE HELPED ME WITH MY GARMIN AND SHOWED ME HOW
TO USE FACEBOOK. THEN THERE WAS THIS GUY WHO WAS LIKE, A
WORLD-CLASS ATHLETE. HE'D RIDE HIS MOUNTAIN BIKE IN ALL
THESE RACES. HE WAS REALLY STRONG AND I COULDN'T KEEP UP
WITH HIM ON THE UPS, BUT I COULD CATCH HIM ON THE DOWNS.
I HIKED WITH HIM FOR ABOUT A MONTH. OTHER THAN THAT, IT
WAS A BUNCH OF KIDS. THEY WERE A LOT FASTER THAN ME, BUT
THEY WOULD GET OFF THE TRAIL AND SPEND TIME IN TOWNS
AND I WOULD CATCH UP AND PASS THEM AGAIN, SO I SAW
THEM ABOUT FIVE OR SIX TIMES THAT WAY AND WE GOT PRETTY
CLOSE. I'VE LOVED EVERYTHING. I'VE MET MY FIRST FRIEND
WHO'S TRANSGENDER, SO THAT WAS COOL! I DIDN'T KNOW
ANYTHING ABOUT THEM AND THEN I GOT TO KNOW THIS GUY AND
THE WHOLE STORY ABOUT HOW IT HAPPENS, WHAT YOU DO, WHAT
YOU CALL IT. SO IT JUST OPENS MY EYES. IT OPENS MY EYES TO
ALL THE TRAIL PROVIDES FOR YOU." - ARTHUR, 71, MAINE

The amount of camaraderie and kindness I've experienced on
trails is exponentially higher than any other area of everyday life.
Every person that passes on the trail says, *hello*. Where else do you
see that? Not in the grocery store or on a city sidewalk, that's for
sure. When you walk into a public room like a coffee shop or the
bank, do you nod and smile at every person you see? When you're

sitting on the subway or riding the bus, do you ask each person around you what their name is and how their day is going? People do that at shelters and campsites. It seems wrong not to. The first thing I always notice when returning from a long-distance hike is the impulse I still feel to say hello to everyone who passes me, and the strange feeling of biting my tongue because that's not deemed normal in the "real" world. On the trail everyone greets a stranger like a friend, because they are all fighting towards the same common goal. We all want to see each other at the finish line, and no one turns a blind eye if they notice someone struggling. If an accident were to happen to me anywhere, I'd actually prefer it be on the trail because I know the type of people that are hiking and the lengths they would go in order to help a stranger to safety. That's something I haven't seen replicated anywhere else.

"THE URGE TO EMBED ONESELF IN A FAMILY - TO HOLD AN ENDEAVOR IN COMMON WITH OTHERS, TO BE PART OF A TEAM, A BAND, A GROUP THAT STRUGGLES TOGETHER TOWARD A COMMON VICTORY - IS AN INDOMITABLE ASPECT OF THE HUMAN MIND AND BRAIN. IN A CULTURE WHOSE MEMBERS ARE RAVENOUS FOR LOVE AND IGNORANT OF ITS WORKINGS, TOO MANY WILL INVEST THEIR LOVE IN A BARREN CORPORATE LOT, AND WILL REAP A HARVEST OF DUST.'
A GENERAL THEORY OF LOVE,
BY THOMAS LEWIS, FARI AMINI, AND RICHARD LANNON

It's hard to put the culture and communities that envelop our long-trails in writing because it seems like one of those things you need to see and be a part of to fully understand. For this reason, my suggestion to those who wish to understand trail culture and community is to get out there if you are able. I don't mean to hike the entire trail, but drop off your hiker, visit and provide trail magic[1] for them so that you can meet the people they're spending time with, or go to whatever trail is closest to you if the one they're on is too far away. Better yet, volunteer with a trail maintenance group near

1 Trail magic is when a person brings treats out to the trail for hikers. It is magic because it is unexpected and unplanned on the hiker's end, and feels magical to stumble upon in the middle of a hiking day. There are things that need to be considered in order to provide trail magic responsibly, which will be covered later in this book.

you and talk to the pros about why they love their trail and want to preserve it.

On my first night of the Appalachian Trail, I approached the Hawk Mountain Shelter and met a group of 12 hikers huddled around a fire. Everyone said hello, asked my name, why I chose to hike the trail, and why I chose to start the day I started. We went around the circle and shared stories from how it just seemed like a good day to start, to how a loved one who had aspired to hike the trail passed away on the same day a year prior and the hiker was now setting off on the anniversary to honor the goals of someone they lost. To my left was a guy who just turned 19, and to my right was a woman in her 60's. By the time we put out our fire to head back to our tents, I had made several friends who I got to know pretty well. People compared the mileages they were hoping to achieve and which days they thought they would make it to the first town. Those with similar goals made plans to split motel rooms and exchanged numbers to stay in touch if they didn't see each other until then.

On the second night I camped with a group of college kids who were on the trail for Spring Break. I knew I wouldn't see them again due to the mileage they were planning, but we still sat around a fire and talked about what their college was like and why they chose this as their spring break excursion. I met another man who snored throughout the night, and we laughed about how that resulted in the trail name[2] *Grizzly* as we ate breakfast the following morning.

Best of all, on my third day hiking, I met a guy named Easy who was having lunch at a shelter 50 mi (80.5 km) into the trail. Our hiking paces were similar enough that we hiked to town together, hiked to the same shelter the night we left town, hiked to the same shelter the night after that, and eventually stood next to each other in front of the Katahdin sign after walking the rest of the 2,192 mi (3,527.7 km) together. I didn't know Easy before the trail, but we got along well, hiked at similar paces, and slowly realized that we would be hiking around each other for a while due to our similar mileage goals. From that day on, I was no longer hiking alone, though I did have the option to stop early or hike further had I wanted to. However, I found a person who would be my rock when I was at my lowest, and to whom I could reciprocate the support. When I was

2 A trail name is an alias that a hiker will adopt on the trail. It is either given by others on the trail or chosen by the hiker.

struggling, he was there to push me further. When he was struggling, I was an ear to vent to. We hiked with multiple groups, but consciously chose to stick together when they merged or separated.

"THE TRAIL COMMUNITY WAS FASCINATING. THE PEOPLE THAT YOU MEET, NOT ONLY ON THE TRAIL, BUT ALSO IN THE TOWNS, ARE SO GENEROUS AND DO SO MUCH FOR HIKERS. TRAIL MAGIC JUST COMPLETELY BLEW ME AWAY. I NEVER EXPECTED THAT... WHEN YOU GET OUT THERE, THE MANTRA OF 'HIKE YOUR OWN HIKE,' TO ME IS JUST, THERE'S NO JUDGMENT. WE'RE ALL IN THIS DOING THE SAME THING, BUT HOW WE CHOOSE TO DO IT IS UP TO US. EVERYONE CAN COMPREHEND WHAT IT'S LIKE TO DO SOMETHING PHYSICAL, BUT IT'S HARD TO UNDERSTAND THE CAMARADERIE AND HOW PEOPLE HELP EACH OTHER. SOMETIMES YOU GET TO SAY YOUR GOODBYES TO OTHER HIKERS AND SOMETIMES YOU DON'T. IT'S JUST LIKE LIFE. AS A PART OF BEING ON THE TRAIL, THE POSSIBILITY EXISTS THAT YOU MIGHT NOT SEE SOMEONE AGAIN, BUT I DIDN'T LOOK AT EVERYBODY THINKING THAT IT WOULD BE THE LAST TIME I'D SEE THEM. IT JUST HAPPENS THAT WAY SOMETIMES. BUT BACK IN THE REAL WORLD YOU'LL START TO THINK THAT WAY. I'LL SEE SOMEONE AND CONSCIOUSLY TELL MYSELF THAT I WANT THAT INTERACTION TO BE MEANINGFUL BECAUSE IT MIGHT BE THE LAST TIME I SEE THEM OR THEY SEE ME. I'M IN GREAT SHAPE, BUT I COULD GET HIT BY A BUS TOMORROW. YOU NEVER KNOW. MY EXPERIENCE ON THE APPALACHIAN TRAIL WAS TRANSFORMATIVE TO ME AS A PERSON. MAYBE IT'S BECAUSE OF MY AGE OR WHAT I'VE EXPERIENCED IN LIFE, BUT IT REALLY MADE ME LOOK AT PEOPLE IN A LESS JUDGMENTAL, MORE COMPASSIONATE WAY. IT'S FASCINATING. THAT'S JUST IT, IT'S NOT JUST A HIKE. IT'S A CULTURE. AND I THINK IT'S A CULTURE FOR LIFE. I REALLY DO."
- GARY, 59, MISSOURI

As much as it may seem like I got lucky meeting Easy, the same happened to me and a group of four guys on the PCT when the friend I started with had gone home. The same also happened with countless groups around me on the AT. When Chris McCandless, subject of the book, *Into The Wild*, journaled, "happiness is only real when shared,"[39] he had a point. For the most part, hikers want

to share the experience with those around them. They want to wake
up early together to see the sun rise at McAfee Knob. They want to
stand at the top of Mt. Whitney and share the summit with their trail
friends. They can also relate to each other about how tough it can be
after hiking through a week of rain or through a sketchy section of
snow. They help those around them because sharing the highs and
lows of the experience is part of what makes a long-distance trail
such an amazing adventure.

'THE TRAIL ISN'T AS DANGEROUS AS PEOPLE MAKE IT OUT. FROM
WHAT I'VE SEEN, EVERYBODY SEEMS REALLY INCREDIBLE, LAID-
BACK, AND HELPFUL. NOBODY THAT I'VE RUN INTO WOULD LET
YOU SUFFER. IF YOU WERE TO RUN OUT OF FOOD, PEOPLE WOULD
GIVE YOU FOOD. THERE'S ALWAYS THIS EXTREME URGE TO HELP
PEOPLE AND FEELING THAT NO ONE HAS TO GO AT IT ALONE.
I REALLY LIKE THAT. EVERYBODY IS JUST ALWAYS WATCHING
EACH OTHER'S BACK. THAT'S A BIG DEAL FOR ME.'
- ANDY, 44, MASSACHUSETTS

Even with limited reception, hikers find a way to communicate
with those around them. My group knew what each other's trekking
poles looked like, so if we stopped for any reason we'd use them to
let each other know. One trekking pole in the ground meant that I'm
here, but don't come looking because I'm using the bathroom. Two
trekking poles meant I've stopped for a break, follow this side trail to
come meet me. When there were two poles, we'd always leave them
in the ground until the last member of our group saw them. It's easy
to get an idea of who is ahead of and behind when you see who left
camp before you and take turns passing each other throughout the
day. When the last person would show up to the poles, they would
take them to the meeting spot.

This may have just been what our group did, but it's not the only
way people can communicate on the trail without cell coverage.
One thing that always surprised me was the speed at which news
can travel amongst hikers. We're much more informed about what is
happening on the trail than most people give us credit for.

Facebook groups exist for each year's hikers that can be posted
to with updates on trail conditions, anything worth being aware of,

and information on things to stop and see along the way. Hikers help each other with gear questions and selections, worried parents and spouses check-in to see if anyone has seen their hiker when they've gone a while without hearing from them, and people will post if they find a piece of gear left behind on the trail to try to return it to the owner. When available, ridge runners[3] and trail angels keep hikers in their areas informed about the stretch of trail they are on, like if there is an up tick in wildlife or upcoming dry stretches.

"I EXPECTED HIM TO SEE A LOT OF UNIQUE INDIVIDUALS IN TERMS OF THEIR WALKS AND WAYS OF LIFE. I EXPECTED HIM TO RUN INTO A LITTLE MORE VAGRANCY... PEOPLE UP TO NO GOOD, SO TO SPEAK. BUT HE HASN'T. ACTUALLY, HE'S RUN INTO SOME PEOPLE THAT HE'S BECOME REALLY GOOD FRIENDS WITH. HE'S BEEN ABLE TO BROADEN HIS FRIEND GROUP ACROSS THE COUNTRY WHICH HAS BEEN REALLY NEAT." - TABATHA, 34, FLORIDA

Even hikers going in the opposite direction are helpful in assisting with communication. At Rocky Top on the Appalachian Trail, I accidentally hiked past the turn-off to the shelter I told Easy I'd meet him at for lunch. I stopped when I realized and asked someone hiking south to let Easy know that I was okay and would meet him at the peak instead. All I had to do was describe what he was wearing, and when they passed him, they let him know.

On the PCT, I would get to camp a few hours later than the rest of my group, as I was the weakest hiker among us. However, I always knew where to meet them because we would pick our campsite the night before and confirm it when we came together again for lunch. They knew my hiking pace and could estimate when I would show up. One night I took longer than anticipated, and they confessed that they were going to wait 30 more minutes before someone was going to hike back to make sure I was alright.

The night before we made it to the Canadian border, three of us got separated because the two of us who were behind got caught in a hail storm and had to set up tents. The next morning we saw our third

---

3 Ridge runners travel along designated sections of the Appalachian Trail, talking to hikers, collecting information from them, and sharing the information with others. We met ridge runners who were very informed about the stretch of trail they were watching, and were friendly and willing to help if we needed it.

friend a few miles ahead. We hadn't shown up to the break spot we
agreed on, so he set up his tent and waited for us there.

There are always people on the trail who are willing to keep
tabs on those around them and can tell when something is a cause
for concern. Hikers exchange phone numbers and social media
accounts so they can stay in touch if they get separated and make
an effort to help each other when they can. If someone is on their
own in town, hikers often extend their plans to include them. We
met a guy in Pearisburg, Virginia, who didn't have anyone to split
a motel room with, so we rearranged our room plan to include him
that way he wouldn't need to pay for a room on his own. We met
again in Lincoln, New Hampshire, and were ecstatic to see him after
several months apart. There's a joy to having a familiar face show up
unexpectedly and getting to see that hiker again

'MY DAUGHTER MET A FEW GUYS AND FINISHED THE HIKE WITH
ONE OF THEM. THE KID SHE WAS HIKING WITH WASN'T THERE
WHEN I MET HER IN THE 100-MILE WILDERNESS. WHEN IT GOT
DARK WE DECIDED TO SET UP CAMP. I ASKED IF SHE WAS
WORRIED ABOUT HER FRIEND AND SHE SAID, 'NO. SOMEBODY,
WHETHER ITS A SOUTHBOUNDER OR A NORTHBOUNDER, WOULD
KNOW IF THERE WAS A PROBLEM.' I DIDN'T REALIZE HOW THAT
REALLY WORKED UNTIL I WAS ON THE TRAIL, BUT IF THERE'S
SOMETHING WRONG, IF SOMEONE'S HAVING A PROBLEM, THE WORD
CAN TRAVEL REALLY QUICK.' - DON, 64, MASSACHUSETTS

There is also something beneficial to being on an equal playing
field with everyone around you where any type of category that
might separate us in real life doesn't seem to exist. To be able to
sit around a campfire with people who range in age from teenagers
to old-timers, who come from different backgrounds, countries,
upbringings, and walks of life, provides a perspective into how other
people are experiencing the world that we may not get anywhere
else. A college student can sit next to someone who is retired and ask
questions about what they did in their career and what they wish they
had done differently. Hikers compare how they grew up in different
countries which allows a perspective into worlds that exist outside
our own. We can learn what those around us have struggled with in

their lives and how we can do things differently to better ourselves when we return home.

"PEOPLE NEAR THE TRAIL ARE USED TO SEEING HIKERS. WE'RE SMELLY AND DIRTY, BUT WE BOOST SOME OF THESE SMALL TOWN'S ECONOMIES FOR SEVERAL MONTHS, AND PEOPLE ARE HAPPY TO SEE US. HIKERS ON THE TRAIL FEEL LIKE MIRROR-IMAGES OF MYSELF. EVERYONE'S ON THE SAME ADVENTURE AND YOU RUN INTO PEOPLE WHO ALL HAVE THE SAME THING ON THEIR MIND, KEEP GOING. YOU TALK TO PEOPLE FROM ALL OVER THE WORLD. I GOT TO MEET PEOPLE FROM OTHER COUNTRIES WHO I DIDN'T THINK I WOULD HAVE AS MUCH IN COMMON WITH AS I DID. THERE'S POLITICAL TURMOIL AND RACIAL DIVIDES AND THINGS LIKE THAT IN THE REAL WORLD, BUT YOU GET OUT TO TRAIL AND IT ISN'T LIKE THAT. NO ONE SAYS THEY DON'T WANT TO HANG OUT WITH SOMEONE BECAUSE THEY'RE IN A CERTAIN GROUP, EVERYONE JUST COMES TOGETHER, HELPS EACH OTHER OUT, AND WANTS TO MAKE SURE THAT EVERYBODY IS OKAY. I SAW HIKERS TAKING CARE OF OTHER HIKERS AND GIVING OTHER HIKERS FOOD OUT OF THEIR OWN FOOD BAG IF THEY WERE RUNNING SHORT. IN PARTICULAR, ONE TIME I ALMOST HAD HEAT EXHAUSTION IN THE DESERT AND THESE SECTION HIKERS PRETTY MUCH TOOK CARE OF ME. THEY GOT ME WATER AND MADE SURE THAT I WAS OKAY. EVERYONE I MET OUT THERE WERE GOOD PEOPLE." - EMILIO, 29, TEXAS

In *We Need to Talk: How to Have Conversations That Matter*, Celeste Headlee states, "We are separating the entire population into groups of us (those who agree with us) and them (those who don't). If you only speak to people who agree with you, you shut out the possibility of new perspectives, discoveries, and information."[40] That being said, stigmas and stereotypes are less prevalent on the trail. There are no social ladders or chains of command, just people who are working towards the same monumental feat and are joined together by that common goal. These aren't scary people or crazed lunatics, they are doctors, professors, psychologists, environmental consultants, financial advisors, writers, students, retirees, and all-around incredible people who make hiking a long trail worth the struggle.

CONCERNS FOR AN OLDER HIKER

If you are the spouse, child, family, or friend of an older hiker, you may hold a deeper concern for safety than you would for a 25-year-old. Many hikers take on a long-distance trail after retiring, as they usually have both the time and budget for such a trip. Trails like the Appalachian Trail that have easy, frequent access to towns and roads often see more older hikers. Long-distance trails aren't exclusive to the young or in-shape, and choosing to embark on a long-distance trail could be a great decision for older hikers. Staying active helps both their brains and bodies remain strong.

In *Spark: The Revolutionary New Science of Exercise and the Brain*, Ratey dives into the benefits of staying physically active at an older age. "Older adults who reported having a strong history of aerobic exercise clearly had better preserved brains, according to MRI scans... Those with improved fitness had an increase in brain volume in the frontal and temporal lobes... The idea that just six months of exercise remodels these crucial areas of the brain is incredibly heartening. In the scans, the exercisers' brains looked as if they were two to three years younger than they were... The major implication is that exercise not only keeps the brain from rotting, but it also reverses the cell deterioration associated with aging."[41] If six months of exercise are all it takes to remodel crucial areas of the brain, a long-distance hike is just the thing to keep an older hiker sharp. While you may be reluctant to accept your hiker taking on a trail, keep in mind that a challenge like this will boost resilience.

Encourage your hiker to start training as early as possible to build endurance. It may take longer to adjust to carrying a fully-loaded pack and allowing time to incrementally add weight can help prevent injury. Early training can help a hiker learn how frequently to rest, what pain and discomfort to expect, and what recovery methods remedy each pain best. Typically older hikers are less susceptible to peer pressure and better able to "hike their own hike" Those who have waited their whole lives to tackle a long-distance trail may be more keen to taking side-trails and stopping to smell the flowers than those in pursuit of high-miles or speed.

While a low pack weight may be important to prevent wear on an older body, items are usually more willingly added to ensure comfort. These could be medications, additional first aid supplies, or extra layers for comfort when resting at breaks or at night. While not always the case, many retirees have a bigger budget and can afford appropriate, comfortable, and lightweight gear that allows space and weight for additional smaller items. Because time lines are often more flexible after retirement, many hikers can also afford to take their time on miles, breaks, and rest stops in town. This is beneficial as more zero days for recovery might be required, and a bigger budget can allow the town-time without guilt.

Put the hike to the back of your mind for a moment and think about your biggest concerns and fears for your loved one. For many, these might be developing diseases like Alzheimer's or dementia. Science proves that an active lifestyle naturally helps suppress the onset of these diseases. "In a 2001 study published in the Archives of Neurology, Danielle Laurin of Quebec's Laval University analyzed the relationship between exercise and physical activity among a group of 4,615 elderly men and women over the course of five years. Laurin found that women over sixty-five who reported higher levels of physical activity were 50 % less likely than their inactive peers— women and men alike—to develop any form of dementia."[42]

Another common concern is that loneliness can lead to apathy and depression. By introducing themselves into a community that not only encourages exercise and activity, but fosters friendships and an ability to socialize with others of all ages and walks of life, your loved one is preventing loneliness and the undesirable effects that come with it. A recent study from the Rush Alzheimer's Disease Center, "showed that people who feel lonely—those who identify with statements such as 'I miss having people around' and 'I experience a general sense of emptiness'—are twice as likely to develop Alzheimer's... Apathy can become a defining characteristic... Depression and a lack of motivation can set in as people feel they're just waiting to die."[43]

Taking on a long-distance hike and setting a precedent for an active lifestyle encouraged by community will serve your loved one well even after returning from the hike. Planning future trips will keep the hiker's brains active, the exercise will prevent physical deterioration, and the trail community will stave off loneliness.

"THE AVERAGE SEVENTY-FIVE-YEAR-OLD SUFFERS FROM THREE CHRONIC MEDICAL CONDITIONS AND TAKES FIVE PRESCRIPTION MEDICINES, ACCORDING TO THE CENTERS FOR DISEASE CONTROL (CDC). AMONG THOSE OVER SIXTY-FIVE, MOST SUFFER FROM HYPERTENSION, MORE THAN TWO-THIRDS ARE OVERWEIGHT, AND NEARLY 20 % HAVE DIABETES... PEOPLE WHO ARE OBESE ARE TWICE AS LIKELY TO SUFFER FROM DEMENTIA, AND THOSE WITH HEART DISEASE ARE AT FAR GREATER RISK OF DEVELOPING ALZHEIMER'S... WE'VE HAD THE MEDICAL PROOF THAT EXERCISE PROTECTS AGAINST THESE DISEASES FOR DECADES, YET, ACCORDING TO THE CDC, ABOUT A THIRD OF THE POPULATION OVER SIXTY-FIVE REPORTS THAT THEY ENGAGE IN NO LEISURE-TIME ACTIVITY."[44]
SPARK: THE REVOLUTIONARY NEW SCIENCE OF EXERCISE AND THE BRAIN BY JOHN RATEY

When fearing for an older hiker taking on a long-distance trail, consider the alternative fear of a sedentary lifestyle, and examine how a trail might have more benefits than risks. Older hikers on the trail are some of the most hardcore out there - pushing through body aches and pains that come with decades of use, side effects from life changes, like menopause, and using extra caution to stay safe and healthy.

I've met older hikers who have tackled a long-distance trail in one season. Others prefer section hiking. One relayed starting from the beginning of the Appalachian Trail every summer, and seeing how far he could make it each time. For each of these hikers, the sense of community, as well as the noticeable difference in how they felt when they were on the trail, drove them back year after year.

THE DEBATE ON CARRYING PROTECTION

"Are you going to carry a gun?"
This seems to be one of the more popular questions that family and friends will ask. Having a loved one head into the wilderness with strangers makes the question of carrying protection understandable, though after 5,000 mi (8,046.7 km) on long-distance trails, I believe it is unnecessary.

My particular stance is that, no, I do not need to carry a gun on the trail. While every now and then a tragedy does occur, the likelihood of being harmed by another person on the trail is far less likely than other places. I am more likely to face injury driving my car to work. I am more likely to be attacked by another person in a city than on a trail in the woods. That being said, I understand that not everyone's views are the same, so while I'll defend my stance, I'll also share opinions from people who do carry a gun on the trail, and hikers who have carried a gun and decided to stop.

Had I wanted to carry a gun on a long-distance trail, I would need to do extensive research. Gun laws vary state-to-state, and for trails like the Appalachian Trail, which spans 14 states, the Pacific Crest Trail, which covers three states, or the Continental Divide Trail, which goes through five states, the hiker would need to learn each state's specific laws on how the gun has to be carried, how it has to be concealed, if it can be loaded or not, and other requirements that go into carrying responsibly. Does your hiker have experience holding, shooting, and caring for a weapon? While anyone can theoretically pick up a gun and pull the trigger, it takes some training to operate a firearm safely and accurately.

The last gun I fired was a Red Ryder BB gun that my brother and I would shoot at a water jug on the back deck when I was young. The goal was to hit the "O" in "Poland Spring," but I rarely hit the jug. For me to bring a gun on the trail, I'd want to practice firing accurately, otherwise I'd potentially provide a weapon to my attacker. I'd also be concerned about how I'd respond in a high-stress, adrenaline-filled situation, given that operating a gun is not second-nature to me. I'd be worried about fumbling, doing something wrong under pressure, and risking an accident to myself or another hiker in the process. And to be honest, in a dangerous situation, I think I'd freeze up before pulling the trigger.

"ABSOLUTELY NOT. I AM 100 % ANTI HAVING A GUN ON THE TRAIL. I THINK IT CAUSES MORE POTENTIAL DANGER THAN IT DOES SAFETY, ESPECIALLY WITH SOMEONE LIKE ME WHO MIGHT PANIC AND NOT REMEMBER HOW TO USE IT PROPERLY. THE AMOUNT OF ACCIDENTS THAT COULD HAPPEN WITH A GUN MAKE IT TOO RISKY FOR ME. AS FAR AS ANIMALS, MOST GUNS YOU'D CARRY WOULDN'T EVEN BE POWERFUL ENOUGH TO TAKE DOWN A BEAR OR SOMETHING. I'M JUST PRETTY MUCH AGAINST IT ALL TOGETHER." - NIKKI, 40, WISCONSIN

For states that do not allow concealed-carry in a holster, having a gun seems useless. The common argument against carrying a gun on the trail is that if it's stored inside of the hiker's backpack, it's not quickly accessible when needed. This also applies to states that don't allow the weapon to be loaded. If someone wants to attack me, I can't call a time-out to load my weapon. In talking to hikers who conceal-carry in everyday life, I asked if in those states they would consider sending the gun home and learned that even that seems like a hassle. A gun cannot be mailed from the post office, but must be sent from a gun shop or a location with a Federal Firearms License (FFL).

Furthermore, on wetter trails, moisture-management can be an issue. I spoke with a hiker who conceal-carries on a day-to-day basis. He explained that the gun he brings hiking is one of the lightest on the market, but also metal-based. He spoke about how on a trail like the Appalachian Trail, he would have to carry a cleaning kit and perform regular maintenance to avoid degradation and rust. This adds a time-consuming task when free time is already limited.

As for wildlife, all of the concealed-carriers I spoke to pointed out that the weapon they'd take on the trail wouldn't be a high enough caliber to protect against an animal attack. If anything, it would just make the animal angry. Animal attacks on long-distance trails are incredibly rare. Most hikers will view a bear-sighting on the AT or

PCT as a special moment, while hikers on the CDT carry bear spray that is more effective in a grizzly encounter than a gun. On top of everything, carrying a gun means carrying more weight and we've already established that an over-loaded hiker faces a higher chance of injury. The number one reason that hikers—gun enthusiasts and those with anti-gun beliefs alike—choose to forgo carrying a gun is that it just isn't worth the weight.

But I'm still worried about my hiker's safety. Just because something bad doesn't happen often, doesn't mean it can't happen to my hiker.

I understand. It is perfectly reasonable to worry about the safety of a loved one embarking on an adventure that is new to you both. As I mentioned earlier, it's hard to understand the culture of a long-distance trail if you have not spent time on one yourself. The unknown causes fear, and we naturally want to combat that fear by making sure our loved ones are as prepared as possible. A gun may or may not be a part of your hiker's safety plan. Ultimately the hiker has to decide. Ideally that decision will follow reflection on personal experience with guns, research on laws in each state of the selected trail, and considerations on weight.

If your hiker is not already a concealed-carrier, has rarely held a gun, or has never held a gun, think about if this is the most sensible option, and try to understand the reasoning if your hiker is against it. I carry pepper spray in my fanny pack on all of my long-distance hikes instead. I have never had to use it, but for me it seems like enough to buy time to get away from a situation if I need to. I also carry a knife, which primarily ends up being used to spread peanut butter on bread. But again, it helps me sleep at night and doesn't weigh much.

One effective way your hiker can take personal responsibility for his or her safety is by taking self-defense courses. Learning situational awareness and self defense could be more useful than fumbling for a weapon that the hiker doesn't have experience with. Gifting a course to your hiker—or, even better, taking it together—is one way to ease your mind regarding safety while simultaneously showing support for the hiker.

If you are still interested in more opinions on this topic, countless articles have been written online by people on both sides of the topic. Google will have no shortage of drama and debate.

"I INITIALLY CARRIED A FIREARM BECAUSE OF THE IDEA OF TAKING PERSONAL RESPONSIBILITY FOR MY SAFETY. 90 % OF THE TIME I CARRY ONE ANYWAYS. THAT WAS THE MENTALITY. I CARRY THIS ANYWAY. I'LL CARRY IT ON THE TRAIL, AND I'LL BE ABLE TO ESCAPE A SITUATION IF I NEED TO. I KNOW IT'S RARE. I WAS AWARE OF THAT GOING INTO IT. I'VE OPEN-CARRIED ON TRAILS BEFORE. NO ONE HAS LOST THEIR MIND OVER IT. IF SOMEONE FEELS UNCOMFORTABLE AND I'M NOT ABLE TO BREAK THE ICE I TRY TO GIVE THEM SPACE.
THE PRIMARY DECISION WHEN I DON'T CARRY IS THAT THE TWO TIMES I HAVE CARRIED OVER LONG-DISTANCES INCLUDED INCLEMENT WEATHER. MY WEAPON IS ONE OF THE LIGHTEST YOU CAN CARRY. IT ISN'T A POLYMER-BASED FRAME, IT'S METAL-BASED, AND IT DOESN'T HOLD UP WELL TO MOISTURE. I'D HAVE TO CARRY A CLEANING KIT AND DO MAINTENANCE OR THINGS WOULD START TO RUST. WHEN PEOPLE TALK ABOUT GUNS ON THE TRAIL, THEY TALK ABOUT HOW IF YOU HAVE TO DIG THROUGH YOUR PACK TO GET TO IT, YOU WON'T GET TO IT IN TIME. ANYTHING MORE ACCESSIBLE USUALLY MEANS THERE'S A MOISTURE ISSUE. TO CARRY IT WITHOUT A MOISTURE ISSUE, YOU'D PROBABLY HAVE TO USE A DYNEEMA FANNY PACK THAT YOU COULD UNZIP AND IMMEDIATELY HAVE ACCESS TO. THERE'D PROBABLY BE SOME HOLSTER MODIFICATION TO CARRY IT 100 % SAFELY. THAT'S IN THE REALM OF CUSTOM WORK... IT COMES DOWN TO PERSONAL CHOICE. THERE ARE GOOD RESOURCES ABOUT THE LAWS STATE-TO-STATE, BUT I'VE ALREADY MADE THE DECISION THAT I'M NOT GOING TO BE SHIPPING A GUN BACK AND FORTH. THAT'S MORE OF A BARRIER THAN IS WORTH IT TO ME. I THINK SITUATIONAL AWARENESS IS THE NUMBER ONE THING A HIKER CAN HAVE. ESPECIALLY WHEN TALKING ABOUT THE HUMAN ELEMENT. I THINK IF PEOPLE COULD HAVE SITUATIONAL AWARENESS AND EVEN A LITTLE BIT OF TRAINING, THAT'S PROBABLY MORE OF A LIFE-SAVER."
- JOSH, 35, FLORIDA"

I'M A SECOND AMENDMENT SUPPORTER, BUT I HAVE MIXED
EMOTIONS BECAUSE THE LAWS ARE DIFFERENT IN EVERY STATE.
YOU HAVE TO KNOW THEM IN EVERY STATE THAT YOU'RE GOING
THROUGH. THAT BEING SAID, I PROBABLY WILL CARRY A GUN
ALONG THE WAY. I'M LICENSED TO CARRY IN FLORIDA, AND
FLORIDA HAS RECIPROCITY WITH A NUMBER OF STATES, SO I
HAVE TO RESEARCH IF ANY OF THOSE WILL COINCIDE WITH
THE ONES I'M GOING THROUGH. THERE STILL MIGHT BE QUIRKS
RESPECTIVE TO THAT STATE'S LAWS WITH WHERE YOU HAVE TO
CARRY AND WHETHER IT CAN BE LOADED OR NOT. I DON'T KNOW
SPECIFICALLY, BUT SOME OF THE NUANCES MIGHT BE HAVING
THE CHAMBER EMPTY AND THE MAGAZINE OUT OF THE GUN. I
WOULD PREFERABLY CARRY ON A CHEST HOLDER, LOADED, BUT
COMPLETELY CONCEALED. I USE A SMALL CALIBER 380 SEMI-
AUTOMATIC HAND GUN THAT WEIGHS A POUND AT LEAST. I
HAVE NO CONCERNS WITH THE SAFETY ISSUE, I'VE BEEN AROUND
GUNS MY WHOLE LIFE AND IT CAN'T MISFIRE IF THE SAFETY
IS ON AND THERE ISN'T A ROUND IN THE CHAMBER. LEGAL GUN
HOLDING ISN'T SOMETHING WE BOAST ABOUT. WE DO IT FOR
OUR OWN PROTECTION OR FOR THE PROTECTION OF OUR LOVED
ONES. WE HAVE IT JUST IN CASE, LIKE AN INSURANCE POLICY.
I SUSPECT MORE PEOPLE CARRY THAN WE THINK, THEY JUST
DON'T BROADCAST IT. IT'S HARD FOR ME TO BELIEVE, BUT I
KNOW PEOPLE WHO HAVE NEVER EVEN HELD A GUN IN THEIR
HANDS BEFORE. I IMAGINE IT MIGHT BRING NERVOUSNESS TO
SOME PEOPLE, AND THAT'S NOT SOMETHING THAT I WANT, SO
I WOULDN'T FLAUNT IT... IT ONLY TAKES A FEW SECONDS FOR
SOMETHING OR SOMEONE TO BE ON TOP OF YOU, SO NOT HAVING
IT DIRECTLY ON YOU WOULD NEGATE THE PURPOSE. OBVIOUSLY, I
HOPEFULLY NEVER HAVE TO USE IT. I DON'T EXPECT TO HAVE TO
USE IT." - JOHN, 58, FLORIDA

"MY HUSBAND ALWAYS CARRIES A KNIFE OF SOME SORT, BUT HE
CHOSE TO STOP CARRYING HIS FIREARM FOR COMFORT REASONS
AND WEAPON INTEGRITY, BECAUSE SOMETIMES HE HIKES THROUGH
WATERWAYS AND IT DOES NO GOOD TO HAVE A FIREARM ON YOU
IF IT'S WET. HE ALSO DIDN'T WANT THE EXTRA WEIGHT, SO HE
CHOSE TO ONLY CARRY A KNIFE." - TABATHA, 34, FLORIDA

'MY DAUGHTER IS LICENSED TO CARRY, BUT IT'S TOO HEAVY.
I DON'T KNOW IF IT'S A GREAT IDEA, BECAUSE IF YOU NEED
IT, YOU NEED TO GET TO IT FAST, AND IT MIGHT NOT BE THAT
READILY AVAILABLE. SHE DID CARRY PEPPER SPRAY.'
- DON, 64, MASSACHUSETTS

'MY STEP-DAD IS A POLICEMAN AND WE'RE FROM THE MIDWEST
WHERE PEOPLE THINK THAT WEAPONS ARE THE ANSWER.
THERE WAS A LOT OF TALK ABOUT HOW I WASN'T GOING TO
CARRY A WEAPON. THEY DEFINITELY HAD CONCERNS. I DON'T
KNOW ANYTHING ABOUT HAVING A GUN, SHOOTING A GUN, OR
ANYTHING LIKE THAT, SO I FEEL LIKE THAT WOULD BE A RISK
THAT I WOULD TAKE TO EVEN JUST BE RESPONSIBLE FOR A
GUN.' - KATIE, 25, COLORADO

'GUN ISSUES ARE LESS DOMINANT IN CANADA. FROM A
CANADIAN PERSPECTIVE, ON CANADIAN TERRITORY, I WOULD
SAY ABSOLUTELY, 100 % NO WAY. FROM A CANADIAN ON
AMERICAN TERRITORY, I WOULD SAY ABSOLUTELY, 99 % NO WAY.
I'M SAVING 1 % AS A VARIABLE FOR THINGS I MAY NOT KNOW.
THE FACT OF THE MATTER IS THAT RESEARCH HAS DICTATED
AND SHOWN THAT IF YOU'RE CARRYING A GUN, YOU'RE MORE
LIKELY TO GET HURT THAN IF YOU'RE NOT. I DON'T THINK
IT'S ANY QUESTION THAT IT'S BETTER NOT TO HAVE ONE
ON THE TRAIL. THE TWO MOST DANGEROUS ANIMALS IN THE
BACKWOODS ARE HUMANS AND DOGS. PEOPLE TALK ABOUT BEARS
AND COUGARS, BUT MORE PEOPLE ARE HURT BY HUMANS AND
DOGS THAN ANY OTHER ANIMALS OUT THERE. STATISTICALLY
SPEAKING, THE LIKELIHOOD OF A HUMAN INJURING YOU ON THE
TRAIL IS WAY LESS THAN IN A CITY AND ALMOST ANY OTHER
PART OF THE COUNTRY. UNFORTUNATELY, PEOPLE DON'T RESPOND
TO NUMBERS, THEY RESPOND TO FEELINGS, AND THAT'S ONE OF
THE DANGEROUS ISSUES IN OUR SOCIETIES. ODDS ARE YOU'RE
MORE LIKELY TO GET HURT WITH A GUN THAN WITHOUT IT,
AND ODDS ARE THAT YOU'RE SAFER ON THE TRAIL THAN PRETTY
MUCH ANYWHERE ELSE. THOSE TWO ADDED TOGETHER? IT'S A NO-
BRAINER TO ME.'
- BRUCE, RETIRED POLICE OFFICER, 60, ONTARIO

A NOTE ON CARRYING PROTECTION FROM THE ATC

"IN GENERAL, APPALACHIAN TRAIL CONSERVANCY DISCOURAGES
THE CARRYING OF FIREARMS ON THE TRAIL FOR THE REASONS
NOTED BELOW. ON FEDERAL LANDS ADMINISTERED BY THE
NATIONAL PARK SERVICE (NPS) AND THE U.S. FOREST SERVICE
(USFS), POSSESSION OF A FIREARM MUST BE IN COMPLIANCE
WITH THE LAW OF THE STATE IN WHICH THE FEDERAL LAND IS
LOCATED. MANY HIKERS FEEL THE CARRYING OF FIREARMS IS
UNNECESSARY AND CONTRARY TO THE SOCIAL NATURE OF THE
TRAIL. FIREARMS CAN BE TURNED AGAINST YOU OR RESULT IN
AN ACCIDENTAL SHOOTING AND ARE EXTRA WEIGHT. IF YOU
PLAN TO CARRY, BE SURE TO ACQUIRE TRAINING BEFOREHAND
AND MENTALLY PREPARE YOURSELF FOR USING THE FIREARM.
BECAUSE LAWS RELATED TO CARRY AND CONCEALED CARRY VARY
BY STATE AND LAND UNIT, IT'S BEST TO CONTACT THE FOREST,
PARK, OR STATE LAND UNIT THROUGH WHICH YOU'LL BE PASSING
TO ENSURE THAT YOU ARE AWARE OF THE RELEVANT LAWS AND
HAVE ACQUIRED ANY NECESSARY PERMITS. FIREARMS ARE NOT
PERMITTED IN NPS BUILDINGS, INCLUDING VISITOR CENTERS."[45]

WILDLIFE ENCOUNTERS

If wildlife is treated respectfully and responsibly, your hiker can look back on encounters fondly. Dangerous situations can usually be avoided through attentiveness and proper food storage. In the desert where rattlesnakes are common and brush obstructs the ground, is the hiker wearing headphones or listening to the surroundings? If there is a bear box at the shelter are hikers putting their food bags inside or keeping food in their tents at night?

Wildlife are afraid of hikers, not on a mission to attack. Snakes don't launch the moment they see someone approaching, bears prefer berries to human flesh, and moose just want to be left alone. Seeing a grizzly bear or mountain lion can be scary enough to leave a puddle at your hiker's feet, but when prepared and knowledgeable about how to react, the result will likely be an incredible story.

It's easy to fear for your hiker's safety when it comes to unfamiliar wildlife. If you don't know what to do when you see a bear, how do you know your hiker will? Let's arm you with knowledge about the common animals that a hiker could encounter, along with the National Park Service's recommendations for how to react to each.

The sixth Leave No Trace principle is to respect wildlife and keep your distance. Giving the right amount of space will allow the animal an exit from the encounter and help it remain comfortable with your hiker's presence. The National Park Service asks that we give 75 ft of space to most wildlife, like deer, elk, and bighorn sheep.[46] For reference, that's roughly the length of two school buses. With black bears, moose, and mountain lions, they extend that distance to 120 ft to 150 ft, or four school buses.[47]

Hikers don't always have a say in how much distance is between them and wildlife. When hiking the A.T., I encountered a bear who appeared from behind a tree fewer than 50 ft away. Knowing the right way to respond helped avoid conflict. In *Worried?: Science Investigates Some of Life's Common Concerns,* Chudler and Johnson explain, "Meeting a bear in the wild can be a harrowing experience for the human and likely for the bear. Humans are not part of the

standard bear diet, so there should be no concern about being hunted
down by one of these large animals. However, people do not always
dispose of and secure their food properly. Therefore, bears can
acquire a fondness for human food and lose their fear of people,
increasing the likelihood of bear-human interactions... Even if you
take precautions to avoid a bear, you may still find yourself sharing
a campsite or hiking trail with one. Nevertheless, the likelihood of
being killed or attacked by a bear is very low."[48]

Between 1900 and 2009, only 63 people were killed by non captive
black bears in North America. "Of those 63 deaths, 49 occurred in
Canada and Alaska... In addition, only eight people were killed by
grizzly bears in Yellowstone National Park in 145 years (1872 to
2015). Interestingly, during this time period, six people were killed
by falling trees, and five people were killed after they were struck
by lightning... The rarity of deaths caused by bear attacks is put
into perspective when the number of deaths caused by other animals
is revealed. Between 1999 and 2007 in the United States, hornets,
bees, and wasps were responsible for 509 deaths, and dogs were
responsible for 250 deaths."[49] Despite the facts, people never seem
ask, "but what if you see a dog on the trail?" We are accustomed to
fearing animals like bears, so that is what we cling to.

"I SAW A LOT OF DEER, ONE COYOTE, AND THREE BEARS. THAT
WAS THE FIRST BEAR I EVER SAW IN THE WILD. I WAS ALONE
AT THE TIME. I HAD JUST EATEN A POWER BAR AND STILL
HAD THE WRAPPER IN MY HAND. I STOPPED AND PUT MY HANDS
UP, WAVED MY TREKKING POLES, AND STARTED HITTING THEM
TOGETHER. HE SAW ME AND RAN OFF. WITH THE SECOND BEAR, I
WALKED UP TO A CAMPGROUND AND HE WAS SITTING WHERE WE
PLANNED ON SETTING UP TENTS. WE HAD BEEN MAKING NOISE,
SO HE RAN AWAY. THE THIRD WAS HANGING OUT IN THE BUSHES
BY THE TRAIL. HE RAN PAST ME TO GET AWAY. I HAD NO BAD
ENCOUNTERS WITH ANY ANIMALS." - EMILIO, 29, TEXAS

BLACK BEARS

When encountering a black bear, a hiker should make friendly noises to avoid startling it. Hikers need to be aware of their surroundings to make sure they haven't accidentally come between a mother and her cubs. If a hiker encounters a black  bear from too close a distance, the bear may make loud noises, swat the ground, or bluff charge in an effort to get more space. Hikers should increase their distance by backing up slowly while facing the bear. They should not run or play dead. Allowing the bear to have clear exits will keep it from becoming aggressive. If a bear approaches hikers, they should make themselves appear large by waving their arms or trekking poles in the air, they should shout at the bear, and they should try changing direction as they back away. If the bear is clearly after the hiker's food, the National Park Service recommends separating from the food and continuing to slowly back away.[50] Should the bear attack, which again, is incredibly rare, the hiker should fight back aggressively.

A NOTE ON BLACK BEARS

DID YOU KNOW THAT EVEN THOUGH BEARS ARE BROWN, IT DOES NOT MEAN THEY ARE "BROWN BEARS?" WHILE BEARS IN STATES LIKE CALIFORNIA AND COLORADO ARE OFTEN BROWN IN COLOR, THEY ARE TECHNICALLY BLACK BEARS. "BROWN BEARS" REFER TO GRIZZLY BEARS, ALASKIAN PENINSULA BROWN BEARS, KODIAK BEARS, AND OTHERS FOUND IN AREAS LIKE CANADA, RUSSIA, CENTRAL ASIA, AND SMALL PARTS OF THE UNITED STATES. BLACK BEARS CAN ACTUALLY RANGE IN COLOR FROM BLACK, BROWN, CINNAMON, BLONDE, BLUE-GRAY, OR WHITE.

BROWN BEARS

Many brown bear areas will recommend that hikers carry a can of bear spray in the event of an unfriendly encounter. National Parks even rent cans. When hikers are traveling through an area that recommends bear spray, they
should carry it. Brown bears can be more aggressive than black bears, and the recommendations for a brown bear encounter are slightly different.

If hikers encounters a brown bear, they should make themselves appear large by waving their arms or trekking poles in the air, calmly announce their presence, and move away slowly. The National Park Service suggests moving sideways as this movement is non-threatening to bears.[51] Hikers in brown bear territory should have a can of bear-spray readily available. If a bear decides to charge, they can spray the bear when it is 30 ft to 60 ft away to put a cloud between them.[52] Should a hiker be attacked, the response is different than for that of a black bear. Instead of fighting back, which could increase the intensity of the attack, the National Park Service recommends that the hiker initially play dead. To do this, I would lay on my stomach with my pack covering my back, place my hands behind my neck, and spread out my legs to prevent the bear from flipping me over. A hiker should remain in this position until the bear has left the area. If a hiker uses bear spray, the likelihood of a bear persisting to the point of an attack is rare.

"THROUGH WYOMING AND MONTANA WE'RE DEFINITELY CARRYING BEAR SPRAY. THERE ARE FOUR OF US AND EACH OF US HAS OUR OWN, WHICH IS SUPER IMPORTANT IN CASE WE GET SEPARATED. I WOULD SAY 100 % CARRY IT. IT WILL GIVE YOU PEACE OF MIND. NATIONAL PARKS LIKE GLACIER AND YELLOWSTONE RECOMMEND IT. WE AREN'T WEARING BEAR BELLS OR ANYTHING LIKE THAT, BUT THE BEAR SPRAY IS 100 %."
- KATRINA, 37, ILLINOIS

MOUNTAIN LIONS

Mountain lion sightings are
rare, but not unheard of. The thing
to know about encountering a
mountain lion is that it's important
to give them space, convince
them that you're not prey, and let
them know that you're potentially
dangerous.[53] The National Park Service suggests that most mountain
lions avoid confrontation and that it's more likely that a hiker will
be struck by lightning than to be attacked by a mountain lion.[54]
Should hikers encounter a mountain lion, they should allow a way
for the lion to exit the scenario. Hikers should not run. They should
remain calm, face the animal, make themselves appear larger, and
if necessary, shout and throw objects. Running has the potential to
trigger the instinct to chase, and crouching or bending over could
accidentally make hikers appear like four-legged prey.

There are precautions your hiker can take to avoid encounters.
Mountain lions are most active at dawn and dusk, so hiking during
those hours can be avoided when in an area that is known to have
mountain lions. Wearing brightly colored clothing can keep a
mountain lion from mistaking a hiker for a deer or other prey, and
hiking with others easily makes hikers less desirable targets.

If a mountain lion does attack, hikers should fight back with
anything they can find. People have fended off attacks with sticks,
rocks, and even jackets.

"THERE'S LESS WILDLIFE THAN I EXPECTED. I SAW ONE
RATTLESNAKE AND A COUPLE OF DEER. I WORRIED THE MOST
ABOUT MOUNTAIN LIONS, BUT I NEVER SAW ANY EVIDENCE OF
THEM, TRACKS OR ANYTHING." - NIKKI, 40, WISCONSIN

MOOSE

In Bill Bryson's, *A Walk in the Woods*, he gives a quote on his experience with a moose on the Appalachian Trail, saying, "Hunters will tell you that a moose is a wily and ferocious forest creature. In fact, a moose is a cow drawn by a three-year-old."[55] While Bryson is unarguably a very talented writer, he does a disservice to the reader by painting moose as friendly dummies and discrediting those who describe them aggressively. In actuality, moose can be dangerous. The National Park Service even claim that moose injure more people each year than bears.[56]

Moose are often harder to spot in the wild since they stand very still and blend in to forested areas. Because of this, getting closer than 150 ft before noticing a moose isn't unheard of. The moose I saw on the Colorado Trail and the Appalachian Trail were both closer than that by the time I saw them. The good thing is that it's not too difficult to convince a moose that you aren't a threat.

The National Park Service recommends that if the moose hasn't seen you yet, keep it that way, but if it has, talk softly and back away. If the moose looks like it will charge, the hiker should get behind a tree. The key difference with moose and the other potentially dangerous animals is that it's okay to run from a moose, and they usually won't pursue a runner. If attacked by a moose, the hiker should curl in a ball, protect his or her head, and remain still until the moose moves on. Fighting back in this unlikely scenario will encourage the idea that the hiker is still a threat, and the moose won't back down.

RATTLESNAKES

On the Pacific Crest Trail, I
traveled 650 mi (1,046.1 km)
through the desert without seeing
a rattlesnake. I kept headphones in
when I hiked and was convinced
that they were seeing me, but that I
wasn't seeing or hearing them. I needed to listen to music sometimes
to stay sane, and using a speaker on the trail is one of the easiest
ways to ostracize yourself as *that jerk*. One day while my music was
playing, I heard the loudest rattling over my headphones. I jumped,
ran, and turned to see that a rattlesnake had been laying under the
brush and was now coiled up, shaking its tail at me in annoyance.
Luckily, they don't immediately strike. Usually, they coil and give
warning with their rattle to let you know you're way too close.

According to the National Park Service, 30 % of adult rattlesnake
bites don't inject any venom.[57] However, the best way to avoid
venom roulette is for a hiker to be aware of surroundings, not hike
with headphones, and move away if a snake is spotted. Awareness
is probably the most important, since not all rattlesnakes will rattle.
When bitten by a rattlesnake, best practice is to immobilize the
area, wash it gently, and keep it lower than heart level. Avoiding
movement of the bitten area will slow the spread of venom. The NPS
doesn't recommend using a constricting band because it can cause
more harm. Every year in the United States, 7,000 to 8,000 people
are bitten by venomous snakes, however only five die as a result.[58]
The chance of dieing from a venomous snake in the U.S. is less than
15 in a billion. That is comparable to 15 seconds out of 31 years.

"I SAW A LOT OF RATTLESNAKES. ONE WAS CURLED UP IN A
BUSH BY THE TRAIL I HAD HEADPHONES IN, BUT IT RATTLED
SO LOUD THAT I COULD HEAR IT OVER THE MUSIC IN MY
HEADPHONES, AND I JUMPED AND RAN UP-TRAIL. THAT WAS THE
CLOSEST I GOT TO WILDLIFE." - EMILIO, 29, TEXAS

VENOMOUS VS. POISONOUS

WHEN TALKING ABOUT SNAKES LIKE RATTLESNAKES AND
COPPERHEADS, KNOW THE DIFFERENCE BETWEEN VENOMOUS AND
POISONOUS. THESE SNAKES ARE VENOMOUS, NOT POISONOUS.

VENOMOUS: TOXINS ARE INJECTED THROUGH BITES OR STINGS

POISONOUS: TOXINS ARE RELEASED WHEN INGESTED OR EATEN

"THERE ARE A LOT OF SNAKES, BUT YOU HAVE TO UNDERSTAND
NATURE. THEY'RE MORE AFRAID OF YOU THAN YOU ARE OF THEM.
ONCE YOU GET OVER THAT, KEEP YOUR EYES OUT ON THE TRAIL.
YOU JUST HAVE TO BE AWARE. I THINK FOR AS MANY PEOPLE
THAT ARE OUT THERE HIKING, YOU DON'T HEAR TRAGEDIES
HAPPENING FROM PEOPLE GETTING BIT BY SNAKES OR ATTACKED
BY ANIMALS. I THINK IT'S MORE FEAR THAN REALITY."
- JIM, 58, TRAIL ANGEL IN SOUTHERN CALIFORNIA

HITCH-HIKING

The safety of hitch-hiking near trails is almost always a tough sell for the loved ones of hikers. Hitch-hiking is often the most convenient way to access towns along trails, as hikers aren't usually willing to add on what can be a full day of road-walking each way. Sometimes roads to town don't have water sources. Others are major highways that may be unsafe to walk along. Public transportation to and from road crossings is rare and inconvenient, so often times the choice is to find a hitch or walk. It is a tougher topic to convince a loved one to be okay with. My mom hates the idea of me hitch-hiking, and the one time I chose to hitch alone, I definitely didn't tell her about it. (Sorry, Mom.)

But that's just it, I only chose to hitch-hike alone one time out of probably over 100 hitches, and that was a choice that I consciously made. I could have easily waited to hitch with another hiker, but I was in a rush that day and just didn't feel like it. When I'm hiking with my trail friends, even if we are walking separately, we usually decide when we want to get to town and will leave camp in the morning at times that will help us reach the road with a buddy. If there are several of us, we may hitch in pairs or threes to try to make it easier to get a ride, but we almost always wait for the last person in our group to make sure that no one ends up alone. One safety-conscious tip to share with your hiker is to take a photo of the license plate before getting into a vehicle.

"ONE THING THAT MY FAMILY AND OTHERS NEED TO REALIZE IS THAT THIS IS MY DREAM. THIS IS WHAT I THINK ABOUT ALL DAY LONG. THIS IS WHAT EXCITES ME. THIS IS WHAT MAKES ME HAPPY. THIS IS A GOAL OF MINE. IT'S OKAY FOR YOUR FAMILY TO BE SCARED AND HAVE CONCERNS, BUT IT'S STILL YOUR GOAL AND YOUR HAPPINESS, AND THEY NEED TO UNDERSTAND THAT AND NOT CAST THEIR FEARS ON YOU." - JACKIE, 26, GEORGIA

'THE PCT WAS THE FIRST TIME I'VE EVER EXPERIENCED HITCH-
HIKING. BEFORE I DID IT, I ASSUMED SOMEONE WOULD KIDNAP
AND MURDER ME, BUT THEN I ACTUALLY GOT RIDES AND STARTED
TALKING TO THE PEOPLE DRIVING. A LOT OF THEM LIVE NEAR
THE TRAIL AND SEE HIKERS ALL THE TIME AND JUST WANT TO
HELP OUT. THE FIRST HITCH-HIKE I GOT, I WAS VERY NERVOUS.
I EVEN HAD MY KNIFE IN MY POCKET. THE GUY WHO PICKED US
UP TOLD US THAT HE HAD REALLY WANTED TO DO THE PCT, BUT
HASN'T BEEN ABLE TO FIND THE TIME. IT PUT ME SO MUCH MORE
AT EASE TO SEE THAT HE WAS JUST LIKE ME. I'VE EVEN BEEN
PICKED UP BY A FAMILY. A HUSBAND, WIFE, AND TWO TODDLERS
IN CAR SEATS. THE MOTHER WAS TELLING THE TODDLERS
THAT THEY SHOULD TRY TO BE LIKE US AND EXPERIENCE LIFE
AND USED US AS ROLE MODELS. I THOUGHT THAT WAS SO
INTERESTING. THERE'S WAY MORE GOOD STORIES THAN BAD
STORIES OUT THERE FOR HITCH-HIKING.' - EMILIO, 29, TEXAS

In the beginning I was nervous about hitch-hiking. Hollywood portrays it as the fast-track to a body bag, but the people who have stopped to pick me up from trailheads were almost always locals who knew the trail ran through their area and liked to help hikers. In Northern California, I accepted a hitch from an older lady on her way back from church. It wasn't until she slipped into conversation that she never leaves home without her gun, that I realized she might have been more afraid of us than we were of her.

Hitch-hiking requires trust on both sides. Hikers can be hesitant about taking rides from a stranger, but there were also times that I stood in the pouring rain with the sun setting, desperate to get to town, and perfectly fitting the stereotype of a crazed hitch-hiker. Who would want to give me a ride? But people do—often because they are familiar with the trail in their local area and help hikers season after season.

Keep in mind nothing is forcing a hiker to accept a ride. I have been hitch-hiking before with another hiker and been told by a driver that there was only room in the car for one of us. We politely said we'd prefer to stay together, and he wished us well and drove off. If a driver stops and your hiker is uncomfortable accepting the ride, there

102   SECTION THREE: SAFETY

is always the option to decline without making it awkward.

"We're waiting on our [imaginary] friend who's a bit further behind than we expected when we put our thumbs out, sorry."
"Is this [wrong road]? Ah, shoot. I don't think this is where I need a ride then. Thanks anyway."
"Oh no, I just realized I left my [piece of gear] back at the last stream. I've got to go get it!"

"WHEN MY BOYFRIEND SPOKE ABOUT HOW MUCH HE HITCH-HIKED IT MADE ME A BIT ANXIOUS. I'D NEVER FEEL COMFORTABLE HITCH-HIKING AND IT DID MAKE ME KIND OF ANXIOUS THAT HE WAS DOING THOSE THINGS." - EMILY, 21, KENTUCKY

Hitch-hiking can introduce hikers to amazing people. When I reached Carlisle, Pennsylvania, it started to rain and Easy and I decided to head into town to wait out the weather. Don, a man in a topless Jeep Wrangler, stopped and told us that he lived around the corner and would need to switch cars before taking us to town. He didn't raise any concerns, so we agreed and got in. At his house, we met his wife, Kim, who told us they were having the family over to celebrate the life of her father-in-law who had just passed away. We were given mason jars of ice water and chairs to sit in, and only moments after we arrived, they offered to let us stay until the rain stopped. That afternoon, we learned how to play pickle-ball in the garage with Don and Pop, Kim's dad. We told them stories about our trip and heard about their lives in Carlisle. When the rain stopped, they offered to let us stay for the family barbecue, but we insisted that we still had a few more miles to get through before the sun went down, so they returned us to the trail and gave us their address to send a postcard to once we finished.

This is just one story, but I have many stories about the generosity of strangers met through hitch-hiking, as does almost every long-distance hiker. Yes, there is risk inherently involved with hitch-hiking, but by listening to instinct most hikers remain safe hitch-hiking near the trail.

If you live near a long-distance trail, try stopping by a popular road that intersects the trail to give hikers a ride to town. Tell them you have a loved one who will be hiking, or is hiking, and ask about their experiences with hitch-hiking on the trail. I have accepted many rides from family members of hikers who are paying forward the kindness their loved one received. In North Carolina, a woman was waiting at a trailhead because her husband was hiking through the area during the next few days. She drove us to the grocery store to resupply, waited while we shopped so that she could drive us back to the trail afterwards, and even treated us to Wendy's! The kindness from strangers in the communities around the trail is greater than I expected, which helped alleviate many fears.

"I DIDN'T WANT HER TO DO IT. I DIDN'T WANT HER OUT IN THE WILDERNESS FOR FIVE MONTHS. I DID NOT WANT HER TO. BUT I KNEW IT WAS A DREAM THAT SHE HAD AND I WANTED TO BE SUPPORTIVE OF HER. I NEVER WANTED TO BE THE REASON THAT SHE DIDN'T FOLLOW THROUGH WITH A DREAM. I CERTAINLY DON'T WANT TO BE THE THING THAT STANDS IN THE WAY. I THINK THAT THE PARENTS, FAMILY, WHOEVER, NEED TO BE SUPPORTIVE OF THEIR GOALS AND THEIR AMBITIONS."
- CYNTHI, 55, INDIANA

ENVIRONMENTAL HAZARDS

Weather can be unpredictable and unforgiving. From heavy snowpack and river crossings, to forest fires and extreme heat, there are plenty of weather-related issues that can be cause for concern. Being prepared will be your hiker's best defense. Research and prep-work can ensure a safe and enjoyable experience.

In this section, we'll explore different environmental hazards that could be experienced on long-distance trails, along with how your hiker can prepare and gain experience. On some trails, all of these conditions could be encountered. On others, none will. Snowpack isn't a concern on the Florida Trail. Not all trails have river crossings. Talk to your hiker about which hazards and terrain are relevant, and how they plan to prepare.

"THERE WERE TIMES ON THE TRAIL WHERE I FELT LIKE I COULD DIE, ESPECIALLY GOING THROUGH THE SIERRA NEVADA IN A HEAVY SNOW YEAR. THAT WHOLE AREA WAS DEFINITELY A DANGEROUS SITUATION. BUT AT THE SAME TIME, I FELT LIKE I WAS IN CONTROL. I'VE HAD EXPERIENCE IN SNOW TRAVEL, AND I FELT AWARE OF THE POTENTIAL DANGER. THERE WERE VERY FEW SITUATIONS WHEN I CAME OUT OF IT SURPRISED THAT IT WAS DANGEROUS. MOST OF THE TIME I WAS FULLY AWARE OF WHAT I WAS ABOUT TO GET MYSELF INTO." - JUSTIN, 40, TEXAS

SNOW

Hikers will face more intense snow conditions early in the season than those traveling in the middle of summer. Hikers should have the correct tools and honestly assess their skill levels against the skills that are needed before entering dangerous conditions. Justin's quote can be discomforting, but the important take-away is that he was knowledgeable of the dangers he might face, he had the proper experience, and most importantly, he was not caught unaware in a dangerous situation since he was aware and well-prepared.

When I reached the Sierra Nevada Mountains on the Pacific Crest Trail after a winter of record-breaking snow, I had to give myself a reality check on upcoming conditions. Until that point, I had never considered the idea of flipping north or skipping miles. Other people were doing it, but not me. I'd go straight through. The first 50 mi (80.5 km) of the Sierra Nevada from Kennedy Meadows to Lone Pine are mild, breaking 10,000 ft for the first time on a northbound hike. I was comfortable with the snow I expected in those 50 mi.

In Lone Pine, I talked to friends who attempted to enter the next stretch and turned back, others who had made it through to the next town and hitched back to pick up mail, outfitter employees who were knowledgeable of their area's conditions, and checked online resources for what to expect on the next leg. Our goal had been to reach the Sierra Nevada Mountains late enough that the avalanches and new snow stopped, but early enough that we could take advantage of snow bridges[1] before they melted and became unsafe. The information we received from hikers ahead revealed that the avalanches were still occurring, and they described the river levels as much higher than I had anticipated. What was up to one hiker's thighs would be up to my belly button. I came to the harsh realization that not only was I not experienced in mountaineering—which were skills the upcoming stretch required—but that at 5 ft 1 in tall, I also did not have the physical build to make it through the deep river crossings without the assistance of a group that I trusted to stay with me.

The friend I started the trail with had decided to go home, and the guys we were hiking with had taken off early in the morning to get a jump-start on the daylight. I wasn't ready to make up my mind when they left, and I wasn't a strong enough hiker to catch up to them. I could have found a different group in town, there was definitely a bottle-neck of nervous hikers trying to decide what to do, but ultimately I felt like I would be putting my life at risk when I'd likely end up flipping north after reaching the next town. I didn't want the next 50 mi to ruin my experience of the trail or force me to go home, and I didn't want my stubbornness to blind me to the reality of my

---

1 A snow bridge is when thick snow blankets a river crossing and is solid and strong enough to walk over. These can be useful to get over river crossings without getting wet, but become riskier as the season progresses and snow begins to soften and melt.

capabilities. Maybe I would have made it through. I don't know. In the end, I decided to flip past the dangerous snowpack.

The danger was there, but I chose not to face it. Your hiker will also have the opportunity to assess and re-assess skills, comfort levels, and risk tolerance between each stretch of trail. Options for turning back, delaying departure, and other creative solutions exist to keep hikers safe. An important thing to remember is that the snowpack changes from year to year depending on the winter before it. Trail conditions one year are not indicative of trail conditions in other years.

IS YOUR HIKER READY FOR HEAVY SNOW?

- DO THEY HAVE A GROUP THEY WILL BE TRAVELING WITH, OR DO THEY PLAN ON GOING THROUGH ALONE?
- DO THEY KNOW WHERE TO LOOK FOR UPDATED CONDITIONS AND SAFETY INFORMATION?
- DO THEY HAVE THE PROPER TOOLS TO PASS THROUGH SAFELY?
- HAVE THEY LEARNED HOW TO USE THESE TOOLS AND PRACTICED WITH THEM ENOUGH TO REACT REFLEXIVELY IF NEEDED?
- ARE THEY CARRYING A SATELLITE DEVICE THAT CAN BE USED TO COMMUNICATE IF THEY NEED HELP CHECKING TRAIL CONDITIONS OR HAVE A NON-EMERGENCY ISSUE? DOES IT HAVE AN SOS BUTTON THAT CAN BE PUSHED IN AN EMERGENCY?
- DO THEY HAVE A PLAN THAT SHOWS THEIR INTENDED ITINERARY WITH A BACKUP PLAN AND BAIL-OUT ROUTES IN THE EVENT OF AN ISSUE? HAVE THEY GIVEN A COPY OF THIS ITINERARY TO SOMEONE AT HOME, ALONG WITH AN ESTIMATED TIME-FRAME FOR WHEN THEY WILL BE IN TOUCH AGAIN AND WHEN THEY EXPECT TO REACH THE NEXT TOWN?

Less concern should be placed on the conditions themselves, than the precautions your hiker has taken to make it through heavy snow safely. Ego-driven, strong-willed, or stubborn hikers must work especially hard to be honest about their skills. As long as your hiker has thoroughly evaluated skill-sets, support decisions and express availability to help if needed. Hikers rarely change plans because of concern expressed from those at home. Instead, they may stop sharing plans until after the fact. Sharing your support will help ensure that your hiker keeps you up to date with everything that is happening, as it is happening.

One way to support your hiker in changing conditions is to provide mail support. Sometimes hikers need to add or eliminate gear as conditions change, and having someone at home who can help is immeasurably beneficial. In most heavy snow areas, hikers will need an ice axe and gear for their feet, but these are pieces of gear that will be needed for a short period and then shipped back home.

TOOLS FOR YOUR HIKER'S FEET FOR SAFE SNOW TRAVEL

MICROSPIKES: A SLIP-ON TRACTION SYSTEM USING TINY SPIKES TO AID IN SNOW TRAVEL. THESE ARE GREAT FOR MILD SNOW.

CRAMPONS: A STRAP-ON TRACTION SYSTEM USING LARGE SPIKES TO AID IN SNOW TRAVEL ON ICY OR STEEP TERRAIN. THESE ARE MORE INTENSE THAN MICROSPIKES AND CAN BE USED IN MORE TECHNICAL SNOW CONDITIONS.

SNOW SHOES: THESE ASSIST IN SNOW TRAVEL ON SNOW DEEPER THAN 6 INCHES AND HELP KEEP A HIKER FROM POSTHOLING[1], THOUGH OFTEN TIMES HIKERS PREFER NOT TO CARRY THEM DUE TO THEIR BULKINESS AND WEIGHT NOT BEING WORTH THE HELP THEY PROVIDE.

---

1 Postholing refers to when a hiker's weight is too heavy for the snow to hold, and their foot or leg will break through the snow as a result.

SELF-ARRESTING TOOLS FOR SAFE SNOW TRAVEL

SELF-ARRESTING IS A MOUNTAINEERING TECHNIQUE IN WHICH
A HIKER WHO HAS FALLEN AND IS SLIDING DOWN SNOW OR
ICE STOPS THE SLIDE BY THEMSELVES. IT IS CRUCIAL FOR
YOUR HIKER TO UNDERSTAND AND PRACTICE BEFORE ENTERING
CONDITIONS WHERE THEY MIGHT NEED TO RELY ON AN ICE AXE
OR WHIPPET TO STOP A FALL.

ICE AXE: A MULTI-PURPOSED HAND-HELD TOOL USED TO SELF-
ARREST, GLISSADE (CONTROLLED SLIDING), AND ASSIST IN
ASCENDING AND DESCENDING FROZEN TERRAIN.

WHIPPET: A SKI POLE WITH AN ICE-AXE ATTACHMENT USED FOR
SELF-ARRESTING. WHIPPETS LACK SOME OF THE BENEFITS OF
AN ICE AXE, SUCH AS HOLDING POWER, STRENGTH, AND MULTI-
FUNCTIONALITY. THE ARGUMENT FOR A WHIPPET IS THAT IT
IS IN YOUR HAND WHEN YOU NEED IT, AS OPPOSED TO ON YOUR
PACK.

IT WILL BE IMPORTANT FOR YOUR HIKER TO PRACTICE USING
THEIR TOOL OF CHOICE IN SNOW BEFORE THEY RELY ON IT TO
SAVE THEIR LIFE. IF THEY DO NOT HAVE ACCESS TO THIS AT
HOME, THEY CAN PRACTICE ON THE TRAIL AT THE START OF
THE SNOWY SECTIONS BEFORE DECIDING IF/WHEN THEY WILL GO
FURTHER. THERE ARE IN-PERSON COURSES OFFERED BY COMPANIES,
LIKE REI, AS WELL AS RESOURCES AND DEMONSTRATIONS ONLINE
FOR HOW TO SELF-ARREST IN DIFFERENT SITUATIONS.
YOUR HIKER SHOULD PRACTICE FALLING AND SELF-ARRESTING IN
THE FOLLOWING WAYS:

   - FACE UP, FEET FACING DOWNHILL
   - FACE UP, HEAD FACING DOWNHILL
   - FACE DOWN, FEET FACING DOWNHILL
   - FACE DOWN, HEAD FACING DOWNHILL

SELF-ARRESTING TECHNIQUES DIFFER BASED ON HOW A HIKER
FALLS. THEY SHOULD FAMILIARIZE THEMSELVES WITH EACH
METHOD, AS WELL AS HOW TO SELF-ARREST IN AN EMERGENCY
WITH TREKKING POLES AND WITHOUT ANY TOOLS.

RIVER CROSSINGS

Just after I flipped around the Sierra Nevadas, two young women died in separate river crossing incidents in the section I skipped. They were my height, my build, and each found herself at a difficult river crossing alone. While it's best to wait and cross with others, food supplies limit the number of days a hiker can spend on the trail. In stretches with multiple river crossings, turning back might also mean re-crossing a different river. Undoubtedly, these factors contributed to each hiker's decision to cross alone. The deaths were chilling because either could have just as easily been me. I fit the description in every way, apart from choosing to skip the Sierra, even if it meant having to forgo the title of "thru-hiker."

River crossings can be dangerous, but there are steps your hiker can take to ensure safety, including staying aware of what to expect on each upcoming stretch of trail. The Pacific Crest Trail Association has resources on how to cross rivers safely, and recommends the following:[59]

- Look for hazards and try to cross downstream from them.
- Look for areas where the water is flowing slower than it may be at the trail.
- Remember we float more as water gets deeper, which makes it hard to stay grounded.
- Use features like islands to create a mid-crossing break.
- Look for changes in depth along the bottom of the river.
- Be patient searching for the right place to cross. It may take all day or require extra miles upstream. Scouting a safe crossing can take work, but it is worth it to ensure your hiker's safety.
- Observe features like downed logs to ensure they are sturdy and safe before using them to cross.
- Be certain snow bridges can support your weight before trusting one.
- Take into account the time of day. Crossing early in the morning can ensure the water is at it's safest depth for the day. If the water level doesn't change, search for an area into which less snow drains.
- Stay honest. Assess the risk involved with each crossing and the likelihood of something going wrong. Assess if

your team is ready for the crossing or if they could use a
break. Never be too stubborn to turn back if something is
beyond your skill level.

If hikers fall in the water, they should position themselves on
their backs with their feet facing downstream to break impact with
obstacles while getting to shore. Best practice is to unbuckle hip-
belts before crossing rivers in case a pack needs to be removed
quickly.

If your hiker is going to be on the trail after a heavy winter, courses
in wilderness first aid and swift water rescue might be helpful.
Being prepared and properly trained can help hikers make the right
decisions when risk is high.

RIVER CROSSING TECHNIQUES FROM THE PCTA[60]

ONE PERSON: LEAVE SHOES ON, UNCLIP PACKS, AND FACE
UPSTREAM WITH AT LEAST THREE POINTS OF CONTACT ON
THE GROUND. ONLY MOVE ONE FOOT OR TREKKING POLE AT A
TIME, WHILE KEEPING THE OTHER THREE STABLE. MAKE SURE
PLACEMENT IS SECURE BEFORE MOVING AGAIN, AND TAKE
SMALL, CAREFUL STEPS WHILE LEANING INTO THE CURRENT.

TWO TO THREE PEOPLE: TWO HIKERS CAN LOCK ARMS AND
USE EACH OTHER FOR SUPPORT. THREE PEOPLE CAN FACE
EACH OTHER IN A TRIANGLE WITH THE STRONGEST PERSON
UPSTREAM TO BREAK THE CURRENT. TWO HIKERS STAY WHILE
THE THIRD MOVES.

FOUR TO SIX PEOPLE: WITH THE STRONGEST HIKER IN FRONT
AND WEAKER HIKERS IN THE MIDDLE, LARGER GROUPS CAN
BREAK THE CURRENT IN A LINE, FOLLOWING INSTRUCTIONS
FROM A DESIGNATED LEADER, OR IN A WEDGE WITH A STRONG
HIKER AT THE TOP OF THE WEDGE, AND OTHER STRONG
HIKERS IN THE SPOTS CLOSELY BEHIND. HAVING MEMBERS
DOWNSTREAM TO ASSIST IN THE EVENT OF A SLIP IS A
BENEFIT OF HIKING WITH A LARGE GROUP THROUGH THIS
KIND OF TERRAIN.

FOREST FIRES

Ninety percent of wildfires are caused by humans,[61] so it's important for anyone who spends time in the backcountry to act responsibly. Some trails will require campfire permits, like the California Fire Permit for the Pacific Crest Trail, which consists of an online course on fire safety and responsible campfire etiquette. Information is also available online for your hiker to check applicable areas for threat levels, fire bans, restrictions on certain stoves, and areas of closed trail due to active wildfires.

The fifth Leave No Trace principle addresses minimizing the impact of campfires. To help prevent wildfires hikers can keep campfires small, refrain from building fires in locations that haven't had a campfire before, follow local rules and regulations, and fully extinguish fires before going to bed.

Staying on top of fire weather warnings and existing wildfire closures, as well as having situational awareness, knowing threat levels, and keeping an eye out for red flags, will help your hiker stay out of harm's way and maximize time to respond should something go wrong. It's illegal to enter a fire closure, as they exist to keep hikers far enough from existing wildfires to stay safe. If a stretch of trail closes, trail organizations act quickly to provide alternative routes or recommend a bypass. Your hiker should know how to check for updated conditions and closures before entering areas prone to wildfires. Ask them to share these websites and resources with you if you would like to know how to check as well.

Over the course of my summer on the Pacific Crest Trail, more than 400 total miles of trail closed due to wildfires. Since my group skipped ahead of the Sierra Nevadas, we stayed ahead of most closures. However, being so close to the fires required us to check conditions more frequently than usual. We always knew where we were in proximity to the fires, how quickly the fires were spreading, and how long that gave us to get through nearby areas before the closures would expand.

It was very clear when the trail was closed. Bright pink and orange tape criss-crossed over it, preventing hikers from passing. Fire closure information was printed, often laminated, and stapled to a tree next to the closure. There was usually a map with a circle drawn around the closure and a path to show the alternative route. It

was frustrating when that route added distance or prevented us from
entering a stretch of trail that we were looking forward to, but we
were grateful that the closures were easy to spot and the instructions
were clear.

"IN CALIFORNIA, THE REDDING FIRE WASN'T FAR FROM US.
THERE WAS A LOT OF SMOKE. SOME HIKERS SKIPPED AHEAD
BECAUSE IT MADE THEM FEEL SICK. THE DANGER IS REAL WHEN
IT COMES TO THE FIRES, BUT YOU HAVE TO DO YOUR BEST TO
KNOW HOW CLOSE YOU ARE TO THEM AND IF IT'S SAFE TO GO
AHEAD. IF YOU DECIDE TO SKIP AHEAD BECAUSE OF FIRES, YOU
CAN ALWAYS GO BACK TO DO THE MILES. IT WOULDN'T HAVE
BEEN AN ISSUE IF I NEEDED TO SKIP AHEAD. LUCKILY FOR US,
WE WERE ABLE TO KEEP GOING. THERE ARE A LOT OF ACCESS
ROADS ON THE TRAIL, SO YOU CAN USUALLY TAKE ONE TO A
MAJOR ROAD AND HITCH-HIKE OUT. YOU CAN FIND OUT IN TOWN
HOW SAFE IT IS AND SKIP AHEAD IF NECESSARY."
- EMILIO, 29, TEXAS

There were instances when we saw smoke columns from pre-
existing fires that we weren't aware of. I was far enough away that I
wasn't concerned about the fire spreading to where I was on the trail.
Hikers can keep an eye on smoke columns to see which direction the
fire is traveling. They should not hike towards a fire or the direction
the fire is traveling.

If hikers are close enough to a wildfire that they can see flames
or are concerned that they are in danger, the Pacific Crest Trail
Association recommends that they react by moving quickly. Fires
burn faster uphill, through chutes, saddles, and ridge lines. If
evacuating, hikers should travel downhill and position themselves
below the fire, rather than above it.[62]

When hiking near fires, hikers should be aware of how smoky an
area is and if it is smart for them to be in a state of heavy-breathing
and exercise in those areas. Heavy smoke can be unhealthy and even
life-threatening. If a hiker has health concerns, like asthma, this may
affect whether or not an area is safe for them individually. Keep in
mind that your hiker has the option to bypass an area and return to it
later.

LIGHTNING

On trails like the Colorado Trail, where a hiker can stay above tree line for as far as 38 mi (61.2 km) at a time, lightning can be a concern. Above tree line hikers are exposed and should take storms seriously. The Colorado Trail Foundation lists precautions to take to stay safe.[63] If possible, hikers should be off exposed areas by noon, as afternoon storms are common. Situational awareness and preparation are key for your hiker's safety. Judgment calls often happen on the fly, as clouds can form unexpectedly. If clouds are forming and hikers have a pass coming up, they need to decide if they should wait for the weather to clear, or try to beat it. If hikers are above tree line for a prolonged period, they need to remain conscious of where they can move downhill should they need to for safety.

IF YOUR HIKER CAN'T FIND SAFETY

- AVOID FIELDS, RIDGES, AND HILL-TOPS
- STAY AWAY FROM TALL TREES AND ISOLATED OBJECTS
- SPREAD OUT GROUP MEMBERS TO AVOID A TRAVELING CURRENT
- TRY TO SET UP CAMP IN A VALLEY OR RAVINE
- STAY AWAY FROM WATER, WET OBJECTS, AND METAL

Testing rain gear and having backup layers to replace soaked clothes can be instrumental in cold weather. Hypothermia (described in next section) is a real threat as high elevations can become frigid. Hikers should have a change of dry clothes and packs should be set up so that items like sleeping bags and spare clothes remain dry.

COMMON ILLNESSES + PREVENTION

Sickness can force a hiker into town early, require extra zero days to recover, and in worst-case scenarios, end a long-distance hike prematurely. What illnesses do hikers worry about? How are they prevented and treated? This section, written with the assistance of Dr. Ed Corkran, D.O., Elizabeth Keller, RN, BSN, and Keith Michel, RN, BSN, as well as NOLS Wilderness Medicine 6th Edition, outlines seven common illnesses that a hiker might encounter.

7 COMMON ILLNESSES ENCOUNTERED ON TRAILS

1. TICK-BORNE ILLNESSES
   (LYME DISEASE)
2. HYPOTHERMIA
3. DEHYDRATION
4. GIARDIA
5. NOROVIRUS
6. HEAT EXHAUSTION
7. MALNUTRITION

LYME DISEASE

Lyme disease is a bacterial infection that is usually caused by the bite of an infected deer tick. It can be tough to diagnose since it shares many symptoms with diseases like the flu.[64]

SYMPTOMS
- Red rash in the shape of a bull's eye where bitten
- Fever, body aches, stiff neck, fatigue

TREATMENT
- Remove ticks by inserting tweezers between the tick's mouth and hiker's skin. Grasp close to their mouth, remove the head of the tick, and avoid squeezing its body.
- Antibiotics - According to the CDC, if treated early, people usually recover rapidly and completely.[65] Most recover after a few weeks, though some may have longer effects if not treated early. Untreated Lyme disease can become a life-long illness.

PREVENTION:

- Every day hikers should check areas where ticks hide - their legs, around their hairline, behind their knees, around their waist and belly button, and in locations below the belt that may not commonly see the light of day. Sitting on a mat or pad creates an extra barrier between the hiker and the ground which may lessen the likelihood of contact with ticks.
- Apply permethrin, an insecticide, to clothing and gear. Permethrin made a big difference in how often I saw ticks on my body and on my gear. I re-sprayed permethrin roughly every six weeks. I would recommend this for a trail that has a higher risk of exposure to ticks, like the A.T.

HYPOTHERMIA

This isn't as much an illness as it is a medical emergency. Caused by cold, wet environments, hypothermia can occur when the body loses heat faster than it can produce it and core temperature drops dangerously low.[66] The reason it's considered an emergency is because when a person's core temperature drops too low, organs stop functioning, the body shuts down, and the outcome can be fatal. Many symptoms can be misinterpreted as fatigue or dehydration, so it's important for hikers to stay mindful of the possibility of hypothermia.

SYMPTOMS [67]

- Mild: shivering, goosebumps, minor muscular impairments, confusion and sluggish thinking
- Moderate: stumbling, lethargy, obvious altered mental and physical state, forgetfulness, clumsiness, falling
- Severe: shivering ceases, incoherence, weak pulse, muscle rigidity, inability to walk, and blood pressure, heart rate, and respiratory rates fall (shock)

TREATMENT:

- A person with hypothermia should seek professional medical attention. While on trail, others can help until professionals arrive or the hiker is safely evacuated. The goal is to raise the hiker's body temperature back to a safe degree. If possible, the person should be removed from the cold, wet clothing should be replaced with dry clothing, the hiker should be covered with sleeping bags or other layers, and breathing should be monitored. Direct heat can cause harm, so avoid using hot water, though if the hiker is coherent drinking warm fluids is okay, as is giving the hiker something to eat.

- Severe stages of hypothermia are more difficult to treat in the wilderness and can lead to shock or death. Keep the hiker horizontal, monitor breathing and heart rate, and evacuate if the situation is severe.

PREVENTION[68]

- The acronym COLD can be used to remember prevention: Cover, Overexertion, Layers, Dry.
- Cover: Cover skin to prevent heat loss (i.e. hats and gloves)
- Overexertion: Adjust pace and layering so that hikers aren't producing excess sweat.
- Layers: Hikers should make sure layering systems are appropriate for the weather. Clothing material is also extremely important - Merino wool is great for retaining warmth whereas cotton doesn't wick moisture well.
- Dry: Hikers need to stay dry when the weather is cold, so changing out of wet clothing, be it from rain or sweat, is key.

DEHYDRATION

Dehydration is caused when the body doesn't have enough water to function properly. This can be caused by not drinking enough water in addition to losing water through sweating or using the bathroom. Dehydration can occur more commonly in areas with longer water carries, unpredictable water sources, or extreme heat.

SYMPTOMS [69]
* Thirst and dry mouth
* Headache, muscle cramps, rapid heartbeat, rapid breathing
* Dizziness, fainting, nausea, vomiting
* Late signs: dark yellow urine or lack of urination, vision disturbance, delirium, decreased skin elasticity

TREATMENT [70]
* Sip fluids slowly. If possible, it's helpful to drink something containing electrolytes and carbohydrates.
* Vomiting is an example of severe dehydration, and in this case the hiker must stop vomiting for at least an hour before drinking water, otherwise the water will not be absorbed.
* In extreme cases, IV fluids may be administered by a healthcare professional.

PREVENTION
* Drink water! Carrying water alone isn't enough.
* Stay on top of water reports for questionable stretches of trail and carry extra water if resupplying at an unreliable source.
* Increase water intake at higher elevations, in extreme heat, and with high energy expenditure.
* Carrying an extra water bag is a way to prepare for a longer water carry and won't take up a lot of room when unused.
* Stay mindful - Hikers should pay attention to the location of the next reliable water source, be aware of how much water they have left, and fill up at existing water sources.
* Adequate salt intake is critical for maintaining hydration without risking hyponatremia[1].

1 Hyponatremia occurs when sodium levels in the blood are too low. It can cause nausea, headaches, confusion, and fatigue. Hyponatremia comes from drinking too much water and not ingesting enough sodium.

GIARDIA[71]

Giardia is a microscopic parasite contracted through contact with contaminated feces or water from a source where the parasite lives. A hiker can become infected by swallowing the parasite, which reinforces the importance of treating water and applying hand sanitizer after using a privy or shared space.

SYMPTOMS[72]

- Diarrhea, gas, greasy stool
- Nausea, upset stomach, and stomach cramps
- Dehydration, malaise, and fever

TREATMENT:

- Giardia usually works its way out of the system in two to six weeks, though prescription drugs can be obtained if necessary. Garlic can be used to relieve symptoms and alleviate discomfort.[73]

PREVENTION:

- Hikers can reduce the risk of Giardia by treating all water, avoiding potentially contaminated food sources, and washing hands regularly. In town, hikers should use soap and warm water. Between towns, hand sanitizer or disinfecting wipes should be used after going to the bathroom and before eating. Hikers should avoid putting their hands in snack bags when sharing. Pouring snacks into hands will keep germs from spreading.

NOROVIRUS

Unlike the other illnesses mentioned, norovirus is highly contagious. It's a virus contracted through contact with contaminated food, fecal matter, water, surfaces, or people, that can cause vomiting and diarrhea. Norovirus can be a nightmare on the trail due to how easily it spreads.

SYMPTOMS [74]
• Diarrhea, nausea, vomiting, stomach pain

TREATMENT
• Norovirus will work its way out of a hiker's system in one to three days.

PREVENTION
• Hikers should be especially vigilant in *the bubble*[2] or at the convergence of NOBO/SOBO groups. Overcrowding breeds contamination and enhances transmission.
• Avoid norovirus by treating water and washing hands regularly. All water should be filtered.
• Avoid contact with infected hikers. When hikers are infected, they should do their best to quarantine themselves from shelters and other areas where hikers congregate.
• Avoid sharing water bottles, utensils, and other items that could transmit viruses. Hikers should avoid putting their hands in snack bags when sharing. Pouring snacks into hands will keep germs from spreading.
• When possible, choose flowing water sources rather than stagnant ones where viruses can more easily breed.

When I hiked the Appalachian Trail, the group I was with contracted norovirus in Maine. Luckily, we were fewer than 10 mi (16.1 km) from town, so we stopped at a hostel to rest. Hiker hostels are familiar with norovirus, and go above and beyond to prevent the virus from spreading while not turning away infected hikers in their time of need. When we arrived at Shaw's Hiker Hostel in Maine,

2 The bubble describes a majority of the season's hikers who are clumped together. This occurs since most hikers start within the same 2-3 months due to weather windows.

the owners had completely taken control of the situation, having seen the first case of infection a few nights prior. They designated a bunk house and bathrooms specifically for the sick, as well as separate areas for those who were not infected. The hostel owners meticulously wiped down surfaces with bleach, and ran endless loads of sheets, towels, and loaner clothes through the wash. At first we had worried that they wouldn't let members of our group stay if they were sick, since word spreading about a hostel with norovirus can negatively impact business, but when I mentioned it to the owner he responded:

"We are a hiker hostel. Our purpose is to provide help and aid to hikers. How could we turn them away when that need is at its greatest?"

This belief and behavior highlights how the trail community always seems to be looking out and trying to keep hikers safe. Just because you won't be there to keep an eye on your hiker, doesn't mean no one else will.

"TRY NOT TO TOUCH YOUR FACE. THAT'S HOW YOU INFECT YOURSELF. IF YOU ARE SICK, DON'T STAY IN A SHELTER. STAY IN YOUR TENT AND STAY AWAY FROM COMMUNAL AREAS. THAT'S HOW OTHER PEOPLE GET SICK. YOU HAVE TO QUARANTINE YOURSELF, OTHERWISE THAT BACTERIA OR VIRUS CAN SPREAD."
- KEITH, 29, NEW JERSEY

HEAT EXHAUSTION[75]

Heat exhaustion occurs when a hiker's body is overheating. It's caused from exposure to high temperatures, especially combined with high humidity and heavy physical activity. Dehydration can also lead to heat exhaustion. Hikers with thyroid-hormone medications, amphetamines, or antihistamines are at a higher risk for heat exhaustion. Alcohol consumption can also make a hiker more vulnerable.

SYMPTOMS [76]

- Cool, clammy skin with goose bumps
- Thirst
- Dizziness, fainting, weakness, fatigue, and headache
- Low blood pressure when standing, vertigo
- Nausea, muscle cramps, and vomiting
- Elevated pulse and breathing

TREATMENT

- Drink fluids, preferably with electrolytes, find cooler temperatures (look for shade), and rest.

PREVENTION

- Use sunscreen, as sunburn will affect the body's ability to cool down.
- Stay hydrated.
- Wear loose-fitting, lightweight clothing.
- Don't hike during the hottest parts of the day. On the PCT we'd rest every afternoon between noon and 2 P.M. to keep activity levels low during extreme heat.
- Keep an eye on medications or other variables that might create a higher risk of heat exhaustion.

MALNUTRITION

Malnutrition, caused by a lack of nutrients or poor diet, can affect
the performance of hikers, leave their bodies more susceptible to
illnesses, and cause wound-healing to take longer. Hikers might
notice symptoms if they aren't eating enough of the right foods,
which is why many hikers spend ample time researching their diets
and anticipated calorie needs while planning. According to the World
Health Organization, there are four sub-categories of malnutrition:
wasting, stunting, underweight, and deficiencies in vitamins and
minerals.[77]

The first, wasting, describes low weight-for-height, and results
in severe weight loss usually due to under-consumption. Many,
but not all, long-distance hikers will lose weight along the journey.
Oftentimes that weight-loss can be dramatic. Losing weight on the
trail doesn't necessarily mean a hiker is malnourished, but paying
attention to food choices and choosing high-calorie, healthy options
over empty calories can keep hikers feeling strong.

SYMPTOMS

- Appetite loss, tiredness, irritability, lack of concentration
- Loss of fat, muscle mass, and body tissue

TREATMENT + PREVENTION

- Increase calorie intake with foods that are high in fat, protein,
  and carbohydrates. In extreme circumstances, hikers can
  spend extra nights in town to put some pounds back on before
  continuing to hike.

As mentioned, not everyone loses weight on a long-distance hike,
and the amount of weight loss can vary. On the Pacific Crest Trail,
I lost 28 pounds, while on the Appalachian Trail, I gained four.
It depends on the types of food a hiker eats, the mileage they are
making, and the hiker's weight and muscle-mass pre-hike. Some
people start a trail with substantial extra weight. Some start a trail
with minimal muscle. On the A.T., I was hiking 15 mi to 20 mi per
day and relying heavily on my trekking poles, which greatly exerted
my upper body and caused muscle gain. Whereas, on the PCT, I was
hiking 25 mi to 28 mi per day but the trail was less demanding.

CALORIE-BOOSTING MEAL SUPPLEMENTS

HERE'S A LIST OF ITEMS TO ADD TO A HIKER'S RESUPPLY BOX OR CARE PACKAGE THAT WILL GIVE THEM AN EXTRA BOOST:

OLIVE OIL PACKETS: ROUGHLY 250 CALORIES PER OUNCE (2 TBSP), AND AN EASY WAY TO ADD HIGH-FAT CALORIES TO ANY MEAL.

POWDERED MILK: AT 600 TO 650 CALORIES PER CUP, POWDERED MILK IS HIGH-PROTEIN, HIGH-FAT, AND HIGH-CARB. IT CAN BE USED IN MORNING COFFEE, EVENING HOT CHOCOLATE, OR ADDED TO MEALS, LIKE PASTA SIDES OR MAC+CHEESE, FOR FLAVOR.

POWDERED BUTTER: ROUGHLY 100 CALORIES PER OUNCE. THIS IS A HIGH-FAT OPTION TO ADD TO MEALS.

CHIA SEEDS: 140 CALORIES PER OUNCE AND HIGH IN FAT, CARBS, PROTEIN, AND FIBER. CHIA SEEDS CAN BE ADDED TO MEALS LIKE OATMEAL OR POURED IN WATER. I LIKE TO ADD CHIA SEEDS TO MY WATER WITH MIO ENERGY FLAVORING TO ADD CALORIES TO MY DIET EVEN WHEN I'M NOT EATING.

NUTS: ALMONDS, PEANUTS, AND WALNUTS ARE BETWEEN 165 TO 185 CALORIES PER OUNCE, AND HIGH IN FAT, CARBS, AND PROTEIN.

PEANUT BUTTER PACKETS: ROUGHLY 185 CALORIES PER OUNCE AND HIGH IN FAT, CARBS, PROTEIN, POTASSIUM, AND FIBER.

CHOCOLATE: A 100 GRAM BAR OF 70 % TO 85 % DARK CHOCOLATE CAN CONTAIN ROUGHLY 600 CALORIES OF FAT, CARBS, AND MINERALS LIKE MAGNESIUM, IRON, AND ZINC.

VITAMINS: NOT CALORIE RICH, BUT ADDING VITAMINS CAN HELP WITH THE FOURTH SUB-CATEGORY OF MALNUTRITION.

COMMON INJURIES + PREVENTION

Injuries, like spraining an ankle or breaking a bone, can halt a hike for weeks, months, or even the rest of the season. However, some minor injuries can be avoided and worked through on the trail. This section reviews six common injuries that a hiker might face. It was written with the assistance of Megan Timler, DPT, Elisabeth Young, PT, DPT, Heather Pannill, DPT, ATC, LAT, and Julie Velasquez, PTA.

6 COMMON INJURIES ENCOUNTERED ON TRAILS

1. BLISTERS + HOT SPOTS
2. PLANTAR FASCIITIS
3. ACHILLES TENDINITIS
4. SHIN SPLINTS
5. ILIOTIBIAL BAND SYNDROME
6. CHAFE

People have started long-distance hikes with minimal training. People have started overweight. I know hikers whose first night on a long trail was their first night ever backpacking.

Hikers can certainly use the first few weeks of a long trail as training, but there is also a direct correlation between the amount of training a hiker does in advance and the amount of pain a hiker experiences during the first few weeks on trail. I didn't train much for the Pacific Crest Trail, but I did for the Appalachian Trail. In my opinion, getting my legs in shape was much easier after sessions at the gym when I could go home and sleep in my bed or take a bath, than when I had to sleep on the ground and hike through the pain the next day. Before the AT, I went to the gym four days a week, spending 20 minutes on the stair climber followed by 40 minutes walking on the treadmill. Some hikers will wear their backpacks at the gym and slowly add weight over time.

Some trail discomfort, like blisters and chaffing, may be inevitable. However, the risk of common injuries can be lowered through training, preparedness, and active stretching. Active

stretching or a dynamic stretching warm up will be more effective at
preventing injury than static stretching. Your hiker should remember
that while pain can be reduced with medications like Ibuprofen, too
much "Vitamin-I"[1] can negatively impact health and should be used
sparingly.

ACTIVE STRETCHING: TAKING A MUSCLE GROUP THROUGH ITS
FULL RANGE OF MOTION USING YOUR OWN FORCES
    EX. BENDING FORWARD TO DO A HAMSTRING STRETCH

PASSIVE STRETCHING: SOMEONE OR SOMETHING EXERTING FORCE
ON YOU TO STRETCH A MUSCLE
    EX. LAYING BACK AND SOMEONE ELSE STRETCHING YOUR
    HAMSTRING FOR YOU

DYNAMIC STRETCHING: UTILIZING MOVEMENT, TYPICALLY
THROUGH MULTIPLE JOINTS AND PLANES OF MOVEMENT, IN ORDER
TO MOBILIZE MUSCLE TISSUE ACTIVELY
    EX. MOBILIZING THE HAMSTRING MUSCLE BY DOING A SLOW
    INCHWORM ACROSS THE FLOOR (FORWARD BEND, WALK HANDS
    OUT, WALK FEET TO HANDS, RETURN TO STANDING, REPEAT),
    OR SOME STRAIGHT LEG SWINGS BACK AND FORTH

DYNAMIC STRETCHING TENDS TO BE MORE EFFECTIVE IN
PREPARING MUSCLE TISSUE FOR ACTIVITY BECAUSE YOU'RE
INCREASING BLOOD FLOW AND WARMING THE TISSUE WHILE ALSO
MOBILIZING AND STRETCHING IT.

Cold streams and alpine lakes are great for post-hike leg recovery,
especially if followed with passive stretching to maximize muscle
recovery. An "ideal" hiking day for someone who is injured could
start with a light warm up (lunges, leg swings, skipping), followed
by hiking. Afterwards, the hiker can take a "hiker ice bath" with cold
water if it's available, and finish the day with static stretching.

---

1 Hiker lingo for Ibuprofen

BLISTERS + HOT SPOTS

Blisters and hot spots are caused by pressure, heat, friction, and moisture.[78] Breaking in a new pair of shoes or getting used to full days of hiking can invite blisters and hot spots. On the PCT, I tried every type of blister treatment and was always frustrated that solutions like moleskin, band-aids, and blister pads would roll off, leaving an uncomfortable, sticky mess bunched up inside my sock likely causing new irritations.

PREVENTION

- Hikers can avoid blisters and hot spots by keeping feet dry. Sock liners are great for adding an extra layer between a hiker's skin and shoes, and help with wicking moisture. Remember to switch out and dirty, crusty socks as well, as they can cause unwanted rub.
- Take shoes off at breaks to allow feet to air dry to reduce moisture on the feet and also allow socks to dry.

TREATMENT

- After trying nearly every remedy on the shelf, I finally found a solution that stuck. Leukotape is a sports tape that I put directly on my blisters. It sticks better than surgeon's tape or kinetic tape. It's the only thing I carry for blisters and hot spots, though blister pads or bandages could be applied with a layer of Leukotape over the top to hold them in place. Leukotape is hard to find in stores, but is sold online. It usually comes in a roll that weighs more than anyone would want to carry. I take a tube of Chapstick and wrap Leukotape around it until I have the amount I want, then leave the rest in a hiker box. Another option is to have a few pre-rolled chapsticks at home that someone could send in a care package.
- Hikers should rinse off dirt, dry the area before taping, and change the tape daily to let the skin underneath breathe. Some hikers—me included—prefer to drain blisters before covering them.

PLANTAR FASCIITIS

Plantar fasciitis occurs when the plantar fascia, or tissue that runs between the heel and toes, is inflammed.[79] The inflammation can cause stabbing pains during initial movement and after exercise. Dr. Megan Timler, DPT, says that a very common telltale sign of plantar fasciitis she sees at the clinic is pain with the first few steps first thing in the morning. Hikers who are between the ages of 40 and 60, or are overweight, are at a greater risk for developing plantar fasciitis.

PREVENTION

- Choose shoes with good support.
- The main cause of many knee, ankle, and foot injuries is a weakness of the posterior hip muscles (glutes). They stabilize the pelvis and leg when putting weight on each while walking. Glute strengthening and single leg stability training prevents tissue irritation.

TREATMENT [80]

- Rest, icing the area, and stretching.
- A cork ball or similar can be used to roll out feet at the end of the day.
- Pain relieving medication like Ibuprofen can help with inflammation.
- Seeing a physical therapist who can recommend strengthening exercises or additional treatment options.
- Often hikers unfamiliar with zero drop shoes place greater strain on the plantar fascia. If pain occurs, try increasing the heel drop of the shoes to decrease stress.

ACHILLES TENDINITIS[8]

Achilles tendinitis is caused by overuse and repetitive strain on the Achilles tendon, or the band of tissue connecting the back of the calf to the heel bone. Hikers might experience aches, tenderness, or stiffness in the Achilles area. Hikers are more susceptible to Achilles tendinitis if they are older, male, have flat arches in their feet, or are using worn down shoes.

PREVENTION:

- Slowly increase activity levels.
- Warm up slowly with stretches and a slow pace to ease into the day.
- Choose cushioned footwear with arch support to reduce tension, and avoid a high heel rise, which can be common in certain running shoes and hiking boots. A high heel rise shortens the heel cord which changes the way the foot strikes the ground. A shoe with a flat rise (or zero-drop) is the recommendation from Dr. Megan Timler, DPT.
- Achilles tendinitis can be a strengthening issue, for which repeated calf lowers are the best exercise, even while hiking.
- Replace worn-down shoes and inserts—hikers typically do this every 300 mi (482.8 km) to 500 mi (804.7 km), though it can be done sooner if needed.

TREATMENT:[82]

- Soft tissue massage using your hands, or by rolling the calf muscle on a tennis ball or rock.
- Pain relieving medication, like Ibuprofen, can help with inflammation.
- Icy-Hot can help to reduce pain.
- Often hikers unfamiliar with zero drop shoes are placing greater strain on the Achilles tendon. If pain occurs, they may try increasing the heel drop of their shoes to decrease stress.
- Self-care measures are usually enough, but if pain persists or worsens, a hiker should visit a doctor or physical therapist.

SHIN SPLINTS[83]

Shin splints, Medial Tibial Stress Syndrome, or MTSS, occurs from overuse of the anterior tibialis muscle (which lies on the front of the lower leg), and when there is strain on connective tissue. Hikers with shin splints may experience tender, sore pain on the inner side of the shinbone. Hikers with flat feet or high arches are at a higher risk for shin splints.

PREVENTION

- Slowly increase activity levels.
- Train with exercises that strengthen and stabilize legs, ankles, hips, and core.
- Choose cushioned footwear with arch support to reduce tension, and avoid a high heel rise, which can be common in certain running shoes and hiking boots. A high heel rise shortens the heel cord, which changes the way the foot strikes the ground. A shoe with a flat rise (or zero-drop) is the recommendation from Dr. Megan Timler, DPT.
- Hikers with flat arches might consider adding arch supports.
- Replace worn-down shoes and inserts—hikers typically do this every 300 mi (482.8 km) to 500 mi (804.7 km), though it can be done sooner if needed.

TREATMENT

- Rest, icing the area, and stretching.
- Soft tissue massage using your hands, or by rolling the anterior tibialis muscle on the front of the lower leg on a tennis ball or rock.
- Pain relieving medication, like Ibuprofen, can help with inflammation.
- If pain persists, the hiker should see a doctor, as shin splints have the potential to lead to stress fractures.

ILIOTIBIAL BAND SYNDROME

Iliotibal Band Syndrome, IT Band Syndrome, or ITBS, is caused by overuse of connective tissues on the outer thigh and knee. It stems from weak glutes and the decreased control when bearing weight on one leg at a time. Overuse of the tensor fascia lata (TFL), a muscle at the outside/front of the hip, which is directly connected to the IT band, causes stress and irritation to the ITB. ITBS also occurs from the lateral demands on a hiker's body when carrying heavy loads on uneven terrain. The most common symptom is pain or swelling that worsens when the heel hits the ground. ITBS is more common in females.

PREVENTION[84]

- Lateral hip strengthening can prevent undue lateral stresses to the hips and knees that exacerbate the IT band.
- Slowly increase activity levels.
- Hikers need to train the glutes prior to hitting the trail so the TFL doesn't suffer.
- Warming up slowly with stretches and a slow pace can help a hiker safely ease into the day.
- Rest frequently during activity that puts stress on the IT band.
- Replace worn-down shoes and inserts—hikers typically do this every 300 mi (482.8 km) to 500 mi (804.7 km), though it can be done sooner if needed.

TREATMENT[85]

- IT band-specific stretches to improve flexibility.
- Rest, Ice, Compression, Elevation (RICE).
- Foam rolling focused on the TFL and outside thigh.
- Self-care measures are usually enough, but if pain persists or continues to worsen, your hiker should visit a doctor or physical therapist.
- Pain relieving medication, like Ibuprofen, can help with inflammation.

CHAFE

Chafing is usually caused by skin against skin friction to the point of irritation. Hikers will commonly experience chafing between their thighs, buttocks, and in the groin area, as well as on nipples and armpits. Hot weather, humidity, clothing that doesn't fit right or isn't moisture-wicking, sweat, and extra body weight can all contribute to chafing.

PREVENTION[86]

- Stop hiking when tenderness begins, and address the issue by resting, airing out the affected area, and applying lubrication.
- Use powders, like Gold Bond, to reduce moisture.
- Avoid cotton and clothing with seams or tags that can rub.
- Stay hydrated - salt increases in a hiker's sweat when not properly hydrated, which can also increase friction.

TREATMENT[87]

- Rest.
- Use powders, like Gold Bond, to reduce moisture.
- Lubricate the area to reduce friction - popular options include Body Glide, Chamois Butt'r, and Vagisil.
- Rinse the area to remove salt residue from sweat.
- Wear proper-fitting clothing.
- Apply soothing lotions or Vaseline to reduce pain while resting.

PRE-TRAIL EXERCISES FOR MUSCLE STRENGTH + CONTROL

MEGAN TIMLER, DPT RECOMMENDS SIX PRE-TRAIL EXERCISES
THAT ARE EFFECTIVE IN BUILDING GOOD MUSCLE STRENGTH
AND CONTROL FOR PROLONGED HEALTH. THEY SHOULD BE
STARTED WITH BODY WEIGHT FIRST (NO EXTRA WEIGHT) UNTIL
COMFORTABLE AND PROFICIENT IN THE PROPER FORM. THEY ARE
MOST EFFECTIVE WHEN PERFORMED WITH A SAFE PROGRESSION
LOAD WHILE STILL MAINTAINING CORRECT FORM.

SQUATS: BASIC HUMAN MOVEMENT AND SHAPE THAT TARGETS
  QUADS, HAMSTRINGS, AND GLUTES

DEADLIFT: HIP HINGE WITH BRACED CORE TO LOAD THE GLUTES
  AND HAMSTRINGS

LUNGE: CAN PERFORM AT VARIOUS ANGLES (FORWARD, BACKWARD,
  SIDE-TO-SIDE), INITIATES ONE-SIDED HIP CONTROL

STEP-UP + STEP DOWN: CAN PERFORM AT VARIOUS HEIGHTS,
  DIFFERENT FROM USING STAIR CLIMBER FOR CARDIO AND
  MUSCLE ENDURANCE CONDITIONING
- WHEN PERFORMED SLOWLY WITH FOCUSED CONTROL, THIS
  EXERCISE WILL BUILD ONE-SIDED HIP AND LOWER EXTREMITY
  CHAIN STRENGTH AND STABILITY

SINGLE LEG SIT-TO-STAND: STANDING UP FROM A SEATED
  SURFACE USING ONLY ONE LEG
- VARY THE HEIGHT OF SEATED SURFACE TO CHANGE THE
  DIFFICULTY (HIGHER SURFACES = EASIER, LESS DISTANCE TO
  TRAVEL)

SINGLE LEG DEADLIFT: ONE-SIDED VERSION OF TRADITIONAL
  DEADLIFT
- BUILDS STRENGTH AND STABILITY OF PELVIS AND TRUNK IN
  SINGLE LEG STANCE (NEEDED FOR WALKING)

SECTION FOUR
STAYING IN TOUCH

WAYS TO COMMUNICATE WITH YOUR HIKER

How often to expect communications from your hiker has many variables. Setting expectations beforehand will keep everyone on the same page about minimum requirements to limit concerns, along with next steps if the hiker fails to maintain communication. Be open with what you need to stay comfortable with your hiker being on the trail, and try to remain flexible and understanding, as sticking to a plan can be difficult.

"WHEN IT COMES TIME TO COMMUNICATE WITH THE HIKER, PEOPLE ON THE HOME-FRONT MIGHT TRY TO FILTER WHAT THEY SAY. WITH ME, THE HIKER, AS THE DAD OF TWO KIDS, I'M ALWAYS CONCERNED ABOUT WHAT COULD BE GOING ON AT HOME. WELL, THERE WERE THINGS GOING ON, BUT THEY DIDN'T NECESSARILY WANT TO CONVEY THINGS LIKE A BILL PAYMENT OR ANYTHING THAT WASN'T TOO CRITICAL. I HAD A SITUATION WHERE MY SON BACKED OUT OF A RESTAURANT AND KNOCKED THE MIRROR OFF HIS CAR, AND ANOTHER WHERE MY DAUGHTER HIT A TIRE AND KNOCKED HER MUFFLER OFF. MY WIFE DIDN'T TELL ME ABOUT THOSE THINGS UNTIL I GOT HOME, AND THAT WAS JUST FINE. I THINK IF YOU'VE GOT A SUPPORT GROUP OF PEOPLE AT HOME, TELL THEM TO REMEMBER THE HIKER'S MINDSET AS WELL. AFTER YOU'RE ON THE TRAIL FOR TWO WEEKS YOUR LIFE BASICALLY COMES DOWN TO FOOD, WATER, AND SHELTER. WITH EMPHASIS ON FOOD. THAT'S JUST THE TRUTH."
- GARY, 59, MISSOURI

It's no secret that embarking on a long-distance hike is considered by some to be a selfish endeavor. The hiker needs to remain focused on their mission in order to be fully immersed in the experience. When hikers aren't able to do this, it is harder for them to stick out the tough times, and they can come home feeling resentful that they weren't able to experience the trail the way others around them did.

Hikers are in pain all of the time. We're worried about pace, if we're rationing money correctly to make it the whole way, and if we'll have time to get our chores done so that we can relax and recharge. Having someone at home who is upset because we aren't spending that time on the phone can be frustrating, though not always the fault of the person at home. Sometimes people at home really need their hikers, but the nature of long-distance hiking makes it difficult to be fully available emotionally or physically. We aren't trying to be short, distant, or rude, we're just trying our best to get through each day with enough energy left to get through the next.

"WE LIVE IN A WORLD WHERE WE'RE SO CONNECTED TO PHONES THAT WE NEED IMMEDIATE CONTACT FOR SATISFACTION. THERE'S THE IDEA OF NEEDING TO SPEAK WITH THEM BECAUSE YOU'RE USED TO TALKING TO THEM EVERY DAY." - ROB, 34, OHIO

One of the best ways to be supportive at home is through patience and understanding. Cut your hiker slack where you normally wouldn't. Allow your hiker to get away with a short text message when you'd prefer a long phone call - at least you know he or she is okay. If your hiker feels overwhelmed by the amount of communication requested, he or she may become reluctant to reach out when there is reception. Being in touch less often is hard, but it's temporary. No one I've interviewed has reported negative changes in their hiker after returning from the trail. People have talked about ways that hikers have become better people, better parents, better spouses, and better family members, but no one reported hikers coming home worse than they left.

Being separated for so long can be difficult, but there are ways to communicate with your hiker, even if it's just to see that he or she is okay and making progress. Texting, phone calls, and FaceTime are obvious options. We will also cover how carrying a satellite device can add another method of communication when cell reception is lacking. But what other options are there?

I was surprised by the number of supporters who talked about using the Find My Friends[1] app to track their hikers. This could be an

---

1 Keep in mind the Find My Friends app only works on Apple devices, like iPhones.

option for a hiker who is not carrying a satellite device, as it is a free app that can allow tracking options. It may be preferential on less-remote trails, like the Appalachian Trail, where cell reception is more readily available.

"SELFISHLY, THERE WERE DEFINITELY A FEW TIMES WHERE I WISHED I COULD PICK UP MY PHONE AND HAVE HIM BE THERE. BUT, WITH THE NATURE OF THE TRAIL AND NOT KNOWING WHEN THERE'D BE SERVICE, I NEVER FELT ANGRY WITH HIM. I NEVER MADE HIM FEEL BAD THAT HE WAS OUT THERE HIKING WHEN HE COULD BE HELPING ME WITH WHATEVER PROBLEM I WAS HAVING. ONE TIME HE GOT SERVICE AND WAS SITTING OUTSIDE SOME CONVENIENCE STORE, AND PEOPLE KEPT COMING UP TO HIM. I WAS HAVING A REALLY BAD DAY AND HAD THINGS I WANTED TO TALK ABOUT, AND THESE PEOPLE KEPT INTERRUPTING US. HE'S A FRIENDLY GUY AND DIDN'T WANT TO TELL THEM THAT HE WOULD TALK TO THEM LATER, SO IT WAS AN HOUR AND A HALF PHONE CALL WHERE WE MAYBE ONLY TALKED FOR THIRTY MINUTES. I REALLY NEEDED HIM AND HE WAS TOO ENVELOPED IN THE PEOPLE OF THE TRAIL TO PAY ATTENTION TO ME. THAT WAS A PROBLEM. IT WAS DIFFICULT FOR ME TO TALK TO HIM ABOUT, BECAUSE IT IS AN EXPERIENCE, MEETING ALL THESE PEOPLE, HAVING TRAIL FRIENDS, AND THE TRAMILY OR WHATEVER. THAT WAS HUGE FOR HIM. I DIDN'T WANT TO MAKE IT ABOUT ME, BUT THAT WAS DEFINITELY A TIME WHERE I JUST WANTED HIM TO WALK AWAY FOR TWENTY MINUTES." - EMILY, 21, KENTUCKY

Because Find My Friends uses a phone's location services to operate, there may be delays if your hiker has location services turned off when the app is closed. It isn't practical for hikers to leave apps that use location services running all the time, as it can drain a phone battery. Hikers who have used the app reported delays in updating their location on the home-end while their phones were on airplane mode. Many hikers keep their phones in airplane mode while on the trail in order to preserve battery. If you choose to track your hiker this way, remember that it will only update your hiker's location if they have cell reception or WiFi. However, because the app updates automatically, it can be useful even if your hiker forgets to check in. I'd recommend it more as a way to loosely follow your hiker than to track in real-time. Hikers have also mentioned using the app to see where other hikers are on the trail. Remember that the app isn't perfect and may mark your hiker in a slightly inaccurate location. One hiker reported that his mom sent a screenshot that showed him in a lake. Flukes like this should be expected with a free app, so don't rely on it too heavily.

"I THINK KEEPING A MAP IS A GREAT WAY TO BE CONNECTED ENOUGH WITHOUT BEING TOO IN THEIR FACE. AT NIGHT I CAN PULL UP FIND MY FRIENDS AND COMPARE WHERE SHE IS TO THE APPALACHIAN TRAIL INTERACTIVE MAP ONLINE. THE INTERACTIVE MAP HAS ALL THE SHELTERS AND PARKING LOTS ON IT, AND I'VE KEPT UP WITH WHERE SHE IS EVERY DAY IN AN EXCEL SPREADSHEET." - RYAN, 31, LOUISIANA

Social media is great to keep an eye on your hiker's progress without needing to feel like you're texting or calling too frequently. Instagram, Facebook, and YouTube are the main platforms that hikers seem to use, but many hikers will also blog their hikes with individual sites set up using platforms like Wordpress, or through long-distance-focused media companies, like TheTrek.co.

I started the Pacific Crest Trail with the intention of blogging my hike, but learned quickly that there wasn't anything I wanted to do less than type paragraphs on a tiny phone when I reached camp. I switched to vlogging on YouTube and found that my parents loved it because they could actually see me. It put them at ease to see that I was still in one piece, to share the views, and to get a glimpse of me hiking. Watching me interact with hikers they saw in my videos helped my parents feel like they knew them too, and made them more comfortable with me being on the trail.

"I BLOGGED MY HIKE FOR THE TREK LAST YEAR AND THAT WAS ONE OF THE HIGHLIGHTS OF MY LIFE. I'VE NEVER BEEN A WRITER OR ANYTHING, BUT HAVING THAT, WHERE PEOPLE I DIDN'T EVEN KNOW COULD READ AND COMMENT... IT WOULD JUST MAKE MY DAY." - ARTHUR, 71, MAINE

If you want to see videos of your hiker, but he or she is uncomfortable or uninterested in posting them publicly, there is the option to upload videos to YouTube as *unlisted*, which means the videos would not appear in any searches and would only be viewable through a specific link. Many parents and partners also gave feedback on how following other hikers' social media accounts, blogs, and vlogs, helped comfort them. By following hikers that are in proximity to your hiker, you'll see additional perspectives of the trail, what's coming up next for your hiker, and the other hikers around them. It can also help if your hiker doesn't post as frequently as you'd like. I tend to over-post, so on the A.T. I added a new photo to my Instagram almost every day. Some like to nit-pick posting so often, as being on social media so frequently can be viewed as detracting from the experience. At the same time, I had parents, siblings, and family members of my trail friends follow me in addition to their hiker, because they liked to see photos and videos that included their hikers. I'm not saying this to pat myself on the back, as I could probably do with less phone-time, but to encourage you to follow the friends of your hiker and others nearby if you crave information.

"I FOLLOWED HIKERS AHEAD OF HER ON INSTAGRAM BECAUSE I WOULD SEE WHAT THEY WERE DOING AND KNEW WHAT WAS COMING UP FOR HER. I WOULD TELL OTHER PARENTS TO DO THAT AS WELL." - CYNTHI, 55, INDIANA

Social media aside, there's also the option of snail mail. Several friends sent me care packages, and reading handwritten notes made me feel great, as did digging through the goodies they crammed into boxes. One of the most clever packages I received included homemade cookies that were divided into individual bags for other hikers. I loved that my friend went to the effort of thinking about those around me and packed with sharing in mind. If you'd like to send your hiker a care package, ask for a recommended town and arrival time. Surprise packages can cause stress if the town wasn't a planned stop, or if your hiker doesn't expect to be in town during post office hours. Keep the surprises reserved for what's in the box, rather than where the box is sent.

I also love sending postcards while I'm on the trail - my best friend now has a cork board full of them behind her desk at work. Before I leave for hikes, I'll reach out to those closest to me and gather addresses, then take a photo of the list and save it on my phone. When I pick up postcards on the trail, it's easy to copy down the addresses and send them off. I don't forget to send any because the addresses are all saved together. Handwritten cards feel more personal than texts, and I find that they make those at home happy. It's also nice when I visit friends after a hike and see my postcards on their fridges.

A TIP FOR YOUR HIKER

FAMILIES OF PAST HIKERS HAVE RECOMMENDED POSTING PHOTOS SHOWING RESTFUL ACTIVITIES. IT MAY SEEM BORING, BUT IT REAFFIRMS TO THOSE AT HOME THAT THE HIKER IS FINDING TIME TO REST AND RECOVER.

SATELLITE COMMUNICATION DEVICES

Satellite communication devices like the Garmin InReach or Spot Gen3 are a way for your hiker to stay in touch or call for help even without cell reception. Devices like Personal Location Beacons, or PLBs, will only send out emergency messages, but as the world of satellite communication continues to grow, smaller, lighter devices are hitting the market with features from two-way messaging to GPS tracking. While satellite communication devices still aren't 100 % reliable, they can assist in helping those at home know the hiker is okay when other methods of communication aren't an option. Hikers are more likely to carry a satellite communication device on a remote trail like the Continental Divide Trail than on a populated trail like the Appalachian Trail. The high price tag often causes hikers to treat these as luxury items, which is why many times hikers report their device was a gift from a parent or spouse who wanted the extra measure of communication for their own peace of mind.

Based on a brief survey, the four most popular satellite communication devices amongst long-distance hikers as of 2019 are (in no order), the Spot Gen3, the SpotX, the Garmin InReach Explorer+, and the Garmin InReach Mini. They each have a base cost, followed by different subscription plans based on how many features are needed and how many messages the hiker wants to send. I will briefly go through the features of each to help those who would like to purchase a satellite device understand the differences.

SPOT GEN3

The Spot Gen3 is the most basic of these four options. It allows the hiker to send pre-typed messages, but it doesn't allow incoming messages or the ability to create custom messages. The advantage of the Spot Gen3 is that it is the least expensive of the four, with a base cost of $149.^{99}. It is also the second lightest at only 4.0 oz. This device allows GPS tracking and has an SOS button in addition to sending three messages with GPS coordinates to up to 10 predetermined contacts via either email or SMS messaging. The three messages include one message to show you're okay, one message to say you need help (different from the SOS button), and one custom pre-typed message. Downsides are that there is no screen, no keyboard, no ability to type custom messages while on the trail, and that each pre-typed message has to be entered online. While this is often done before leaving for the hike, it is possible to go online to change the messages, though that is dependent on having cell reception or WiFi.

Feedback from hikers shows that if the device is in a pocket as opposed to on the outside of a pack, or if the hiker is in a canyon or under dense tree cover, the messages might have trouble sending. Without the ability to know that a message has gone through, it's impossible to know if the message needs to be re-sent, and those at home could go longer than expected without hearing from the hiker when everything is actually fine.

SPOT X

The Spot X shares all the features of the Spot Gen3, but unlike the Spot Gen3, the Spot X offers two-way messaging and has a full QWERTY keyboard to type custom messages. The Spot X also allows hikers to link their social media accounts to send updates in addition to email and SMS options. The downside to Spot messaging compared to Garmin messaging is that Spot devices do not show a confirmation that the message has been delivered, while Garmin devices do. This can cause unnecessary concern for families if the hiker is unaware a message didn't transmit. The Spot X has a base cost of $199.99 and weighs 7.0 oz.

GARMIN INREACH EXPLORER+

The Garmin InReach Explorer+ allows two-way messaging and includes message delivery confirmation so that the hikers know if their messages have gone through. This device also includes social media linking and can connect to the hiker's cell phone via bluetooth, allowing messages to be sent and received from the phone instead of needing to type on the device itself - a feature that neither of the Spot devices have. Garmin devices use 66 satellites worldwide, while Spot only use 24. This seems to contribute to faster message delivery with Garmin devices. In addition, this device allows hikers to download topographic maps. The downside is that Garmin InReach Explorer+ is the most expensive and heaviest of the four options. The base cost is $449.[99] and it weighs 7.5 oz.

GARMIN INREACH MINI

This is the newest of the four devices to hit the market and I've already seen many hikers on the trail using it. The main draw for this device is the size and weight - 2.04 in by 3.90 in by 1.03 in and only 3.5 oz! While you can also download GPS maps with this device, it does not have a screen and needs to be paired with a smart phone in order for maps to be accessed and custom messages to be typed. I would personally only choose the InReach Explorer+ over the InReach Mini if I didn't have a smart phone to pair it with. The other benefit of the InReach Mini over the InReach Explorer+ is that the Mini is less expensive at $349.[99].

Because the reliability of satellite communication devices isn't perfect, it's important to have an idea of where your hiker is on the trail and when to expect your hiker in town. Talk ahead of time about how often you expect to receive communication via these devices and how long you should wait without receiving a message before you begin to worry. You can compare where they are in their message against where they expected to be on their itinerary to see if they will get to town earlier or later than anticipated.

Ask your hiker to take the device on a practice hike to get a feel for how quickly messages are sent back and forth when there is a clear sky versus dense tree cover or inclement weather. Have your hiker test where their device is stored and if that affects how the messages send. The top complaint about satellite communication devices seems to be that when they are spotty it can cause family and friends at home to worry. Try to remember that if your hiker didn't have a tracker, less frequent contact would be normal and no cause for heightened concern. Follow the pre-established plan when the gap between messages is longer than feels comfortable and don't jump to the assumption that there is a problem. Dead batteries and rainy skies may be the only obstacle your hiker is facing.

A NOTE ON SATELLITE COMMUNICATION DEVICES FROM THE PCTA

"THESE DEVICES CAN PROVIDE WONDERFUL REASSURANCES FOR PEOPLE AT HOME. BUT JUST AS OFTEN THEY ARE THE MAIN SOURCE OF ANGUISH AND ANXIETY. EXAMPLE: YOU'VE BEEN GETTING 'I'M FINE' MESSAGES ON A REGULAR BASIS, THEN NOTHING. THE REGULAR MESSAGES CREATED AN EXPECTATION OF CONTACT. WHEN DAYS GO BY, YOUR EXPECTATION ISN'T BEING MET AND PANIC SETS IN. HOW DO YOU INTERPRET THE LACK OF NEW INFORMATION? YOUR MIND SPINS HOPELESSLY OUT OF CONTROL. WAS YOUR SON OR DAUGHTER ATTACKED BY A BEAR? WHILE POSSIBLE, THAT'S HIGHLY UNLIKELY. FAR MORE FREQUENTLY, YOUR SON OR DAUGHTER JUST FORGOT TO SEND A MESSAGE. THEY GOT TIRED OR, MOST LIKELY, DISTRACTED BY THE BEAUTY OF THEIR TRIP. THEY MIGHT HAVE TURNED THEIR UNIT OFF TOO QUICKLY AFTER SENDING THE MESSAGE, NOT GIVING IT ENOUGH TIME TO TRANSMIT. MAYBE THE UNIT'S BATTERIES RAN OUT. OR PERHAPS THEY'RE RUNNING LOW AND THEY DON'T REALIZE IT. MAYBE THEY LOST THE DEVICE OR LEFT IT SITTING ON A LOG 15 MILES BACK ON THE TRAIL. MAYBE IT BROKE WHEN THEY DROPPED IT. MAYBE THEY PRESSED THE BUTTON, BUT THE SATELLITE SYSTEM THAT COMMUNICATES WITH THE UNIT DIDN'T TRANSMIT THE MESSAGE. PERHAPS THEY PRESSED THE BUTTON WHILE UNDER DENSE TREE COVER OR IN A DEEP CANYON."[88]

"I CARRY AN INREACH WITH THE MOST BASIC PLAN. EACH NIGHT
I SEND A MESSAGE WITH MY LOCATION SO MY WIFE GETS AN
EMAIL SAYING I'M ALIVE AND THIS IS WHERE I'M CAMPING.
THAT WORKED REALLY WELL, ESPECIALLY DURING THE SIERRA
WHEN THERE WERE 9, 10, 11-DAY STRETCHES WITH NO SIGNAL.
THE TIMING ON MY MESSAGES WERE CRISS-CROSSED ONE TIME
WHICH CAUSED HER TO PANIC, BUT THE NEXT DAY HER MESSAGE
CAME THROUGH AND I RESPONDED. OTHER THAN THAT, IT'S BEEN
GREAT TO LET THEM KNOW I'M ALIVE AND WELL." - JUSTIN, 40,
TEXAS

"I HAVE THE GARMIN INREACH AND I SEND MY SISTER A
MESSAGE EVERY NIGHT. IF I FORGET SHE REPRIMANDS ME, WHICH
IS SO FUNNY BECAUSE SHE'S YOUNGER, BUT I THINK GETTING
A CHECK-IN EVERY NIGHT GIVES HER A HUGE PEACE OF MIND.
I USUALLY GIVE A TIME FRAME, LIKE I'LL TELL MY FAMILY
I'LL BE OUT OF RECEPTION FOR FIVE DAYS." - KATRINA, 39,
ILLINOIS

"ONE SURPRISE WE HAD WAS WHEN MY HUSBAND WAS ON A
SECTION HIKE AND A TROPICAL STORM HIT. I WAS PREPARED
FOR NORMAL WEATHER, BUT NOT THAT. HE ENDED UP HAVING A
MALFUNCTION WITH THE SPOT DEVICE AND WAS ABLE TO DRY IT
OUT, BUT I WASN'T ABLE TO TALK TO HIM FOR LONGER THAN I
EXPECTED, WHICH WAS A SHOCK FOR ME THAT I DIDN'T PREPARE
MYSELF FOR. I HAD TO LEARN TO BE A LITTLE MORE FLEXIBLE
AND UNDERSTAND THAT IF I DIDN'T HEAR FROM HIM FOR A DAY
OR SO, IT WASN'T NECESSARILY A BAD THING AND I NEEDED TO
GIVE HIM SOME EXTRA LEEWAY, WHICH ENDED UP TAKING SOME
STRESS OFF OF HIM AS WELL." - TABATHA, 34, FLORIDA

"I HAVE A GARMIN INREACH MINI. I GOT IT BECAUSE IT WAS
SMALL, HOOKED ON MY PACK EASILY, AND PAIRS TO MY PHONE
WITH BLUETOOTH SO IT'S EASY TO TYPE TEXTS. YOU CAN PAY
MORE TO HAVE MORE OPTIONS AND YOU CAN TURN IT OFF WHEN
YOU'RE NOT HIKING AT ALL." - NIKKI, 40, WISCONSIN

PLANNING A VISIT

Planning a visit to see your hiker on the trail can change your understanding of a long-distance hike. For many, being able to see the trail itself, view the hiker in action, and meet other hikers can be the best way to feel at ease with the hiker being out there.

How a hiker will respond to friends and family visiting isn't consistent. Some love visitors, while others want to keep the experience their own. Don't forget that you may not be the only person who wants to visit your hiker. It can be difficult for hikers to coordinate one visit, let alone several, and overwhelming your hiker with expectations might cause stress.

When is the best time to visit if you want to hike a bit of the trail? While folks at home might think the answer would be when the weather is nicest, when their hiker reaches their home state, or when a three-day weekend turns up at work, most hikers reported that the easiest time to have a visitor was at the beginning of the hike.

Even if your hiker wants to start the trail alone, meeting them in the first few days or towns may work best. Your hiker won't have their trail legs[1] yet, which will eliminate many pacing issues that become problematic further into the trail. It will also be more enjoyable to do low miles when that is the mileage your hiker would be doing anyway, rather than when the itch to go fast has hit. While it won't kill a hiker to slow down for a day halfway through, there are other factors that could come into play.

If your hiker has formed a trail family and you want to visit for a few days in the later portions of the hike, slowing down could mean losing hiking partners. While many friends would be okay with slowing down for a day if someone's family is in town, sometimes they can't afford that choice. The further into the trail a hiker gets, the narrower the window to make adjustments and still meet goals. Hikers go slower at the start of hikes not only because they aren't in shape for big miles yet, but because they have the time to afford moving slowly. As time passes, hikers pick up the pace to make up for dilly-dallying, to stay on-target as the end of a weather window approaches, because their funds run thinner than anticipated, and to return to obligations at home—like university or work.

"THERE WERE A LOT OF POSITIVES AND NEGATIVES FOR HAVING MY FRIEND COME HIKE WITH ME ON THE TRAIL. THE POSITIVES WERE THAT I GOT TO SEE MY FRIEND AND HE BROUGHT US A RESUPPLY IN THE 100-MILE WILDERNESS; THAT WAS REALLY AWESOME AND IT WAS GOOD TO SEE HIM. THE NOT-SO-GOOD PART WAS THAT WHEN I ORIGINALLY TOLD HIM TO COME, IT WAS GOING TO BE THREE DAYS OF 13-MILE HIKES, WHICH PRETTY MUCH ANYBODY CAN DO. THAT'S WHAT WE STARTED OFF IN GEORGIA DOING. BUT BECAUSE EVERYTHING GOT COMPRESSED AT THE END, IT FORCED HIM TO HAVE TO DO A 20-MILE DAY AND A 21-MILE DAY, AND THAT'S UNFAIR TO ASK OF SOMEONE WHO HASN'T BEEN HIKING FOR 2,000+ MILES. HE WAS OKAY FOR HALF OF THE FIRST DAY, BUT THEN WE HAD A LITTLE MOUNTAIN TO CLIMB AND AFTER THAT HE WAS GETTING CRUSHED. IT TOOK US SO MUCH LONGER THAN I THOUGHT. IT'S NOT HIS FAULT, BUT THAT'S JUST HOW IT WAS." - KEITH, 29, NEW JERSEY

---

1 Hikers use the term "trail legs" to describe when their legs have become machines accustomed to hiking long distances and tackling terrain at paces and lengths that are hard to match by someone who has not been hiking all day, every day.

If your hiker's trail family gets ahead, there's still the option of making new friends, but your hiker may have formed connections that would be hard— or impossible—to replace. Being separated from a hiking family could make staying in the groove of hiking more difficult. Losing the close bond and mutual dependency that hiker-groups develop can be really tough.

If you're a supporter who is uncomfortable with your hiker being alone, keep in mind that possibility if your visit is too far into the journey. Developing a trail family is important for many hikers and a hiker's desire to have visitors may change if the visit can cause your hiker to fall too far behind their group on the trail. A visit that seemed like a good idea pre-hike may not seem like the best option as the time approaches. It's important for potential visitors to understand the possible impacts of a visit—positive and negative—and to support and decision made by the hiker.

A tip to remember is that you can pick the time you visit, or you can pick the place, but you will have difficulty trying to coordinate both exact dates and locations any further than a few weeks in advance. I'm not saying it's impossible to visit your hiker later along the trail, but the amount of time they'll be able to spend with you might be limited or less-flexible.

What if you aren't able to visit your hiker at the start of the hike, but still want to find a way to visit? By remaining flexible, you can plan to meet in a specific town. The hiker likely won't be able to finalize the exact date until the week or two before, but by meeting in town, you can spend time together on a zero day or near-o day when the hiker isn't as concerned about miles. In fact, visiting in town could be helpful, as the ability to have you drive them to the grocery store, post office, or to any other necessary chores, will be much appreciated.

If you'd rather pick a specific date, as it may be something you need to request from work in advance, try seeing if your hiker would be happier having you come on a holiday, like the 4th of July. The likelihood of the hiker's group wanting to take a day off might be higher. There were several times on the trail where multiple friends' parents were in town because they had all planned their visits for the same holiday. This is a great scenario because your hiker doesn't need to worry about their trail family waiting if other families are visiting as well. It could also be nice to meet the families of the people with whom your hiker is spending time.

If you want to visit for several days but your hiker isn't keen on taking more than a day off from hiking, there are still ways to maximize time together. It can be hard to validate a visit for only one day, so knowing ways to spend time with your hiker while allowing him or her to stay focused could help better the experience. Having a copy of the hiker's ideal itinerary during the time you're considering visiting, as well as a list of the road intersections that cross the trail during that stretch can help you coordinate visits or even trail magic. If you have a car, and there are roads near your hiker's intended campsite, you could hike in to visit at the campsite. You'll gain massive points if you bring a treat, like fresh fruit or soda, for your hiker to enjoy. Knowing you will be at camp could give your hiker extra motivation to get there and spend time with you. Better yet, it will submerge you into the trail experience without requiring anything too physically demanding. If your hiker is planning on camping four miles from the closest road intersection, you'll have all day to make those miles.

My friend Nian visited me on the Appalachian Trail the day we reached Max Patch, a popular bald in North Carolina. The parking lot was only a quarter-mile from the top of Max Patch, so we agreed to push there by sunset. Because Nian only had to walk a short distance, he decided to bring dinner for us. Not only was I thrilled to see him, but watching the sun set with southern barbecue was one of my favorite nights on the trail. On top of that, I got to spend the entire evening with him as well as breakfast the following morning, and it didn't affect my miles.

Another way to be an MVP is to offer to slack-pack your hiker. Slack-packing is when your hiker only carries the essentials for a day hike, leaving extra food, camping gear, and other items with a support person until meeting back up later in the day. It's a treat for your hiker to carry less weight, and with less weight hikers can move faster and further. Keep in mind, your hiker may decline this offer, as some purists view slack-packing as cheating.

One final suggestion: if your hiker is with a trail family, see if there are any Airbnb's available in town. Often renting an Airbnb that sleeps many people will be the same price, if not less expensive, than getting hotel rooms for you and your hiker. When my parents visited us in Duncannon, Pennsylvania, we were a bit behind schedule, so my group hoped to near-o in town and then get back out the following morning. My parents got an Airbnb that slept everyone. Knowing they would be there to drive us to the grocery store and that everyone would sleep in a bed gave us the extra push to get to town.

One can only hope that your hiker would be happy to see you along their journey, but there are some who prefer to save the reunions for after they finish. Seeing familiar faces from home has the potential to create homesickness and can put your hiker into a funk once you've left. Your visit could serve as a reminder of what your hiker is missing at home, and any previous struggles to stay focused may be amplified.

A TIP FOR VISITING YOUR HIKER IN TOWN

IF YOU KNOW THAT YOU'LL BE VISITING YOUR HIKER IN TOWN, ASK IF THEY'D LIKE TO LEAVE AN OUTFIT FOR YOU TO BRING. I WAS JEALOUS WHEN I SAW A HIKER COME TO DINNER WEARING JEANS AND A CUTE TOP, BECAUSE I MISSED WEARING CLOTHES THAT DIDN'T PRIORITIZE FUNCTION OVER AESTHETICS. BRINGING AN OUTFIT TO LOUNGE OR SLEEP IN WOULD ALSO BE A TREAT. REMEMBER THAT YOUR HIKER IS WITHOUT SIMPLE LUXURIES, SO IF THERE ARE SMALL THINGS YOU CAN DO THAT WILL BRING THEM SOME COMFORT, THEY WILL BE APPRECIATED.

The same is true for having your hiker visit home—sometimes it helps, and sometimes it's a detriment. After we stayed with my parents in New York it was hard to find the motivation to get back on the trail. We dragged our feet for the week that followed. Rediscovering the comforts of home was a painful reminder of what we didn't have. The following days when I felt sore or when the weather turned sour, I couldn't keep my mind from drifting towards the idea of returning home and being done with it all. Of course, that wasn't what I actually wanted, but it had felt like a tease to be given all of my comforts back only to watch them be taken away again.

Another reason a hiker may be apprehensive to have a visitor is wanting to keep the trail *their thing*. Because it's so hard to relate to what hiking a long-distance trail is like, having visitors spend a few days on the trail and then go home and act like they fully grasp the experience can be frustrating to the hiker. The idea of having to share an experience like this with a person who only gets a taste of it might be something your hiker would prefer to go without. Try to understand this isn't about how your hiker feels about you, rather how they feel about this experience. There may be fear that sharing it could take away from it.

"I PICKED HER UP FOR HER SISTER'S BIRTHDAY. WHEN I TOOK HER BACK I SPENT THREE DAYS WITH HER AND INITIALLY WAS LIKE, 'I DON'T KNOW IF I COULD DO THIS FOR FIVE OR SIX MONTHS. I DON'T KNOW WHAT THE ATTRACTION IS.' BUT BY THE END OF THE THREE DAYS I WAS HOOKED. I WENT OUT TWO MORE TIMES. I DID MT. MOOSILAUKE AND THE 100-MILE WILDERNESS WITH HER. IT WAS THE PEOPLE AND THE TRAIL ITSELF. BEING OUTSIDE. THE WHOLE THING. THE YEAR AFTER, I HIKED MASSACHUSETTS AND 30 MILES OF NEW HAMPSHIRE. THIS YEAR I'VE BEEN OUT TWICE. IT'S FUNNY, YOU FINISH THE HIKE AND CAN'T WAIT TO GET HOME, THEN TWO DAYS LATER YOU'RE TRYING TO FIGURE OUT YOUR NEXT WAY OUT AGAIN. I CAN'T SAY ENOUGH ABOUT IT. THERE'S NO POLITICS, WHICH I THOUGHT WAS GREAT. IT WAS JUST PEOPLE WITH SIMILAR INTERESTS. DOWN TO EARTH, GREAT PEOPLE. I ENJOYED MEETING PEOPLE JUST AS MUCH AS HIKING. I'VE MET SOME LIFE-LONG FRIENDS. I'VE DONE ABOUT 250 MILES NOW, AND I'VE GOT FIVE LIFE-LONG FRIENDS." - DON, 64, MASSACHUSETTS

"I KNEW THAT IF WE HAD BEEN HIKING FOR FIVE MONTHS IT WOULD BE WEIRD HAVING SOMEONE VISIT WHO HASN'T BEEN ON THE TRAIL. EVEN BEING IN THE MINDSET OF THRU-HIKING WOULD MAKE IT DIFFICULT - HAVING SOMEONE VISIT THAT HAS BEEN AT HOME WITH THEIR COMFORTS, HASN'T BEEN RAINED ON FOR DAYS, HASN'T BEEN SLEEPING IN LOW TEMPERATURES. IT WOULD BE WEIRD TO HAVE TO ADJUST TO THEIR COMFORTS WHEN WE'VE GOTTEN RID OF OURS." - JACKIE, 26, GEORGIA

"WHEN I GOT TO VERMONT, MY WIFE CALLED AND ASKED IF I GOT HER PACKAGE. I TOLD HER NO. SHE SAID TO CHECK THE FRONT PORCH, AND THERE WAS MY FAMILY. MY WIFE, TWO KIDS, AND MOTHER-IN-LAW ALL SURPRISED ME. I WAS SHOCKED. IT WAS LIKE WORLD'S COLLIDE. I DIDN'T KNOW HOW TO REACT. I ONLY TOOK EIGHT ZERO DAYS THE WHOLE TRAIL, BUT I TOOK TWO THAT DAY. PEOPLE ALWAYS ASK, 'WHAT'S THE HARDEST DAY?' SOME SAY IT'S THE CLIMBS IN THE WHITES OR THE WILDCATS, OR THE MAHOOSUC NOTCH. THE HARDEST DAY FOR ME WAS THE DAY I HAD TO SAY GOODBYE TO THEM. WE'RE TALKING ABOUT THE VERMONT/MASSACHUSETTS STATE LINE. THE NEXT ZERO DAY WAS AFTER I SUMMITED KATAHDIN. I WAS SO DRIVEN. SEEING FAMILY KEPT ME GOING, BUT IT WAS TOUGH. THE MENTAL ASPECT WAS TOUGH. IT MADE ME HOMESICK. WHEN THEY TOOK ME BACK TO THAT GRAVEL ROAD WE SAID GOODBYE, GAVE HUGS AND KISSES, AND I SAID THAT I WAS GOING TO HEAD NORTH, I WAS NOT GOING TO TURN BACK AROUND, AND I WAS GOING TO RIP THE BAND-AID OFF. I COULD HEAR THE CAR DOOR CLOSING AND THE ENGINE STARTING. I COULD HEAR THEM DRIVING DOWN THE ROAD. IT BROKE MY HEART. IT WAS REALLY TOUGH. THAT WAS THE HARDEST DAY ON THE TRAIL, BUT I STUCK TO IT. AS MUCH AS I BATTLED IN MY BRAIN ABOUT HOW MUCH FURTHER I HAD TO GO, MY LEGS KEPT MOVING, AND AS LONG AS MY LEGS KEPT MOVING I KNEW I WAS GOING TO FINISH. I TOLD MYSELF TO KEEP WALKING. THAT'S THE PSYCHOLOGICAL ASPECT OF IT. THERE'S A MENTAL ASPECT THAT A LOT OF PEOPLE CAN'T COMPREHEND, BUT BEING COMMITTED TO SOMETHING FOR THAT MANY MONTHS, AWAY FROM YOUR FAMILY, AWAY FROM YOUR HOME; THAT'S TOUGH." - GARY, 59, MISSOURI

"I TOOK TWO ZERO DAYS AND A NEAR-O DAY FOR EACH VISIT. IT WAS GOOD ENOUGH THAT I COULD GET SOME REST, I WASN'T FALLING TOO FAR BEHIND FROM THE PEOPLE I WANTED TO BE HIKING WITH, AND I DIDN'T GET TOO COMFORTABLE THAT I DIDN'T WANT TO GET BACK ON TRAIL." - KATIE, 25, COLORADO

DESIGNATED AT-HOME COORDINATOR

This coordinator is someone off-trail who has a copy of the hiker's itinerary, handles mail (resupply boxes, swapping out gear, or sending replacement gear), and acts as a point-of-contact for hiker updates. Designating an at-home coordinator will ensure that someone knows roughly where the hiker is, if the hiker is late to contact, or if something feels wrong. It will also be a help to your hiker when they inevitably need something mailed. This was my most important person while I was on the trail, and I relied on my at-home coordinator to send needed supplies on time. This person may be responsible for the following:

KEEP UPDATED ITINERARIES: THE HIKER CAN LEAVE A SAMPLE ITINERARY BEFORE STARTING, AND SEND UPDATES.

MAIL: HOW INTENSIVE THIS TASK IS DEPENDS ON IF THE HIKER WILL BE SENDING RESUPPLY BOXES OR IF THE PRIMARY TASK IS SWAPPING OUT GEAR.

KEEP IMPORTANT INFORMATION: IN THE EVENT OF AN EMERGENCY, HAVING A PERSON AT HOME WHO KNOWS THE HIKER'S TRAIL NAME, HAS A PHOTO/DESCRIPTION OF THE HIKER, AND KNOWS THE NAMES AND PHONE NUMBERS OF REGULAR HIKING PARTNERS IS CRUCIAL. LEAVING COPIES OF IMPORTANT CARDS LIKE A DRIVER'S LICENSE, CREDIT CARD, AND INSURANCE CARD CAN ALSO HELP IN THE EVENT OF A LOST WALLET OR CELL PHONE.

KEEP OTHERS INFORMED: WITH LIMITED TIME OFF-TRAIL AND LIMITED DOWN-TIME WHILE HIKING, IT'S A HASSLE TO SEND THE SAME MESSAGE TO SIX DIFFERENT PEOPLE, SO HAVING ONE PERSON IN CHARGE OF RECEIVING UPDATES THAT CAN BE RELAYED TO OTHER FRIENDS OR FAMILY HELPS TAKE STRESS OFF THE HIKER.

WHO TO CONTACT IF SOMETHING IS WRONG

No one wants any hiker to face trouble, but in the event that something feels wrong it's helpful to know who to contact. If there's an emergency, you can always call 911 and a dispatcher will redirect you to the correct contact. However, it's important to differentiate when a hiker is too busy to check in, versus when they have gone too long without checking in, to avoid calling for a search that isn't necessary. This is why it matters to have a person at home who your hiker will send updates to and inform when they are going into stretches where communication may be less frequent. Setting an expectation for how long you will wait before worrying will hold your hiker accountable to regular check-ins.

The first step you can take in a non-emergency is to check the hiker's activity compared to the time frame provided. Is your hiker late to check in? If so, try calling and texting. If your hiker has a satellite device that tracks progress, check to see where it last tracked your hiker. If he or she has social media accounts, check those. Your hiker may have been unable to call, but posted an Instagram or Facebook update since your last contact.

If you do not have success through these searches, search the trail name and the year to find the appropriate Facebook group. For my AT hike, it would have been, "Appalachian Trail Thru-Hikers Class of 2019," though names may vary year-to-year. Try posting on the appropriate Facebook group with a photo of your hiker (preferably from the trail), your hiker's trail name, and a short sentence or two saying when you last contact was, where your hiker was on the trail, and asking if anyone has seen him or her recently. I've seen posts like this with comments from other hikers saying when and where they last saw the hiker in question.

If this doesn't provide answers, the next step would be to call the sheriff in the county of your hiker's last known location. Explain your concerns and the steps you've already taken, and tell the sheriff you would like to file a missing persons report. The exception to this would be if your hiker was last in a National Park, as they have

their own Search and Rescue (SAR) teams. In that case, you would
call the National Park. If necessary, Search and Rescue will be
able to dispatch a team to look for your hiker. Should they decide
that a search is warranted, the photo of your hiker and photos and
descriptions of your hiker's gear will be useful.

HAVE YOUR HIKER PREPARE THEIR AT-HOME COORDINATOR WITH
THE FOLLOWING INFORMATION:

- NAME AND NICKNAME, TRAIL NAME, OR OTHER ALIASES
- PHONE NUMBER AND PHONE PROVIDER
- PHOTO OF DRIVERS LICENSE/PASSPORT AND INSURANCE CARD
- PHYSICAL DESCRIPTION: HEIGHT, WEIGHT, AGE, HAIR
  COLOR, EYE COLOR, NOTABLE SCARS, TATTOOS, AND ANY
  OTHER CHARACTERISTICS THAT COULD BE USED FOR
  IDENTIFICATION
- RECENT PHOTOS OF THE HIKER ON THE TRAIL
- LIST AND PHOTOS OF GEAR, CLOTHING, AND SHOES,
  INCLUDING COLOR, BRAND, MODEL, AND SIZE
- LIST OF MEDICATIONS, ALLERGIES, AND ANY OTHER NOTABLE
  MEDICAL CONDITIONS
- LAST UPDATED TRIP ITINERARY, LAST KNOWN LOCATION,
  ANTICIPATED CHECK-IN DATE, ANTICIPATED LOCATION OF
  HIKER
- ANY KNOWN FACTORS THAT MAY AFFECT THE HIKER'S
  ABILITY TO BE IN CONTACT: BAD WEATHER, MEDICAL
  CONDITIONS, DIFFICULT TERRAIN, ETC.
- NAMES AND PHONE NUMBERS OF OTHER HIKERS LAST KNOWN
  TO BE WITH YOUR HIKER
- SEALED ENVELOPE OF PASSWORDS, VARIOUS ACCOUNT
  DETAILS, AND LIVING WILL

Hikers' appearances could change on the trail, especially if they
grow out their hair or beards. Having updated photos of what your
hiker looks like on the trail will be more useful than ones from home.
It will be easier to recognize a person by trail appearance than from a
photo in a business suit.

"I THINK A WEEK IS THE SPECIAL NUMBER. I KNOW IT'S HARD FOR PARENTS TO UNDERSTAND THIS, BUT SOME HIKERS DON'T WANT TO TALK. THEY DON'T WANT TO BE ON THEIR PHONES AND THEY DON'T WANT TO COMMUNICATE. THEY LIKE JUST BEING OUT THERE. SO I THINK WAITING SEVEN DAYS IS OKAY. BEFORE THEY LEAVE FOR THE TRAIL, MAKE A RULE. SAY THEY NEED TO COMMUNICATE AT LEAST ONCE EVERY SEVEN DAYS. FOR SOME PEOPLE I KNOW THAT WOULD BE WAY TOO LONG, BUT FOR ME IT WOULD BE A WEEK. THERE USUALLY WON'T BE SEVEN DAYS WHERE THE HIKER WON'T HAVE SERVICE, SO I THINK IT'S REASONABLE FOR BOTH THE HIKER AND THE PARENT." - ROB, 34, OHIO

Waiting while SAR does their job can be frustrating and stressful. Luckily, there are measures you can take during this time to help spread the word about your missing hiker and create awareness on the trail. Work in conjunction with SAR and law enforcement to ensure actions don't interfere with or cause confusion in their search plan. Put together a flier with photos and descriptions of the hiker, his or her gear, clothing, and who to contact with information. Create a Facebook page to share your flier and additional updates. Share your flier to other sites like Reddit or Instagram, as well as to the trail Facebook page to which you initially posted. Contact local television stations, radio stations, newspapers, etc. and ask them to help spread the word. Contact local outdoor organizations, ranger stations, forest service or Bureau of Land Management (BLM) offices, etc. as well.

Once you've spread the word, try to coordinate with SAR so that you or others can assist with the search. SAR will keep track of what areas have been searched and what areas still need to be combed through. Post on your newly created Facebook page with updates on upcoming searches and ask for volunteers to help. Most importantly, stay hopeful, stay optimistic, and stay involved.

"Hello all... My name is Sally and my son Sherpa is a missing hiker from the awesome Class of 2016. You will see me on here saying Mom things from time to time. Please know I only have yours and your family's well being in mind."

Every year, Sally Fowler makes a post on the current class' Pacific Crest Trail Facebook page that begins this way. Her son Sherpa went missing in Washington on the PCT in October, 2016; a risky time to still be in the Cascades due to the potential for winter storms. She is a parent who has gone through a worst-case scenario, and offers advice to the current year's hikers on what they can do beforehand to take responsibility for themselves if something happens to them on the trail. It's a topic that can be tough to read, as no hiker wants to consider being the exception, but important, as Sally has shared first-hand examples of things her son, Sherpa, could have done to limit the struggles she faces in his absence.

As a long-distance hiker, her suggestions are not always ones I want to follow. Because hikers spend so much effort trying to convince those at home that nothing bad will happen to them, handing over things like a living will or a sealed envelope with passwords and account details, seems like a quick way to ruin any progress made towards comforting those at home. These aren't documents or materials that a parent or loved one wants to see, but Sally explains how privacy and HIPPA laws can prevent a hiker's family members from accessing information or making medical decisions for the hiker without certain items in place. She also explains that having access to passwords and account details, like the hiker's bank account or phone account, will help track phone activity or recent purchases and can lead to clues that narrow down areas to search.

Sally admits that her "invincible" son probably wouldn't have taken her advice, as he considered himself a *grown-ass man* and didn't have any intention of going missing. However, she also reinforces that if your hiker is going to take this adult journey, they should also take some adult steps beforehand.

"The Will is very important. Even if you have nothing. Leave who you want to be your beneficiary and power of attorney. Without this, if you are over 18 and end up in a hospital and your parents or loved one calls to check on you, the hospital does not have to and may not tell them anything at all about you or your condition. You can go online and find out how to do your Will and you don't have to spend a lot of money to do it."

This is not meant to crumble any reassurances we may have built in the pages prior to this section, rather it is a reminder that bad things can happen to good people at any phase of life in any location. While most people will never need to use this information, having it available is the least a hiker can do to protect loved ones from additional hardships and struggles in a worst-case scenario. Sally tells hikers that if they think life is hard, they haven't dealt with a death. She signs off asking hikers to keep an eye out for her son when they get to Washington, noting that he would want to be found.

SECTION FIVE
SUPPORT

BEFORE THE HIKE

Your hiker is likely to face some pre-trail anxiousness as they become consumed with preparations. Researching, selecting, and purchasing gear, testing clothing and other purchases, training, getting in shape, assembling resupply boxes, subletting their apartment, moving items into storage, and closing out tasks at home is enough to overwhelm anyone. Your hiker is probably growing apprehensive, especially if they have spent a long amount of time preparing. A long-distance hike has a way of feeling so far away, that when the start-date approaches, it can cause a person to second-guess if they are ready.

"ONE ISSUE AFFECTING ME IS PRE-HIKE ANXIETY. I'M TORTURING MYSELF OVER WHICH SHIRT TO BRING. I'M DOING TESTING, BUT MY LOVED ONES DON'T GET THE PASSION I HAVE FOR THE GEAR SELECTION THAT I'M GOING THROUGH. AMPLIFY THAT BY 100 FOR SOMEONE WHO'S NEVER DONE THIS BEFORE. THEN AMPLIFY THE ANXIETY ABOUT THE LOGISTICS ON THE TRAIL, WHERE TO STOP, HOW TO FILL UP, WHAT FOOD TO PREPARE. OH MY GOODNESS, IT'S OVERWHELMING. I WAS WORKING ON THIS SPREADSHEET ABOUT POTENTIAL PLACES TO RESUPPLY. I KNOW IT'S GOING TO BE LOOSEY-GOOSEY, BUT IT'S FUN JUST TO GIVE ME AN IDEA. MY WIFE ASKED IF I WAS GOING TO BE DOING THIS RIGHT UNTIL MARCH, BUT IT'S IMPORTANT TO ME AND IT HELPS RELIEVE MY ANXIETY ABOUT THE WHOLE THING. I DON'T THINK OUR LOVED ONES APPRECIATE ALL THE STRESS THAT A PERSON HAS WHEN PLANNING FOR THIS." - BRUCE, 60, ONTARIO

Having those around your hiker also questioning if they are prepared can add to the stress he or she might be feeling, but there are constructive ways to put your hiker at ease. Most hikers I spoke to said the best support they received was simply having others express interest and enthusiasm.

'I'LL BUMP INTO PEOPLE, AND THEY'LL SAY, 'OH, I HEARD
YOU'RE DOING THIS!' IT KEEPS THE STOKE HIGH, WHICH IS
NICE BECAUSE ALL OF THE LOGISTICS AND PLANNING CAN GET
STRAINING. YOU START STRESSING ABOUT MONEY AND CAN GET
DRAGGED DOWN ABOUT THAT, BUT JUST TALKING TO SOMEONE
AND HAVING THEM TELL YOU THEY'RE GOING TO TUNE IN
WHENEVER THEY CAN AND TO LET THEM KNOW IF THEY CAN DO
ANYTHING KEEPS THE STOKE HIGH.' - ZACH, 23, MICHIGAN

If you are looking to give more than a pat on the back, try offering to help with a portion of the research. Some things will need to be researched by your hiker, but small tasks, like comparing two pieces of similar gear, can be done by anyone. Your hiker will be able to use your notes to assist with decisions and will appreciate being able to cross something small off the to-do list. Make sure your hiker is receptive to this before you dive in. Unsolicited advice may not be appreciated and could add stress if your hiker is already overwhelmed.

If your hiker would prefer to do the research, try offering to go on a practice hike together. This allows the hiker an opportunity to test gear. Day hikes allow hikers to test out packs and assess if the base weight is too heavy. Overnight trips will help hikers test their shelters and sleep systems. Taking time for the two of you will be a great way to bond before your hiker leaves. Ask questions about how gear selections were made, what features are most liked, and if everything is working as desired.

One supporter went to the hiker's family and friends and had each person record audio clips talking to the hiker, giving encouragement, and reaffirming confidence in the hiker's ability to complete the trail. The supporter compiled the files and sent them to the hiker as a holiday present. The hiker kept the recordings on his phone and listened to them during low-points on the trail when he didn't have reception to call home.

The support you show your hiker in the months leading up to the trail doesn't need to be time consuming or labor intensive. Even offering to be there during organizing and planning can be calming. Having someone willing to sit and read, do homework, or work on the computer while the hiker is doing trail homework can make the tasks less overwhelming.

SMALL TASKS THAT ANYONE CAN HELP WITH

YOUR HIKER MAY HAVE SO MUCH TO RESEARCH AND PREPARE THAT IT'S HARD TO KNOW WHAT TYPES OF HELP TO ASK FOR. HERE ARE SOME SPECIFICS YOU CAN OFFER ASSISTANCE WITH:

- COMPARE SPECS (WEIGHT, COST, SIZE, WARMTH) OF VARIOUS GEAR ITEMS. SEE THE GEAR LISTED IN SECTION ONE FOR IDEAS OF WHAT TO OFFER TO RESEARCH.
- OFFER TO LOOK UP POPULAR BACKPACKING FOODS AND OPTIONS TO BUY IN BULK, ESPECIALLY FOR RESUPPLY BOXES.
- GO SHOPPING TOGETHER. THERE WILL LIKELY BE COUNTLESS TRIPS TO OUTFITTERS AND GROCERY STORES AS YOUR HIKER LOOKS INTO GEAR AND RESUPPLY OPTIONS.
- OFFER TO PICK UP FLAT-RATE BOXES FROM THE POST OFFICE IF YOUR HIKER WILL BE SENDING RESUPPLY BOXES. GO TO A CRAFT STORE AND GET DUCT-TAPE THAT IS COLORFUL OR HAS A PATTERN THAT WILL STAND OUT AGAINST OTHER BOXES.
- OFFER TO RESEARCH POST OFFICE OR HOSTEL ADDRESSES TO WHICH YOUR HIKER CAN SEND BOXES.
- OFFER TO RESEARCH OPTIONS TO GET TO/FROM THE TRAIL.
- LOOK UP DAY HIKES OR OVERNIGHTS NEARBY THAT WOULD BE FUN TO PRACTICE ON AND OFFER TO GO WITH YOUR HIKER.
- OFFER TO GO WITH YOUR HIKER TO THE GYM AS A WORKOUT BUDDY IF YOU DON'T WANT TO GO ON A PRACTICE HIKE.
- MEET FOR DINNER, ASK HOW PREPARATIONS ARE GOING, AND LISTEN TO EVERY EXCRUCIATING, INTRICATE DETAIL.
- COMPARE PRICES OF STORAGE UNITS IN THE AREA IF YOUR HIKER NEEDS TO FIND ONE. IF YOU HAVE A TRUCK OR LARGER VEHICLE, OFFER TO HELP MOVE BELONGINGS INTO STORAGE.
- OFFER ASSISTANCE WITH PET CARE.
- OFFER TO KEEP AN EYE ON YOUR HIKER'S HOUSE, YARD, OR CAR.
- OFFER TO COLLECT MAIL RECEIVED WHILE THE HIKER IS AWAY.

Be aware that your hiker may be experiencing doubt and putting on a brave face to reassure others. Constantly bombarding your hiker with worries about preparedness can do more harm than good. Try not to cause second-guessing. Help your hiker build confidence rather than being the reason it wavers.

"MY MOM WANTED TO GET A GIFT FOR MY BIRTHDAY AND ASKED IF I HAD A WAY TO CHARGE MY PHONE. I TOLD HER I WAS GOING TO GET A SOLAR CHARGER BUT HADN'T BEEN ABLE TO START RESEARCHING IT YET. SHE OFFERED TO DO THE RESEARCH AND ENDED UP GETTING ME ONE. DOING THE RESEARCH WAS HER WAY OF SHOWING SHE SUPPORTED ME, BUT IF SHE HADN'T USED MY BIRTHDAY AS AN EXCUSE I NEVER WOULD'VE ASKED. I HAVE NO DOUBTS IN MY ABILITY TO DO THIS TRAIL, BUT WHAT'S STRESSING ME OUT AND OVERWHELMING ME IS THE IDEA THAT I HAVE TO DO IT 'RIGHT.' I HAVE TO DO SO MUCH RESEARCH. IT'S LIKE THERE'S LEG WORK BEFORE THERE'S EVEN LEG WORK. HAVING MY MOM OFFER TO RESEARCH SOMETHING, THAT WAS THE GIFT. IT'S STRESS OUT THE WINDOW AND I DON'T HAVE TO THINK ABOUT IT." - LILY, 33, WASHINGTON

IS YOUR HIKER PREPARED?

AS THE TIME LEADING UP TO THE TRAIL DRAWS NEAR, HIKERS
MAY START TO QUESTION IF THEY ARE PREPARED. GIVE YOUR
HIKER THIS CHECKLIST IF THEY NEED REASSURING.

- [ ] I HAVE RESEARCHED MY TRAIL
- [ ] I HAVE APPLIED FOR ALL NECESSARY PERMITS
- [ ] I HAVE RESEARCHED + PURCHASED THE GEAR I NEED
- [ ] I HAVE TESTED MY GEAR + CLOTHING
- [ ] I AM SURE I WILL BE WARM ENOUGH
- [ ] I WILL BE ABLE TO KEEP IMPORTANT ITEMS DRY
- [ ] I HAVE THE MAPS I NEED + KNOW HOW TO READ THEM
- [ ] I AM PREPARED FOR VARYING TERRAIN + WEATHER
- [ ] I KNOW THE PACE I MUST MAINTAIN TO FINISH
  WITHIN MY WEATHER WINDOW
- [ ] I HAVE ESTIMATED MY BUDGET + SAVED ACCORDINGLY
- [ ] I HAVE RESEARCHED FOOD STORAGE + PURCHASED THE
  CORRECT OPTION
- [ ] I AM COMFORTABLE WITH THE AMOUNT OF RESUPPLY
  BOXES I HAVE CHOSEN TO SEND
- [ ] I UNDERSTAND WHAT WILDLIFE I MIGHT ENCOUNTER +
  HOW TO REACT TO KEEP ENCOUNTERS FRIENDLY
- [ ] I HAVE DESIGNATED AN AT-HOME COORDINATOR WHO
  HAS MY SAMPLE ITINERARY, PHOTOS OF MY GEAR, +
  OTHER NECESSARY INFORMATION
- [ ] I UNDERSTAND THE LEAVE NO TRACE PRINCIPLES +
  WILL ACT AS A ROLE MODEL ON MY CHOSEN TRAIL
- [ ] I HAVE TRAINED + AM COMFORTABLE WITH THE
  FITNESS LEVEL I WILL START AT
- [ ] I HAVE SPOKEN TO THOSE AT HOME ABOUT HOW OFTEN
  TO EXPECT COMMUNICATION + REPERCUSSIONS FOR
  FAILING TO CHECK IN

DURING THE HIKE

Let your hiker know you're available if he or she is having a hard time and would like to call someone at home. Most of the time when I'd call friends it wouldn't be due to homesickness or wanting to quit, but because I was struggling to stay focused, as the boredom would nag me to sit down, check my phone, or do anything other than continue to hike. Calling a friend while I hiked who could talk about things that had nothing to do with hiking was a great break from the usual chatter at camp and reaffirmed that my connections at home weren't drifting. My friends tried not to make me feel like I was missing out on anything, and hearing them vent about their jobs or stressors at home was a reminder of how lucky I was to be on the trail, which was sometimes easy to forget. It also gave them the ability to talk about their problems to someone who was eager to listen.

> "MY PARENTS GOT A MAP A MONTH BEFORE I STARTED AND THAT WAS REALLY COOL BECAUSE THEY WERE ABLE TO KEEP TRACK OF WHERE I WAS. IT ENCOURAGED ME TO CHECK IN WHEN THEY'D SAY THINGS LIKE, 'OH, WE SEE YOU ON THE MAP.' 'YOU'RE HERE.' 'YOU'RE NOT THAT FAR FROM LA.'" - ELLIOT, 25, ARKANSAS

Tracking progress on something like a wall map[1] is another way of letting your hiker know that you are supporting from afar. My parents marked my PCT progress on a wall map and pinned notes that showed the dates I reached towns. My maps were always zoomed in, so I didn't always know where I was in the grand scheme of the state or country. Having someone point out cities and features that were part of the big-picture was always nice.

On the Appalachian Trail, Easy would call his dad and tell him which mile we had just finished, and his dad would respond with the

---

1 There are wall maps available online for long-distance trails that show the trail in its entirety, with towns and notable landmarks labeled.

percent of trail we had completed. In the beginning, we were hearing numbers like 9 %, or 12 %. Hearing that number rise helped us feel like we were making progress. Despite being able to look it up ourselves, whenever I wanted an update I'd ask Easy to call his dad. It was fun to have someone else tell us, and it was something special that Easy shared with his dad.

On the PCT, a friend's parents used her sample itinerary to tell her how many days she was falling behind. She constantly stressed about needing to go faster, even though the estimates were predicted from the couch. Make sure that if you're tracking your hiker's progress, it's done in a way that encourages progress rather than criticizes it.

"I TOOK PICTURES WITH EACH OF THE KIDS, FRAMED THEM, AND GAVE IT TO THEM SO THAT THEY'D HAVE A PICTURE OF US TO LOOK AT WHILE I WAS ON THE TRAIL. I ALSO BOUGHT ONE OF THOSE WALL MAPS OF THE TRAIL SO THAT THEY COULD USE PINS TO TRACK ME AS I HIKED. THERE ARE LOTS OF OPPORTUNITIES TO CALL HOME AND STAY IN TOUCH. IT WON'T BE LIKE YOU WON'T HEAR FROM THEM FOR FIVE MONTHS." - JUSTIN, 40, TEXAS

Tracking progress can also be turned into a game. Keep a spreadsheet of progress, and make predictions with friends and family on what dates your hiker will reach certain destinations, when they'll get sick of certain foods, or when they'll see certain animals. One of the guys I hiked the PCT with told us that his co-workers had a pool predicting what day he'd finish and that whoever guessed the closest would win. It was a nice way for him to see that those at home were invested in his success.

If you're close enough with your hiker to talk about money, you could offer to be his or her budget keeper. This is usually done by a parent or spouse, but can be helpful to hikers who have tight budgets or are worried about rationing money. I know hikers who created a joint bank account with someone they trusted. The person would add money from the hiker's funds periodically to ensure the hiker couldn't overspend. If your hiker is confident in tracking spending, you could offer to keep only the emergency fund, to ensure it stays reserved for actual emergencies.

If your hiker is sending resupply boxes and you have the time, you could look up recipes to assemble and send using websites like Pinterest. If you don't have your own dehydrator, there are companies that sell dehydrated ingredients. This can add a change of flavor to what your hiker has been eating. Providing a few extra meals for trail friends will give your hiker a reason to brag about you. Test the meals before you send them to make sure they're palatable, and ask for feedback on what your hiker would like in the next box. If you know you'll never have the time to put together a recipe, offer to send a few backpacking meals.

"SHE DEHYDRATED MEALS AND WROTE INSTRUCTIONS, LIKE HOW MUCH WATER TO USE. SHE WOULD ALSO WRITE LITTLE NOTES, LIKE ONE TIME ON A CURRY MEAL SHE WROTE, 'HOPE YOU DON'T GET DIARRHEA!' IT MADE ME SMILE. IT WAS DIFFERENT FROM WHAT I USUALLY ATE, WHICH WAS REALLY NICE, AND SHE GOT BETTER AT MAKING MEALS AS THE TRAIL WENT ON. I WOULD TELL HER, 'MAYBE USE A LITTLE MORE CHICKEN,' OR, 'CAN YOU THROW SOME SALT AND PEPPER IN THE NEXT ONE?' THEY JUST GOT BETTER AND BETTER. SHE SENT EXTRAS THAT I COULD GIVE TO MY FRIENDS AND THEY LOVED IT." - KEITH, 29, NEW JERSEY

If you are looking to provide monetary support, bear in mind that $20 feels like a lot more at the end of a hike than it does in the beginning. Hikers aren't struggling to validate a night in a bed at the start of their hikes the way they are towards the final third. Make your hiker a homemade voucher beforehand that can be redeemed for a bed at a hostel, or reach out during the second half of the trip and ask if you can cover a meal as a treat. Offering something as simple as a $15 bunk could mean more than you'd expect.

Something that didn't cost any money was receiving pictures of friends or family watching my trail videos. Seeing that they enjoyed following my trip made me feel supported. I loved that they wanted to watch and were pro-actively asking for links to videos.

Finally, if your hiker calls to talk, show support by devoting your full attention to the conversation. Should your hiker need to vent, be ready to listen, and use supportive responses that allow your hiker to maintain control of the conversation. In *We Need To Talk, How to Have Conversations That Matter*, "Derber describes two kinds of responses in conversations: a shift response and a support response. The first shifts attention back to yourself and the second supports the other person's comment… Shift responses are a hallmark of conversational narcissism. They help you turn the focus constantly back to yourself. But the support response encourages the other person to continue the story. It lets others know you're listening and interested in hearing more."[89]

SHIFT RESPONSE
HIKER: I'M SO BORED, IT'S HARD NOT TO CHECK THE TIME
     CONSTANTLY.
SUPPORTER: YEAH, WORK HAS BEEN SO DULL TOO. IT IS
     HARD.

SUPPORT RESPONSE
HIKER: I'M SO BORED, IT'S HARD NOT TO CHECK THE TIME
     CONSTANTLY.
SUPPORTER: MORE-SO THAN USUAL? HOW DO YOU NORMALLY
     PASS TIME?

If you're finding it difficult to get your hiker to open up, try looking at the way you are wording your questions. Instead of saying, "Were you cold last night?" Ask, "How was the temperature last night?" By asking open-ended questions, you're ensuring that your hiker has to say more than, "yes," or, "no."

Headlee says, "There's an old trick that reporters use to get people to say interesting things. We start our questions with one of six words: who, what, where, when, why, and how… They can't be answered with a simple yes or no. The most uncomplicated questions often elicit a complicated response, just as a detailed question can result in a one-word answer."[90]

OPEN-ENDED QUESTIONS TO ASK YOUR HIKER

- HOW HAS THE WEATHER BEEN THIS WEEK?
- HOW FAR IS THE NEXT TOWN YOU HAVE TO REACH?
- WHAT KIND OF THINGS ARE NOTEWORTHY IN THE UPCOMING
  STRETCH?
- HOW MANY HIKERS ARE YOU SEEING EACH DAY?
- WHAT WAS THE MOST CHALLENGING PART ABOUT THE
  STRETCH YOU JUST FINISHED?
- WHAT ARE YOU LOOKING FORWARD TO IN THE NEXT TOWN?
- HOW IS YOUR GEAR HOLDING UP? HAVE YOU ADDED/REMOVED
  ANYTHING RECENTLY?
- WHAT KINDS OF MEALS ARE YOU MAKING YOURSELF?

"MY GRANDPA PASSED AWAY AND THAT WAS REALLY DIFFICULT.
I DIDN'T HAVE MUCH SERVICE AND WASN'T ABLE TO GO HOME.
IT WAS A REALLY CHALLENGING TIME MENTALLY. RECEIVING
TEXTS FROM FAMILY HELPED. MY MOM ALSO SENT A PACKAGE
WITH NOTES. THOSE WERE THINGS I NEEDED." - VICTORIA, 29,
GEORGIA

"I'M REALLY LUCKY BECAUSE I HAD A GREAT SUPPORT SYSTEM.
MY BOYFRIEND SENT RESUPPLY BOXES. MY MOM SENT CANDY.
EVERYONE WAS VERY SUPPORTIVE. THERE WASN'T DOUBT OR
NEGATIVITY AROUND WHAT I WAS DOING. I CAN'T IMAGINE
HIKING WITHOUT SUPPORT. I JUST CAN'T IMAGINE WHAT THAT
WOULD BE LIKE. I DEFINITELY FEEL LIKE I GOT LUCKY." -
KATIE, 25, COLORADO

"MY BIGGEST BARRIER WHEN IT COMES TO SUPPORT IS
ACCEPTING IT. I HAVE FAMILY THROUGH NEW ENGLAND THAT
WANT TO HIKE WITH ME FOR A COUPLE OF DAYS, AND I KNOW
THATS AMAZING AND A LOT OF OTHER HIKERS WOULD LOVE
THAT, BUT I DON'T REALLY LIKE HIKING WITH OTHER PEOPLE.
SO IT'S MORE ACCEPTING THE SUPPORT THAT'S HARD, RATHER
THAN A LACK OF IT BEING OFFERED." - LILY, 33, WASHINGTON

TRAIL MAGIC + TRAIL ANGELS

Trail angels are those who help hikers in one form or another. This can consist of taking hikers in and offering them a place to stay, giving rides to/from trailheads, holding resupply boxes for hikers to pick up, providing trail magic, and more. As a rule, trail angels don't charge for their services, but may accept donations.

Trail magic consists of the food, drinks, and other treats that are brought to the trail for hikers to enjoy. It's magic because it's unexpected and unplanned. It can be as simple as cold water on a hot day, or as vast as a cooked meal, chairs to sit in, and blankets to keep warm. It's important that anything scented or edible isn't left unattended and that all trash is packed out. People conducting magic should ensure that they're being responsible and following Leave No Trace principles.

While trail magic can boost morale, too much can take away from the experience or make hikers take it for granted. I notice that I appreciate trail magic most when I've gone a while without any. There were stretches of the A.T. where my group encountered magic two to three times a day. We talked about how it didn't feel as special. It's nice to stop and take a break when coming upon trail magic, so the stretches saturated with magic felt strange because I couldn't afford the time to take a break at each one, and felt bad passing over them, knowing the person had probably looked forward to helping hikers and spending a brief time sharing stories.

Being a trail angel and providing trail magic to individual hikers is a wonderful and appreciated service. But a more-lasting impact on the trail community as a whole is to perform trail maintenance.

TRAIL MAINTENANCE + DONATIONS

Our long-distance trails were built and maintained by volunteers. By participating in trail maintenance, you are giving back to every hiker that walks through the trail, and to the trail itself. Volunteers of all ages and skill-sets can help keep our trails operable. On the Appalachian Trail alone, over 200,000 hours of work are volunteered each year.[91] Volunteering on local trails can help maintain routes that may not be as well funded. A reader who lives near the Buckeye Trail noted that people rarely choose it for a long-hike due to the lack of maintenance. Searching the trail name and, *volunteer, trail crew,* or, *trail maintenance,* online will guide you towards information on how to get involved.

Seeing the visible difference in a trail after your hard work provides a deeper appreciation for the amount of effort that goes into maintaining every step of a long-distance trail. Volunteering has also been shown to significantly lower the risk of hypertension and increase life expectancy.[92] In addition to being good for your mental and physical health, volunteering will allow you to meet passing hikers and interact with professionals who have been involved in the community and can answer your questions.

If you don't live close to a long-distance trail but are still looking to give support, consider donating to a trail organization. Trail websites (like, PCTA.org for the Pacific Crest Trail Association) will have direct donation links. Donations are used to fund urgent needs of the trail, provide proper training and support to trail maintainers, and to protect the trail and the land around it.

HOMESICKNESS + WANTING TO QUIT

"Don't quit on a bad day."

This is one of the most common phrases your hiker will hear. Hikers are told to make sure they're dry, full, and well-rested before quitting a trail, since the desire to quit is often caused by a lack of one of these three things. If your hiker wants to quit because of a mental struggle, you might be able to help change that mindset. Helping your hiker think positively and remember why he or she started the trail is extremely helpful. When needed, let your hiker vent for as long as needed, and help assess the root of the problem and potential solutions.

"I WAS AT WORK SO I MISSED HER CALL. WHEN I CALLED BACK AN HOUR LATER SHE TOLD ME THINGS WERE GREAT AND SHE LOVED IT. IT WASN'T UNTIL A FEW MONTHS LATER THAT SHE TOLD ME THAT WHEN I DIDN'T ANSWER, SHE CALLED HER LITTLE SISTER BAWLING HER EYES OUT, SAYING SHE COULDN'T BELIEVE SHE WAS DOING THIS, AND ALL THIS STUFF. HER LITTLE SISTER TOLD HER TO SUCK IT UP. BUT SHE TOLD ME SHE WAS GREAT AND EVERYTHING WAS GOOD. I HAD NO IDEA THAT AN HOUR PRIOR SHE WAS CRYING." - DON, 64, MASSACHUSETTS

If your hiker is feeling homesick, see if it's possible to plan a visit. I hiked with a girl who met her parents once a month along the entire trail. She knew these visits were coming, which pushed her to reach those towns. Knowing she'd be seeing family kept her from missing home too much.

If a visit with your hiker isn't feasible, try to FaceTime so you can still see each other face-to-face, or assemble a care package to send with hand-written notes or homemade treats. Having a box to look forward to in an upcoming town could give your hiker extra motivation to get there. This could also be a great time to collect audio recordings from friends and family with words of encouragement. Use a voice recording app on your phone and send the files to your hiker via text or email.

But what if the hiker isn't just homesick? What if he or she wants to quit? Many factors can make a hiker romanticize going home. If your hiker wants to quit because of pain or discomfort, suggest slowing down in a way that doesn't make it sound like a punishment. Seek to engage in collaborative problem solving with your hiker - not to take over and control the situation. Your hiker will likely be more receptive to suggestions if you share ideas, but acknowledge you know your hiker will independently make the final decisions. Don't be judgmental or resort to subtle shaming.

In *We Need To Talk, How to Have Conversations That Matter*, Headlee writes, "Sometimes we use facts to respond to emotion... but they're completely unhelpful to your friend who needs emotional support. A conversation is not a college lecture course or a TED talk. No matter how awkward it may feel to be on the listening end... escaping into logic is rarely the right response... Approaching emotional problems with logic is a strategy that is doomed to fail."[93]

While it may seem best to offer logical solutions, sometimes your hiker just needs someone to listen. If your hiker isn't seeking advice, listen graciously and ask open-ended questions such as, "Why do you think you're feeling this way?" Or, "What do you think would make you feel better?" Talking it out and receiving empathy could be the only solution needed. Headlee goes on to say, "Empathy is very different from compassion. Compassion is the ability to say, 'I feel for you.' Empathy is the ability to say, 'I feel with you.'"[94]

Maybe your hiker is open to receiving advice. If this is the case, ask questions about how your hiker feels, and encourage options that seem comfortable. If your hiker is doing 15 mi days and his or her body is hurting, ask if the people doing 12 mi per day look like they're having a more enjoyable time. Suggest making a friend who is doing lower miles and staying at that pace for a few days. Not making a change feel permanent might seem more acceptable to an unreceptive hiker.

If your hiker doesn't want to slow down, suggest waking up 15 minutes earlier to stretch, and stretching again before bed. Active stretching or a dynamic stretching warm up will be more effective at preventing injury than static stretching. Lunges, leg swings, and skipping are good for morning warm ups, and static stretching can be used in the evening. This could help a hiker who doesn't want to slow down, but needs to mitigate pain to improve morale.

If pain is causing your hiker to dwell on comforts at home, encourage thoughts about the future. In several weeks the comforts will likely have lost their novelty. If your hiker chooses to stop hiking, will he or she feel resentful of trail friends who continued? Will he or she feel jealous or left out? Suggest temporarily enjoying comforts by taking a zero day and splurging on a hotel or motel room. If your hiker is craving real food, suggest eating at a restaurant. Several days in town might leave your hiker satisfied enough to return to the trail. If your hiker's pain ask has to do with faulty or incorrect gear, suggest tapping into the emergency fund to replace the item(s) causing discomfort. It can be frustrating to admit to making the wrong gear choice, but remind your hiker that this is what an emergency fund is for.

Maybe your hiker is ready to throw in the towel because of bad weather. If your hiker has spent day after day sloshing through rain or snow, suggest spending a few days in town until the bad weather passes to rebuild morale. Drying out and warming up in town along with thoroughly cleaning clothes can greatly change a hiker's outlook. There's a good chance your hiker will feel better once the sun comes out.

Perhaps your hiker wants to go home due to loneliness or feeling like he or she hasn't made a close group of friends. Maybe your hiker got separated from a group. In this case, suggest slowing down or spending a few days in town. There could be hikers 50 mi to 100 mi behind your hiker that might be great hiking companions. By slowing down or taking a few zeros, other hikers around them have a chance to catch up. How will your hiker know if the perfect hiking partner is a few days behind if your hiker only keeps pace with one group? It could also be helpful to suggest listening to podcasts or audiobooks to distract your hiker from thoughts of home. If you both listen to the same podcasts, it can give you a reason to call each other after new episodes and might give your hiker something to look forward to.

Finally, if your hiker wants to come home because the budget is running thinner than expected, try to re-offer keeping funds and sending increments weekly. This will be most helpful when your hiker is initially beginning to worry about money rather than after too much has been spent to recover.

Many times quitting not only feels like failing, but like a hiker has let down those at home. If family and friends took time to track progress or help with preparations, the hiker might feel guilty not following through with the commitment to reach the end. Let your hiker know that you have confidence in his or her ability to do this, and encourage waiting another day before making a final decision. If your hiker's mind is made up, reassure him or her that the support-system at home won't be disappointed or upset by this decision.

WHEN TO SUPPORT YOUR HIKER QUITTING

SOMETIMES YOUR HIKER MIGHT HAVE A REASON TO QUIT THAT IS MORE THAN JUST A MENTAL BLOCK. HERE ARE SOME EXAMPLES:

INJURIES: INJURIES NEEDING LARGE AMOUNTS OF RECOVERY
  TIME, SUCH AS A BROKEN BONE OR BAD SPRAIN.
UNSAFE WEATHER: IF YOUR HIKER IS PUSHING A WEATHER
  WINDOW AND FEELS LIKE THEY ARE ON THE TRAIL AT A TIME
  THAT IS BECOMING UNSAFE, IT MAY BE WISE TO HEAD HOME.
IT'S REALLY NOT FOR YOUR HIKER: MAYBE YOUR HIKER HAS
  GENUINELY GIVEN THE TRAIL HIS OR HER BEST SHOT AND
  GONE THROUGH THE OPTIONS OF WORKING THROUGH MENTAL
  OBSTACLES, ONLY TO REALIZE THAT THIS ISN'T WHAT WAS
  ENVISIONED, NOR SOMETHING THAT IS APPEALING.
CIRCUMSTANCES BEYOND CONTROL: EMERGENCIES CAN POP UP
  AT HOME THAT ARE BEYOND A HIKER'S CONTROL, SUCH AS A
  FAMILY MEMBER BECOMING SICK OR PASSING AWAY. HIKERS
  ALSO MIGHT GET OFF-TRAIL IF THEY RECEIVE A JOB OFFER
  THAT IS TOO GOOD TO PASS UP. IF YOUR HIKER DECIDES TO
  FOCUS ON LIFE AT HOME, THE TRAIL MIGHT HAVE TO WAIT.
  THIS IS A GOOD REMINDER OF WHY IT MAY BE SMART TO
  SHIELD YOUR HIKER FROM THE MINOR INCONVENIENCES OF
  HOME-LIFE. IF A HIKER FEELS GUILTY FOR BEING ON THE
  TRAIL, HE OR SHE MIGHT FEEL OBLIGATED TO RETURN HOME.

"I NEVER CALLED HOME WANTING TO QUIT, BUT THERE WERE CERTAINLY UPS AND DOWNS. DURING SOME OF THE LOW-POINTS, BEING ABLE TO TALK TO FAMILY DEFINITELY HELPED. KNOWING HOW MUCH THEY SACRIFICED FOR ME TO DO THE TRAIL HAS GIVEN ME EXTRA MOTIVATION TO SEE IT THROUGH. ONE OF THE HARDEST THINGS IS HEARING ABOUT ISSUES THAT HAVE CREPT UP AT HOME. SOMEONE'S UNHAPPY, THE CAR GOT A FLAT, WE'RE TRYING TO FIND THE MONEY TO REPLACE SOMETHING. THOSE ARE THE TIMES THAT I FEEL MOST GUILTY FOR BEING ON THE TRAIL. BUT THEY REASSURE ME THAT THEY'RE GETTING THROUGH IT, SO I'VE GOT TO SEE IT THROUGH TOO." - JUSTIN, 40, TEXAS

"MY BROTHER GOT A STRESS FRACTURE AND GOT OFF-TRAIL FOR THREE WEEKS. WHEN HE FINALLY WENT BACK, HE LOST HIS TRAIL FAMILY AND WASN'T CONFIDENT IN HOW HE'D HOLD UP. HE CALLED OUR MOM MORE AND WE TRIED TO MESSAGE HIM FREQUENTLY TO KEEP HIS HEAD UP. AT THAT POINT, MY MOM WAS WORRIED HE'D GET OFF-TRAIL. SHE DIDN'T WANT HIM TO. SHE WANTED HIM TO FINISH. I THINK IT WAS HELPFUL HAVING OUR SUPPORT EVEN IF WE WEREN'T THERE." - VICTORIA, 29, GEORGIA

"MY FRIENDS HELPED REASSURE ME THAT I MADE THE RIGHT DECISION. I GOT OFF THE TRAIL TO WORK ON MY RELATIONSHIP AND NOW WE'RE MARRIED AND HAVE A CHILD ON THE WAY. WHEN I THINK ABOUT THE REASONS I GOT OFF, I KNOW I MADE THE RIGHT DECISION, BUT IN THE MOMENT IT WAS REALLY HARD. THERE WERE NIGHTS WHEN I WISHED I HAD STAYED ON THE TRAIL. IT WAS SUPER DIFFICULT." - JOSH, 30, GEORGIA

"WHEN I QUIT THE CDT THE RESPONSE WASN'T AS POSITIVE AS WHEN I FINISHED THE A.T. OR PCT. PEOPLE OFFER CONDOLENCES AND SAY IT'S STILL GOING TO BE THERE, BUT IT'S HARD BECAUSE YOU HAD A GOAL. NO MATTER WHAT, EVEN IF IT'S SOMETHING OUT OF YOUR HANDS, YOU FEEL LIKE YOU FAILED." - ELLIOT, 25, ARKANSAS

HOW TO RESPOND WHEN A HIKE ENDS EARLY

First, understand that while your hiker may be done with the trail at the moment, he or she might not *feel* done. If your hiker got off-trail for a reason other than realizing long-distance hiking isn't enjoyable to him or her, your hiker might not be satisfied saying goodbye to the trail for good. Many hikers go back at some point to try and finish. This might be during the same season, the following summer, or in upcoming years. Hikers may regain determination as they process what went wrong and ways to avoid the same mistakes again. What you say and do during this time can help your hiker look past feelings of failure. The trouble is that a statement might come across as supportive to one hiker, and hurtful to another.

"It's still a lot. That's more than I ever walked!"

"You tried what less than 0.01 % of people have attempted."

These sound the same to me, but the first was given as an example of something that didn't help the hiker feel better, while another reported that the second quote felt supportive.

"WELL-INTENDED BUT ULTIMATELY COUNTERPRODUCTIVE COMMUNICATIONS INCLUDE:

- 'SNAP OUT OF IT!'
- 'YOU'LL BE FINE.'
- 'THERE, THERE. IT'S NOT THAT BAD.'
- 'SURE I UNDERSTAND, I EXPERIENCED THE SAME PROBLEMS MYSELF.'
- 'JUST TRY A LITTLE HARDER.'

THESE STATEMENTS CAN ALL FEEL DISTANCING, PATRONIZING, AND JUDGMENTAL."[95]

WHAT TO DO WHEN SOMEONE YOU LOVE IS DEPRESSED BY MITCH GOLANT, PH.D., AND SUSAN K. GOLANT

Multiple hikers noted it felt good to hear that friends and family were proud of them for trying and for what they did accomplish. Others were hurt by the same sentiments, arguing that it felt like their feelings of failure were being invalidated. The only way to know how your hiker will react is to listen and modify support accordingly.

Try not to tell your hiker what he or she should have done to prevent the hike from ending early, or that you knew your hiker would never make it. I was shocked to hear that hikers had family tell them, "I told you so." Instead, remind your hiker that the trail will be there if he or she wants to try again, and that your hiker will have a leg up on other hikers by knowing what to expect.

POST-TRAIL DEPRESSION

"UP NORTH IN THE YUKON TERRITORY, YOU'RE IN GOD'S COUNTRY. IT'S THIS PRISTINE ENVIRONMENT AWAY FROM EVERYTHING. ALL THE PROBLEMS OF THE WORLD DON'T SEEM TO EXIST. THEN YOU GET BACK TO THE CITY AND THROWN INTO THESE LITTLE PROBLEMS THAT JUST DAYS AGO DIDN'T MAKE SENSE. IT'S HARD TO ADJUST GETTING BACK INTO THE REAL WORLD. BEING A COP, WE'RE WELL-TRAINED IN MENTAL HEALTH DISORDERS, SO DEPRESSION IS SOMETHING I'M AWARE OF AND KNOW THE SYMPTOMS FOR. WHEN I CAUGHT ONTO IT, SELF-AWARENESS WAS VERY IMPORTANT. REALIZING THAT I DON'T WANT TO GET OFF THE COUCH. I'M HAVING TROUBLE ANSWERING PHONE CALLS. I DON'T EVEN HAVE THE ENERGY TO DO THE DISHES. WHY IS THAT? WHY DON'T I HAVE THE ENERGY TO DO THE DISHES? A LITTLE SELF-AWARENESS AND YOU REALIZE, 'OKAY, LET'S GET OUT OF THIS.' LOVED ONES NEED TO BE AWARE THAT THIS IS A REAL THING. THIS ISN'T BOGUS. IT'S NOT A SOFT AND TOUCHY-FEELY THING THAT DOESN'T EXIST. IT'S REAL. A LITTLE BIT OF LOVE AND SUPPORT DOESN'T HURT. I'M ALSO A BIG ADVOCATE OF PROFESSIONAL HELP." - BRUCE, 60, ONTARIO

What is post-trail depression and why does it occur? In the weeks to months after hikers return from the trail, they will experience a period of re-adjusting that can cause them to feel sad or unenthusiastic for things around them. *What to Do When Someone We Love is Depressed,* by Mitch Golant, Ph.D., and Susan K. Golant, states, "It's important not to confuse sadness owing to grief and loss with depression... Sadness, disappointment, loss, grief, and mourning—like joy, satisfaction, accomplishment, and elation—are among myriad feelings that are normal... But there are occasions when the blues can become depression. When and how that happens usually depends upon how much one ruminates on one's state."[96]

Post-trail depression is named because its symptoms resemble many of those associated with clinical depression. It can be caused from the changes occurring as hikers re-adjust, the added stressors and expectations from others, and the lack of goals and purpose. For starters, they are facing withdrawal from a lack of nature. After spending so much time outside with fresh air, natural sounds, and natural light, being cooped up indoors can feel restricting, claustrophobic, and suffocating. Hikers are also facing situations where they are around more people in closer spaces, which can cause feelings of anxiousness. Hikers lack the camaraderie, the sense of adventure, and the sense of purpose that they had on the trail.

"I DIDN'T REALLY BELIEVE IN POST-TRAIL DEPRESSION. I HAD READ ABOUT IT, BUT I THOUGHT IT WAS SILLY. LIKE, YOU GET TO GO HOME. THAT'S AWESOME. AND GOING HOME IS AMAZING, BUT I THINK I MISSED MOVING EVERY DAY, AND EVERY DAY HAVING SUCH A PURPOSE. YOU WOKE UP IN THE MORNING AND EVERYTHING YOU DID HAD A PURPOSE. I THINK I FELT A LOSS OF THAT." - KATRINA, 37, ILLINOIS

Josh Stone, M.Ed., LAPC, therapist, and Appalachian Trail thru-hiker, notes how a lack of purpose is possibly the biggest factor of post-trail depression. The hikers have exited a scenario where they always felt purpose - heading from one end of the trail to the other, getting to a destination for lunchtime and breaks, reaching a specific campsite by the evening, accomplishing a goal, seeking adventure, and experiencing the "here and now-ness" of life on the trail. Josh points out that many of his clients experience depressive symptoms for loss/lack of purpose in their lives, so why wouldn't this be the same for individuals coming off-trail? Hikers lose their purpose, their goal, and their driving force. They are left stagnant, confused, and questioning, "what now?" Golant and Golant reinforce that, "the blues are a mood we should take very seriously. Although it is not depression, it is a step along the continuum that can lead towards depression."[97] There is are many factors that can attribute to your hiker catching *the blues*.

IT COULD BE BENEFICIAL TO NOTE THE SIMILARITIES BETWEEN
POST-TRAIL DEPRESSION AND CLINICAL DEPRESSION. WHILE
BOTH HAVE "DEPRESSION" IN THE NAME, POST-TRAIL DEPRESSION
DOES NOT ALWAYS RESULT IN MAJOR DEPRESSIVE DISORDER.
IT IS TITLED BECAUSE IT SHARES MANY OF THE SAME
FEELINGS OF CLINICAL DEPRESSION, HOWEVER THE DIAGNOSTIC
AND STATISTICAL MANUAL OF MENTAL DISORDERS (DSM-5)[98]
CLASSIFIES MAJOR DEPRESSIVE DISORDER AS FIVE OR MORE
OF THE FOLLOWING SYMPTOMS DURING A 2-WEEK PERIOD. YOUR
HIKER, WHO WILL LIKELY BE MOURNING THE TRAIL, WILL
LIKELY EXPERIENCE SOME OF THESE SYMPTOMS, BUT MAY NOT BE
CLINICALLY DEPRESSED.

1. DEPRESSED MOOD THROUGHOUT MOST OF THE DAY, NEARLY
   EVERY DAY
2. DIMINISHED INTEREST OR PLEASURE IN ACTIVITIES, NEARLY
   EVERY DAY
3. SIGNIFICANT WEIGHT LOSS OR WEIGHT GAIN, OR DECREASED
   APPETITE
4. INSOMNIA OR HYPERSOMNIA NEARLY EVERY DAY
5. PSYCHOMOTOR AGITATION OR RETARDATION, NEARLY EVERY
   DAY
6. FATIGUE OR LOSS OF ENERGY, NEARLY EVERY DAY
7. FEELINGS OF WORTHLESSNESS OR INCREASED GUILT (WITHOUT
   SIGNIFICANT REASON), NEARLY EVERY DAY
8. DIMINISHED ABILITY TO CONCENTRATE, OR INDECISIVENESS,
   NEARLY EVERY DAY
9. RECURRENT THOUGHTS OF DEATH OR SUICIDAL IDEATION
   (THIS IS UNLIKELY WITH POST-TRAIL DEPRESSION, BUT SEEK
   PROFESSIONAL HELP IF OCCURRING)

"SAY YOU CAN'T CONCENTRATE, CAN'T SLEEP, FEEL WORTHLESS,
AND AREN'T INTERESTED IN ANYTHING? THAT'S FOUR.
TECHNICALLY, YOU AREN'T DEPRESSED. WHAT ARE YOU,
THEN? JUST MISERABLE? MY POINT IS WITH ANY DEGREE OF
DEPRESSION, YOU NEED TO SNUFF IT OUT COMPLETELY."[99]
   WHAT TO DO WHEN SOMEONE YOU LOVE IS DEPRESSED
   BY MITCH GOLANT, PH.D., AND SUSAN K. GOLANT

It can feel like there is too much information for hikers to process as decisions and tasks become more complicated than the choices they were making on the trail. They may face periods of frustration as they struggle to remember multiple things at once, or make complex choices. Transitioning from waking up and falling asleep by the sun to being surrounded by fluorescent lights that don't follow a natural cycle can cause trouble sleeping. Hikers might experience sensory overload as they are overstimulated with loud noises, flashing lights, overlapping conversations, and intense smells. They could become quiet, timid, or reclusive in response.

Many hikers achieve a level of happiness on the trail that they will be unable to replicate in their off-trail lives. They may become homesick for the trail in the same ways that they'd been homesick for the comforts of every-day life. Hikers might grieve the trail and a lifestyle that has ended. They might feel empty, or like a part of their lives are missing. Problems and issues left behind at home are still there, and it can feel as though nothing has changed, while at the same time, everything is slightly different. These conflicting feelings can cause confusion and frustration. Depressive tendencies can result from living in this "conflicting emotional state," rather than evaluating the internal conflict and working through it. Avoidance, explains Josh, can increase symptoms of depression.

"ON THE TRAIL, I FEEL LIKE I REACHED A LEVEL OF HAPPINESS THAT I DIDN'T EVEN KNOW EXISTED. NOW I'M BACK BELOW THAT AGAIN. I MISS IT A LOT. LOOKING AT MY VIDEOS, I REMEMBER HOW HAPPY I WAS ON THE TRAIL AND IT MAKES ME FEEL A LITTLE SAD. I KNEW THAT IT WOULD BE A FINITE AMOUNT OF TIME. I KNEW IT WASN'T GOING TO LAST FOREVER. IT'S NOT LIKE I'M SURPRISED BY IT. BUT IT STILL DOESN'T CHANGE THAT IT'S A LITTLE SAD BEING HOME." - KEITH, 29, NEW JERSEY

Financial issues may creep up, especially if a hiker is struggling to find work. This can make it difficult to feel like the hiker gained anything from a long-distance hike. When low on funds and struggling to get back on his or her feet, seeing friends and family who admired and supported the hike impatiently waiting for the hiker to get his or her life together can cause confusion. Friends, family, and former colleagues often support a once-in-a-lifetime opportunity like a long-distance hike. Usually those same people are less supportive of being back at home, jobless, with dwindling funds. This shift in community support can make a hiker feel foolish for having seemingly neglected responsibilities like a career for months at a time.

> "I NOTICE WHEN WE'RE NOT DOING ANYTHING. HE GETS ANTSY WHEN WE WATCH MOVIES. HE HAS TO GET UP AND WALK AROUND. IT'S BEEN ALMOST A MONTH, BUT HE'S STILL FEELING PAIN IN HIS KNEES AND FEET THAT MAKES HIM FEEL LIKE HE NEEDS TO KEEP WALKING." - EMILY, 21, KENTUCKY

When hikers return, their bodies enter a period of recovery that can be uncomfortable. Calluses will cause feet to become itchy and peel. Their legs might experience restlessness and cramp up from a lack of movement. It could be painful for hikers to sit for long, and they may feel pain from simple movements, like going down a flight of stairs.

Your hiker may go through a phase of laziness due to an aversion to return to a job he or she may no longer care for, or a routine that feels too structured. Your hiker may no longer be motivated to address simple tasks which no longer feel important. Time can also become a problem. Readjusting to the concept of following a clock can be difficult when hikers need to be at work or school at certain times, remain there until a set time, and face defined time frames for breaks or meals. Hikers reported being late to appointments and social engagements, as well as feeling antsy sitting too long. They went longer than most do without following a clock, and redefining the boundaries set by time can be difficult.

> "THE HARDEST WAY TO READJUST WAS TIME. I'VE NEVER GOTTEN MY SENSE OF TIME BACK. IT HAS SHIFTED PERMANENTLY. THINGS JUST DON'T CLICK. I'M LATE FOR THINGS. I'VE NEVER BEEN ABLE TO CLICK BACK INTO THE SENSE OF TIME. ONCE YOU DETACH FROM ALL OF THAT, IT'S SO MUCH DIFFERENT. IT'S NEVER BEEN NORMALIZED, EVEN YEARS LATER."
> - ANONYMOUS, 40, CALIFORNIA

Many times, post-trail depression can be triggered by things that make hikers feel like they haven't gained anything from hiking the trail. If they return to their hometown or move back in with their parents, if they don't have an apartment, if they are unemployed, or struggling to find a job, it can feel like the hiker has regressed in life. This can cause a sense of guilt and irresponsibility that causes them to question if completing a long-distance hike was worth the set-backs they are now facing. It can be especially difficult to see that friends and peers have progressed in their careers and lives since the hiker was last home. People have new jobs, new relationships, they have upgraded to new apartments, or moved in with significant others. Journaling can be a cathartic release. Often, minds can become jumbled after something as big as a long-distance hike, and journaling can help clarify thoughts.

During this time, your hiker might experience feelings of social anxiety. It can be hard to talk to people about the trail because it's tough to communicate what it was like. I'm always confronted about my long-distance hikes in the same way.

"Tell me about your trip!"

This phrase can cause me to feel anxious, because it's too vague to answer, but I feel rude saying that. What usually comes out instead is, *"Uh, what do you want to know?"*

Does this well-meaning person want to know my favorite stretch of the trail? My favorite town? What my trail name is and how I got it? Who my friends were and where they're from? The pace I was averaging? What gear I carried? How it held up and any malfunctions? How many bears I saw? What I liked to eat? How my feet held up? What my coldest night was?

I hear a person asking me to tell about my trip and a part of me tenses up because I don't know where to start. I'll usually pick a topic and start talking to avoid the silence that follows, but I start to worry because I don't know if the topic I chose is interesting enough or if that person would rather hear about something else. It's frustrating because I didn't have trouble communicating with others on the trail, but now I find myself struggling through conversations that feel forced.

Frustrations continue as hikers realize that they are no longer surrounded by friends who are free to spend every morning, afternoon, and evening with them. The people they were looking forward to seeing at home are also busy with their own lives. They have jobs, relationships, and personal issues that keep them occupied. Hikers will go from spending day after day around friends to planning around schedules and facing unavailability. It can feel like everyone is too busy and hikers no longer fit in.

Hikers may also feel a lack of connection to friends who they may not share as many similar values or interests with anymore. As your hiker's perception of what he or she wants out of life shifts, there might be friendships that drift and feel distant. Having values that no longer align with those around your hiker could cause him or her to feel lost or without a place in society. This can also highlight that your hiker has changed over the course of the trail. Recognizing and honoring the change is important because it helps hikers understand that the trail was not a static experience. Once hikers recognize that newness, they can identify their new needs and how to meet those needs. For example, going out on regular hikes, joining social groups like hiker meet-ups, or taking shorter outdoor trips that stimulate their new, adventurous selves.

Something that surprised me was that post-trail depression resurfaced the spring after I returned from the PCT. It was triggered by the start of the weather window for the new hiking season, as I saw trail friends posting photos from new trails while I was at a desk. This was the most difficult period of post-trail depression for me, because all of the novelties of home had worn off, and thoughts were constantly creeping into my mind that it wasn't too late to take off again. It was hard to talk to others about this because so much time had passed since I returned from the trail. The only friends who seemed to understand were ones from the trail who were experiencing the same feelings. This relapse lasted until the window to depart on another long-distance trail had closed, and I lost the option to start another hike.

The amount of time it takes a hiker to work through post-trail depression will vary from person to person. Hikers who plan on tackling another long-distance trail the following summer might jump straight back into planning and enjoy the time spent at home because they know it will be temporary. Others who know this is the last time they will be able to afford an extended trip for the foreseeable future might struggle more with those feelings of mourning and grief. It varies hiker to hiker, but understanding what it is and why it occurs will help you understand why your hiker might struggle after the trail.

"YOU GET USED TO THIS CERTAIN STYLE OF LIFE. YOUR ONLY GOAL IS TO GO IN ONE DIRECTION FOR HOWEVER MANY MILES. EVENTUALLY YOU GET TO THE END AND THAT'S ALL YOU REALLY HAVE ON YOUR MIND - WHEN DO I STOP FOR LUNCH? WHEN DO I FEEL LIKE TAKING A BREAK? THEN YOU GET BACK HOME AND REAL LIFE COMES INTO PLACE. ALL OF A SUDDEN IT'S LIKE, I NEED TO GET A JOB, I NEED TO PAY BILLS, I NEED TO FIND A PLACE TO LIVE, I'VE GOT TO PAY RENT, I'VE GOT TO BUY GROCERIES, I'VE GOT TO BUY GAS. I'VE GOT TO DO EVERY-DAY THINGS THAT I KIND OF FORGOT ABOUT. IT'S JUST A WEIRD ADJUSTMENT. IT TAKES SOME TIME TO GET USED TO."
- EMILIO, 29, TEXAS

RECOVERY TIME + EXPECTATIONS

It can be surprising for family and friends to learn that their support is still needed for potentially months after their hiker returns. At this point, you might be tired of hearing about the hike or dealing with your hiker acting selfishly. It can be hard to keep from shaking your hiker and telling him or her to snap out of it.

We get it. You hiked. Move on.

Keep in mind, post-trail depression can be minimized if your hiker has plans in place for when he or she returns home. If your hiker lined up a job, planned a trip, or has any type of goals, it can help smooth the transition by providing a sense of direction. Be patient. Give time to readjust to keep your hiker from feeling overwhelmed. You can do this by allowing your hiker time to be absorbed in his or her thoughts, or to spend time alone when needed. Don't push your hiker to jump back into the real world too quickly. He or she may need time to adjust before returning to work or school. Golant and Golant suggest, "If the bereavement is not excessive or prolonged, a period of withdrawal and sorrowing can help one recover from a crushing blow."[100] Returning home can be a shock, and hikers will appreciate patience and understanding during this transition.

"HE WOULD CRY AND HE WOULD LOOK AT HIS PICTURES CONSTANTLY, WHICH IS GREAT BUT HE WOULD MOURN THEM, NOT LOOK AT THEM WITH EXCITEMENT. IT WAS LIKE HE WOULD WANT TO BE THERE AND NOT AT HOME.' - ALEX, 21, OHIO

Make sure your hiker isn't ruminating in sadness that the hike is over. Self-awareness is key to overcoming a funk. Point out negative behavior, and encourage outdoor activities or other distractions to relieve those feelings. Continue to invite your hiker places, even if he or she is declining offers. This will let your hiker know that their company is, and will continue to be welcome, and that needing time to readjust won't push you away or keep you from reaching out.

Remind your hiker that even if he or she didn't gain something financially from the hike, it was still a huge accomplishment. Reiterate the ways the hike was beneficial. Your hiker may need help to re-find their sense of purpose now that there is no longer a goal to work towards. Try asking for help with tasks and projects, especially those that are outdoors. Completing tasks that are physically exhausting can help your hiker feel useful and provide a way to expend extra energy.

"THE STORIES I HAVE ARE ENDLESS. YOU TELL YOUR FRIENDS AND FAMILY AND THEY'RE REALLY ATTENTIVE THE FIRST TIME. THE SECOND TIME, THEY START TO NOD. BUT THE THIRD TIME, FOURTH TIME, FIFTIETH TIME, THEY'RE ASLEEP. THEY DON'T WANT TO HEAR ABOUT IT ANYMORE. UNLESS YOU'RE TALKING TO ANOTHER LONG-DISTANCE HIKER, THEY DON'T GET IT. THEY DON'T UNDERSTAND WHAT IT'S LIKE." - GARY, 59, MISSOURI

Let your hiker know that he or she can share stories with you, even after time has passed. Hikers can sense when those around them have had enough of the trail, and it can be isolating to feel like no one cares anymore. Encourage your hiker to seek out local outdoor groups, join trail maintenance crews, or attend hiker meet-ups. Having like-minded people with whom they can exchange stories and experiences will allow them to maintain a sense of connection to the trail. It can be a relief to speak with people who relate, and your hiker can reminisce without guilt. It's worth noting that not all hikers want hiker-related interactions after returning home. Finding something to be invested in is what matters. It might be gardening or joining a band or origami. But finding new ways to fill time and new goals to strive for is what matters.

Most importantly, encourage your hiker to stay active and offer to be a workout buddy if you can. In *Spark: The Revolutionary New Science of Exercise and the Brain*, Ratey dives into the notion that exercise is more beneficial than most realize in combating symptoms of depression. "In some ways, exercise is even more important for prevention than it is for treatment. One of the first symptoms of depression... is sleep disturbance. Either you can't get up or you can't sleep or both... First you lose your energy, then your interest in

things. The key is to get moving immediately. And do not stop."[101]
Just because your hiker isn't feeling enough symptoms of depression
for it to be diagnosable, doesn't mean similar steps can't be taken to
feel better.

"IN A LANDMARK STUDY AFFECTIONATELY CALLED SMILE
(STANDARD MEDICAL INTERVENTION AND LONG-TERM EXERCISE),
JAMES BLUMENTHAL AND HIS COLLEAGUES PITTED EXERCISE
AGAINST THE SSRI SERTRALINE (ZOLOFT) IN A SIXTEEN-WEEK
TRIAL... SIX MONTHS AFTER THE STUDY, BLUMENTHAL AND HIS
COLLEAGUES SURVEYED THE PATIENTS TO SEE HOW THEY WERE
DOING AND FOUND THAT EXERCISE WORKED EVEN BETTER THAN
MEDICINE OVER THE LONG TERM. ABOUT 30 % OF THE EXERCISE
GROUP REMAINED DEPRESSED VERSUS 52 % OF THOSE ON
MEDICATION... OF THE PATIENTS WHO WERE IN REMISSION AFTER
THE INITIAL STUDY, JUST 8 % OF THE EXERCISE GROUP HAD A
RELAPSE VERSUS 38 % IN THE MEDICATION GROUP... THE MOST
SIGNIFICANT PREDICTOR OF WHETHER SOMEONE FELT BETTER
WAS HOW MUCH THEY EXERCISED."[104]
SPARK THE REVOLUTIONARY NEW SCIENCE OF EXERCISE AND THE BRAIN
BY JOHN RATEY

Hikers experience chemical changes as they stop producing
the amount of endorphins they experienced with 8 to 12 hours of
physical activity every day. "In Britain, doctors now use exercise
as a first-line treatment for depression, but it's vastly underutilized
in the United States, and that's a shame... About 17 % of American
adults experience depression at some point in their lives, to the tune
of $26.1 billion in health care costs each year."[102] While it may not be
possible to maintain that level of activity, by continuing to train and
staying in shape, hikers can limit post-trail weight gain, continue to
feel motivated, and combat symptoms of depression.

Try suggesting new hobbies, like trail running, hot yoga, cross-fit,
rock climbing, skiing, or cycling. Your hiker might realize that the
struggle to settle back into off-trail life is frustrating for you, and
may feel guilty asking for help. Hikers reported becoming hyper-
aware of the emotions of those around them, so they may refrain
from opening up to avoid becoming a burden. If you notice your

hiker is beginning to withdraw, talk about it.

In her book, *Mood and Food,* registered dietitian Elizabeth Somer explores the relationship between diet and depression, saying, "Certain eating habits, such as skipping meals, may aggravate or even generate negative moods."[103] Golant and Golant suggest focusing on high-proteins foods, dairy products, B vitamins, vitamin C, folic acid, and magnesium, as they manufacture norepinephrine and dopamine.

"[SOMER] MAKES SOME OTHER FOOD RECOMMENDATIONS THAT YOUR LOVED ONE MAY FIND HELPFUL IN COMBATING DEPRESSION:

- BREAKFASTS SHOULD INCLUDE ONE SERVING EACH OF GRAINS, FRUIT, AND LOW-FAT DAIRY PRODUCTS. THIS BOOSTS ENERGY AND IMPROVES MOOD.
- RATHER THAN THREE LARGE MEALS, YOUR LOVED ONE MIGHT BENEFIT FROM FIVE TO SIX SMALL MEALS AND SNACKS SPREAD OUT OVER THE DAY. ACCORDING TO SOMER, PEOPLE WHO SPREAD OUT THEIR DAILY INTAKE 'ARE LESS PRONE TO FATIGUE, INSOMNIA, AND DEPRESSION AND ARE BETTER ABLE TO MAINTAIN DESIRABLE WEIGHT.'
- FAT SHOULD BE LIMITED TO NO MORE THAN 25 % OF COMPLEX CARBOHYDRATES, FIBER, VITAMINS, AND MINERALS IN THEIR DIET BY EATING MORE VEGETABLES, FRUITS, AND GRAINS. DEPRESSION HAS BEEN LINKED TO VITAMIN B6 DEFICIENCIES. BANANAS, AVOCADOS, SKINLESS CHICKEN, SALMON, POTATOES (INCLUDING SKIN), DARK LEAFY GREENS, AND OATMEAL ARE RICH IN THIS VITAMIN.
- MANY PEOPLE EXPERIENCE FATIGUE FROM LOW-GRADE DEHYDRATION. SOMER SUGGESTS DRINKING AT LEAST SIX 8-OUNCE GLASSES OF WATER DAILY.
- IF YOUR DEPRESSED LOVED ONE HAS LOST THEIR APPETITE AND EATS LESS THAN 2,500 CALORIES PER DAY, THEY MIGHT BENEFIT FROM A WELL-BALANCED VITAMIN AND MINERAL SUPPLEMENT THAT PROVIDES 100 TO 300 % OF THE MINIMUM DAILY REQUIREMENTS."[105]

WHAT TO DO WHEN YOUR LOVED ONE IS DEPRESSED
BY MITCH GOLANT, PH.D., AND SUSAN K. GOLANT

Recovery could last anywhere from weeks to months. Some say yearning to be immersed in nature with daily goals and physical challenges never fully goes away. Give your hiker a few weeks to readjust, and encourage new goals after a month if don't already exist. Try to understand that there is no set time for your hiker to bounce back, and do your best to be supportive regardless of how long it takes.

If your hiker is struggling beyond what you know how to handle, research the symptoms and ways to help the behaviors you are noticing. Don't rule out the value of professional help, and don't make your hiker feel ashamed if the support of a licensed professional is necessary.

'I LOST 50 LB, BUT WHEN I GOT HOME I GAINED 100 LB BACK. I GOT TO 270 LB BEFORE DECIDING I COULDN'T LIVE LIKE THAT, SO NOW I'VE LOST ANOTHER 50 LB. IT WAS FRUSTRATING. I DID THE TRAIL WHEN I WAS 49, AND IF YOU KNOW ANYTHING ABOUT BIOLOGY, ONCE YOU GET INTO YOUR EARLY 50'S, THINGS DON'T SEEM TO WORK THE WAY THEY USED TO. I STARTED PUTTING ON 5 LB TO 10 LB A YEAR, BUT I MADE A COMMITMENT TWO YEARS AGO THAT THIS HAS TO END. I CHANGED MY DIET. I BEGAN TO EXERCISE. COMING OFF THE TRAIL, EVERYBODY TELLS YOU YOU'RE IN GREAT SHAPE AND ASKS IF YOU'RE GOING TO RUN A MARATHON, BUT WHAT I'M GOOD AT IS CARRYING 45 LB ON MY BACK AT A 2.5 MPH PACE UP AND DOWN STEEP HILLS. I HAVE NO LEG SPEED. IT WAS FRUSTRATING THAT I WAS STARTING TO GAIN WEIGHT.' - GARY, 59, MISSOURI

"MOST OF THE TIME MY FAMILY WILL TELL ME TO GET MY BUTT
UP AND GET OUTSIDE. THEY'RE UNDERSTANDING ABOUT THE
POST-TRAIL DEPRESSION, BUT THEY'RE ALSO NOT GOING TO
SUGAR COAT IT. THEY'LL SAY, 'HEY, YOU'RE GETTING ANGRY
WITH US. YOU'RE GETTING SNAPPY. GO OUTSIDE.' IT HELPS ME
NOTICE, BECAUSE THERE ARE TIMES THAT I'LL GET MOODY OR
ANGRY, AND I DON'T WANT TO SAY THAT I DON'T NOTICE IT,
BUT I'M SO WRAPPED UP THAT I DON'T REALIZE IT." - BRAD, 28,
OHIO

"WHAT I FOUND WAS THE BIGGEST HELP WAS OPENING UP
AND TALKING ABOUT IT. ABSOLUTELY. TALKING ABOUT HIS
ADVENTURES. IT TOOK ME A WHILE, AS A SUPPORTER TO WANT
TO LISTEN TO HIS STORIES FROM HIS TRIP, BECAUSE I WAS
STILL STUCK IN THE MINDSET OF NEEDING TO DO LIFE HERE AT
HOME. I THINK ONCE I WAS ABLE TO SIT DOWN AND GIVE HIM
THAT, AND LISTEN TO HIS STORIES, HE DIDN'T FEEL AS BAD
ABOUT HAVING LEFT ME AND WE WERE ABLE TO GET BACK IN
SYNC." - TABATHA, 34, FLORIDA

"I DON'T SEE POST-TRAIL DEPRESSION ANY DIFFERENT FROM
POSTPARTUM DEPRESSION OR ANY TIME WHEN YOUR BODY GOES
THROUGH SIGNIFICANT PHYSIOLOGICAL CHANGES. OUR BRAINS
ARE GOING THROUGH CHEMICAL WITHDRAWALS WHEN WE GET OFF
THE TRAIL. UNLESS YOU CAN CONTINUE TO PUNISH YOURSELF
AND DO SOME SORT OF TRAINING OR EXERCISE, OR CONTINUE TO
GO ON HIKES, YOUR BODY IS NOT GETTING THE SAME CHEMISTRY.
YOU'RE GOING TO GO THROUGH WITHDRAWAL. I JUST THINK
IT'S A PERIOD OF ADJUSTING. THERE ARE A TON OF FREEDOMS
ON THE TRAIL AND AN ABSENCE OF A LOT OF STRESSORS. THE
STRESSORS WE HAVE ON THE TRAIL ARE REALLY BASIC. WHEN
WE GO BACK INTO THE REAL WORLD THERE ARE DIFFERENT
KINDS OF STRESSORS." -ANONYMOUS, 40, CALIFORNIA

SECTION SIX
SIGNIFICANT OTHERS

IT WILL BE OKAY

Whether it's one month or five-to-seven, your partner leaving for a long-distance trail can draw concerns for your relationship. As someone who is more involved in the hiker's day-to-day life, the distance can impact you more than other supporters. You'll have to readjust to life, temporarily moving forward without your partner by your side. If you're married or living together, it may mean taking on additional responsibilities and chores.

Some supporters may be hesitant to accept their partner taking on a long-distance trail and could put up a fight in hopes of keeping them home. I've seen this concern addressed in hiking forums and on the trail itself, with the more common response suggesting that in a sound relationship, the partner will be supportive of the hiker's goals and dreams. In a relationship practicing give-and-take, there will be time for you to pursue big dreams, too.

"YOU GO OUT AND YOU'RE WITHOUT PEOPLE FOR A WHILE, AND THEN WHEN YOU COME BACK YOU APPRECIATE RELATIONSHIPS MUCH MORE. MY WIFE DOES RECOGNIZE THAT I'M A MUCH BETTER HUSBAND AFTER I'VE BEEN ON THE TRAIL." - GEORGE, 68, MAINE

While I haven't hiked a long-distance trail with a significant other at home, I've conducted phone interviews and surveys with hikers and supporters in new relationships, long-term relationships, and marriages to gather input from as many perspectives as possible. I have also hiked with many *halves* of relationships, getting to know the perspectives of different partners on the trail as they spoke of their respective relationships either positively, apprehensively, or sometimes, with complete dread.

My overall impression is that those in marriages seem to fair best with their partner being away, while those in newer relationships appear more concerned about surviving the time apart. The duration of a long-distance trail seems more challenging to newer couples that

have not overcome as many obstacles. Think about how long you've
been with your partner. What percentage of your relationship will the
other person spend on the trail? If you've only been dating for a year,
a six-month trail will feel more threatening than it will to partners
who've been together for decades.

Advice in this section was taken from those who have been in
relationships through long-distance hikes, or have partners who are
preparing for a long-distance hike in the upcoming season. Tips and
tricks to help your relationship not only survive the trail, but grow
with it, have been given by hikers who've been in your position and
worked through the same issues you might face. Their advice was
given with you, the reader, in mind.

"MY WIFE IS THE MOST IMPORTANT PERSON IN MY LIFE, SO
UNLIKE EVERYONE ELSE, I HAD TO GET HER APPROVAL. I GIVE
HER STROKES AND PROPS FOR UNDERSTANDING MY PASSION FOR
THIS. WE'VE GOT AN ARRANGEMENT WORKED OUT WHERE SHE'S
GOING TO HAVE HER TURN FOR FIVE MONTHS ON A EUROPEAN
TRIP. SHE WAS THE MOST IMPORTANT HURDLE, BUT ALSO THE
EASIEST." - BRUCE, 60, ONTARIO

When partners and their goals are treated with unconditional
love and support, relationships can grow through the hardships of
the trail. Voice concerns and questions beforehand to ensure each
other's feelings are being considered during the time apart. Headlee
says, "The best conversations happen between two people who are
considering each other. That's the definition of consideration, after
all, to think carefully about the effect of what you say and do and
try to avoid upsetting or harming another person with your words or
actions."[106] Try to communicate any concerns in a considerate way.
Making your partner feel as though pursuing a dream is detrimental
to a relationship with you can lead to ultimatums and arguments.
Communicate early, because those who have been in your shoes
advise ensuring that your relationship is in a strong, stable place
before your partner leaves for the trail. Unspoken concerns or
unresolved arguments can trickle into conversations on the trail and
cause precious time to be spent arguing.

I've met hikers who dreaded calling a partner at home because the conversations would usually result in arguing. It became a cycle; they'd spend time on the phone arguing, and time off the phone annoyed or apprehensive about the next call. Alternatively, those who communicated in a positive manner, catching up on important details, positively affirming each other, and showing genuine interest in their partner's troubles and joys, spoke of them affectionately and longingly. Choosing mature conversation over nitpicking faults will help keep your relationship from faltering.

Entering a long-distance relationship with a partner who you're unhappy with could affect the relationship's chances of success and leave you regretful. However, if both partners can overcome obstacles and show understanding for what the other is going through, this could be an experience you look proudly back on for years to come.

"THIS IS A RELATIONSHIP WHERE WE'RE SUPPORTIVE OF EACH OTHER'S GOALS. IT'LL BE A TRADE-OFF. HE'LL SUPPORT ME WHEN I WANT TO DO SOMETHING, TOO. WE'RE OUR OWN PEOPLE AND WE'RE GOING TO HAVE SEPARATE GOALS. WHILE IT MIGHT NOT ALWAYS ALIGN WITH WHAT WE WANT FROM THE OTHER PERSON AT THAT TIME, ULTIMATELY IT'S HEALTHY AND GOOD FOR US TO DO THIS KIND OF THING." - JOANNA, 27, COLORADO

"IT WAS A LOT HARDER THAN I THOUGHT. I DIDN'T REALIZE HOW MUCH I WOULD MISS HIM. I HAD NO IDEA HOW MUCH I WOULD ACTUALLY MISS HIM AND HOW MUCH HE DOES AROUND THE HOUSE AND WITH THE KIDS. HAVING HIM GONE WAS A LOT. THE KIDS MISSED HIM A LOT TOO. HAVING TO BE THEIR PRIMARY PARENT IS PROBABLY THE HARDEST PART. I THINK IT'S MADE ME REALIZE HOW MUCH I APPRECIATE HIM. I THINK THAT WHEN HE COMES BACK I CAN DEFINITELY SHOW HIM MORE APPRECIATION. IN THE LONG RUN IT WILL DEFINITELY BE SOMETHING GREAT FOR OUR RELATIONSHIP, BEING ABLE TO SUPPORT HIM IN A BIG DREAM WHEN HE HAS CONSTANTLY SUPPORTED ME IN ALL OF MY BIG DREAMS." - KRISTEN, 37, TEXAS

SETTING EXPECTATIONS

Setting expectations before your loved one departs can help avoid unnecessary conflict and ensure you're both on the same page. Keeping feelings silent will only delay arguments, not resolve them. By resolving issues beforehand, you can put fears to rest and reach agreements that keep both sides happy. In *Silent Agreements: How to Free Your Relationships of Unspoken Expectations*, Linda D. Anderson, PhD, Sonia R. Banks, PhD, and Michele L. Owens, PhD, state, "Very few of us look forward to conflict, but avoiding conflict doesn't usually lead to peace. In some cases, such avoidance can even be damaging. When you remain silent out of fear, you're only delaying the inevitable. It's like ignoring a small fire; caught early, it can be put out easily, but if you refuse to take notice of it for long enough, you're going to need an entire fire department."[107] If you know there are issues you have with your partner leaving for a long-distance hike, address them early on rather than waiting until it's time to say goodbye. Allowing time to work through issues will ensure the ability to walk away from, and return to, conflicts until they can be resolved.

THERE WERE TWO YEARS BETWEEN WHEN I SAID I WAS GOING TO DO THIS AND THE HIKE ITSELF, SO IT WASN'T A SUDDEN SURPRISE WHEN I LEFT." - KEITH, 29, NEW JERSEY

Anderson, Banks, and Owens refer to the unspoken rules of your relationships as *silent agreements*. "They grow from the assumptions, expectations, and beliefs that you don't talk about but still hold others accountable for... More often than not, they hinder rather than help your relationships... You proceed as if all parties agree about what is expected in the relationship, about who fulfills which expectations and how they're 'supposed to' do so."[108] Try not to go into the trail assuming that you and your partner have aligned expectations on communication, responsibilities, and other topics that affect your relationship while they're away. There may be a hesitancy to addressing issues, but silent agreements often reveal that thoughts and feelings haven't been fully shared for fear of the relationship ending or having to acknowledge untouched deep emotions.[109]

If you're worried about addressing concerns you may have, try setting a time for your conversation to take place. Establish the root of your concerns beforehand, and express them in a way that encourages positive communication. Preparing for these conversations can help keep your emotions in check and reduce the likelihood of a fight.

"MY HUSBAND HAS BEEN ON THE PCT FOR THE PAST FIVE AND A HALF MONTHS. HE TOLD ME A WHILE AGO THAT HE WANTED TO DO IT, AND IT WAS ACTUALLY MY SUGGESTION THAT HE GO THIS YEAR BECAUSE IT WAS GOOD TIMING FOR OUR FAMILY. I HAVE CONCERNS, BUT OVERALL, WE HAVE THE KIND OF RELATIONSHIP WHERE WE WANT TO SUPPORT EACH OTHER IN GOING FOR BIG DREAMS, SO IT JUST SEEMED LIKE A NATURAL NEXT STEP FOR HIM." - KRISTEN, 37, TEXAS

Learning each other's love languages (ways a person shows and feels love) can help you feel connected with your partner, regardless of the distance. By learning how each of you prefers to receive love, you will better understand ways to give love in return. The ability to communicate this way will continue a connection between you and your partner while separated. *The 5 Love Languages: The Secret to Love that Lasts*, by Gary Chapman, says, "Seldom do [partners] have the same primary emotional love language. We tend to speak our primary love language, and we become confused when our [partner] does not understand what we are communicating. We are expressing our love, but the message does not come through because we are speaking what, to them, is a foreign language."[110] Chapman lists the five love languages as physical touch, words of affirmation, quality time, gift giving, and acts of service.

If there are ways your partner can make you feel more at ease while they are away, vocalize them. Stating exactly what you need instead of making your partner guess can prevent miscommunication and unintentional hurt.

"MAKE THE REQUEST SOMETHING SPECIFIC, NOT GENERAL. DON'T SAY, 'YOU KNOW, I WISH WE WOULD SPEND MORE TIME TOGETHER.' THAT'S TOO VAGUE. HOW WILL YOU KNOW WHEN HE'S DONE IT? BUT IF YOU MAKE YOUR REQUEST SPECIFIC, HE WILL KNOW EXACTLY WHAT YOU WANT AND YOU WILL KNOW THAT, WHEN HE DOES IT, HE IS CHOOSING TO DO SOMETHING FOR YOUR BENEFIT."[112]

THE 5 LOVE LANGUAGES: THE SECRET TO LOVE THAT LASTS BY GARY CHAPMAN.

Physical touch and quality time are challenging love languages when it comes to distance, as they usually require being physically together. This is why it's a great idea to try to meet your hiker during the hike if possible. Chapman says, "You must be creative and committed to staying connected despite the distance. If your love language is physical touch... having photographs of yourself as a couple may remind you of enjoyable times together. Having physical items that belong to one another may also remind you of each other. Perhaps a shirt or the cologne or perfume of your significant other... You also should email, text, write, etc., about how you enjoy being with one another. You might even try keeping a calendar on which you physically mark off the days until you're able to be together again... As for quality time, the time you spend staying in contact, working to encourage one another, sending each other notes and gifts, etc., is quality time... It's not the preferred form of quality time, but it is quality time nonetheless. You must learn to view it and appreciate it as such."[111]

Many supporters already use some of these suggestions, keeping wall maps, tracking progress, sending care packages, and writing letters. However, supporters may not realize that this is a result of how they like to show and receive love.

In addition to setting expectations that ensure both partners feel loved and supported, there may be others to set. For example, how often does your partner expect you to call and check in? How often do you expect calls and check-ins? If these answers are different, address them and come to an agreement to avoid arguments later on. Other common concerns that are beneficial to clarify are areas where less frequent communication may be non-negotiable due to reception, and budget (if you share funds).

Set expectations for yourself, too. What would you like to accomplish while your partner is away? Perhaps there's a hobby which you haven't had time to pursue? Finding ways to fill gaps in your schedule will prevent you from falling into boredom. Designating time for yourself and your goals will keep you from feeling like your life is paused until your partner returns and will prevent jealousy about the time your partner is spending pursuing a dream.

"A BIG PART OF THE EXPERIENCE WAS THE MUTUAL INDEPENDENCE WE WERE EXPERIENCING. I'D NEVER EXPERIENCED A LONG-DISTANCE RELATIONSHIP BEFORE, SO IT WAS CHALLENGING TO GO THROUGH LIFE ON MY OWN AND NOT HAVE HIM THERE OR BE ABLE TO CALL HIM. IT WAS KIND OF DIFFICULT IN THE MENTAL HEALTH ASPECT. I HAVE FRIENDS THAT I CAN GO TO, BUT HE'S MY ROCK. IT WAS REALLY DIFFICULT TO KNOW THAT IF IT'S A WEEK AND I'M NOT HEARING FROM HIM, IT COULD EITHER MEAN HE HAS NO SERVICE OR THAT HE'S FALLEN DOWN A CLIFF. I WISH I'D KNOWN MORE ABOUT WHAT PARTS OF THE TRAIL I'D HEAR FROM HIM. I KNOW FOR MANY HIKERS A BIG PART OF IT IS BEING DISCONNECTED, AND THAT MAKES SENSE, BUT IT BECAME DIFFICULT FOR ME TO DEAL WITH." - EMILY, 21, KENTUCKY

HOW TO GROW WITH YOUR HIKER

The worry that your partner will change as a result of the trail is a concern many share. The root of this concern is usually fear that when the hiker returns you'll no longer be compatible and the relationship will end. And yet how could someone not change after experiencing such a different lifestyle for that long? Change doesn't mean you have to grow apart. Sometimes partners fear that the strong bonds formed with a trail family will seem more powerful than a relationship at home and result in the parter no longer being able to relate.

"THERE ARE SINGLE GUYS AND GIRLS ON THE TRAIL, AND MY LIFE AND [MY GIRLFRIEND'S], AT THAT MOMENT, WERE SO DIFFERENT THAT SHE'D WORRY WHEN THE PEOPLE I WAS SPENDING TIME AROUND BONDED. BUT IT'S A FACT THAT THE PEOPLE YOU MEET ON THE TRAIL, WHETHER IT'S PLATONIC OR NOT, WILL BOND, BECAUSE YOU'RE SPENDING SO MUCH VISCERAL, REAL TIME TOGETHER THAT'S UNINTERRUPTED BY ANYTHING EXCEPT THE NEED FOR MILES, FOOD, WATER, AND SHELTER."
- ELLIOT, 25, ARKANSAS

Many partners at home expressed worries that because the hiker's lifestyle is more similar to that of trail friends', the hiker will grow connections with a trail family rather than the partner. In *A General Theory of Love*, Lewis, M.D., Amini, M.D., and Lannon, M.D. reinforce this inevitable bonding, stating, "Fear's propensity to amplify bonding is what drives high school couples to see scary movies together. An identical mechanism weaves the ties between people who share a traumatic experience, as in wartime or a disaster. Designers of boot camps, and fraternity and sorority initiations, with varying degrees of consciousness exploit the same process to forge affiliations between dissimilar strangers who must be made to cohere."[113] Long-distance hikers all face a level of fear, and in a situation where the hikers are all pushing through pain and frustration in pursuit of a common goal, it's impossible for them to not form a bond. That fear, reliance, and togetherness amplify how they interact in ways that can't be replicated in less immersive scenarios.

The intense bonding between hikers due to shared high-intensity experiences can be hard for a partner at home to accept if the relationship at home does not have an inherent trust and confidence that fosters a pursuit of individual goals and friendships. A partner at home who is not okay with a significant other socializing separately may experience feelings of jealously towards the hiker forming and prioritizing new friendships. Trusting the boundaries in those new relationships can take time to get used to. If pressed, your hiker may give in and spend more time on you, but it may also cause resentfulness towards the partner at home for limiting the ability to experience the trail as immersively as other hikers.

"SHE HASN'T REALLY AFFORDED ME THE OPPORTUNITY TO MEET HER TRAIL FAMILY. EARLY ON IF SHE WOULD'VE AT LEAST MAYBE DONE A FACETIME OR SOMETHING SO I COULD KNOW WHO THESE STRANGERS ARE, WHO ARE WITH MY FIANCÉE EVERY MINUTE OF THE DAY, IT WOULD'VE MADE ME FEEL A LOT MORE COMFORTABLE." - RYAN, 30, LOUISIANA

Partners at home share a desire to be introduced to their hiker's trail friends, whether in-person (if visiting), or via FaceTime or similar video apps. Partners who met the hiker's friends generally felt more comfortable and less concerned. If saying, "hello," to someone your partner is hiking with will prevent an argument, explain how meeting your hiker's friends will ease jealousy and build trust by removing the mystery of who the trail friends are and what they're like.

Remember that this is the hiker's journey, and how much they want to include a partner at home will vary. Some hikers willingly welcomed partners to hike sections of the trail, while others wanted certain milestones—like the start and end—to be kept their own. Before your partner leaves, express the level in which you want to be

included and revert back to amending expectations if your needs and
your partner's don't align.

"BE IN THEIR LIFE AS MUCH AS YOU NEED TO BE, BUT THIS
IS ALSO THEIR JOURNEY AND YOU NEED TO ALLOW THEM THEIR
SPACE. IF YOU TRUST THEM AND THINK YOU'RE GOING TO MAKE
IT AS A COUPLE THEN LET THEM GO, LET THEM DO IT AND
DON'T GET UPSET IF THEY DON'T CALL OR TEXT AS MUCH AS YOU
WANT. YOU CAN GET THROUGH IT." - RYAN, 30, LOUISIANA

Growing with your hiker begins before the trip, as it can be hard to
find time leading up to departure when your hiker isn't preoccupied
with preparations. That time is necessary, but designating time
that's focused on just the two of you can help prevent frustration or
resentfulness. For example, maybe you'll spend a night of each week
helping with research and preparations, and additionally, you'll pick
a weekly date night. If your partner is concerned about saving money
for the trail, suggest dates like going to the park or having a movie/
game night, that allow quality time without spending money. Many
supporters roll their eyes at how obsessed loved ones become with
preparations. However, many also report wishing they'd known more
about the trail and conditions that the hiker would face. Joining in
the preparation can serve a dual purpose—helping your hiker, and
helping you better understand the upcoming trail experience.

In order to see a relationship grow through the trail, neither side
can afford to hold grudges or dwell on past grievances. This may
require more understanding and patience than usual, along with a
willingness to be flexible in expectations. One-sided actions may
seem to benefit one partner, but ultimately harm both. Partners need
to act in ways that benefit both sides of the relationship. I've met
hikers whose partners at home demanded free time be spent on them
rather than allowing the hiker a choice. None of those relationships
lasted. The partners at home didn't understand the limited amount of
down time the hiker had, nor the need to rest and recover from hours
and days of physically and mentally exhausting work. Many times,
the hiker may not have been in the right mental state for a phone call.
Respecting your hiker's choice on the frequency of communications

without placing additional demands may actually encourage the hiker to reach out more. When communications complement a powerful journey instead of feeling like a burdensome obligation, they become more desirable, and sometimes more frequent.

"HE WAS HIKING WITH A GIRL AND MAINTAINING TRUST WAS HARD. BEFORE I VISITED HE TOLD ME THAT HE AND THE PEOPLE HE WAS HIKING WITH WERE GETTING A MOTEL ROOM. I HEARD HER NAME AND THOUGHT, 'YOU'RE SHARING A ROOM WITH A GIRL?' HE EXPLAINED THAT SHE GETS HER OWN BED AND THAT HE AND ANOTHER GUY WOULD SHARE A BED. I KNOW IT'S A PART OF THE TRAIL, BUT I DON'T LIKE THAT. FOR ME, HAVING CONVERSATIONS HELPED A LOT INSTEAD OF MAKING ASSUMPTIONS. BEING HONEST ABOUT HOW I WAS FEELING WAS A BIG PART OF IT. I WASN'T QUESTIONING HIM. I DIDN'T THINK HE WOULD MAKE A MOVE ON HER. BUT I WAS TERRIFIED. IT WAS ONE OF THOSE THINGS WHERE YOU TRUST THEM, BUT YOU DON'T TRUST OTHERS, WHICH ISN'T RIGHT, BUT I DID FEEL THAT WAY. ONCE I MET HER AND GOT TO KNOW HOW FUNDAMENTALLY DIFFERENT SHE WAS THAN MYSELF, I FELT A LOT BETTER. HAD I NOT HAD THE CHANCE TO MEET THE PEOPLE HE'D BEEN SPENDING WEEKS WITH, I WOULD'VE HAD A REAL PROBLEM.'
- EMILY, 21, KENTUCKY

While instances like your hiker sharing a motel room with members of the opposite sex may be uncomfortable, listen to the circumstances before attacking. Understand that the hiker's budget might necessitate splitting costs of rooms with other hikers, and who is in town to split the room with is out of your hiker's control. To the hiker, splitting a room feels no different than sharing a shelter, which is first come, first serve. Hikers often treat hostel or motel rooms similarly, prioritizing sticking with their pack over caring who is in the bed opposite.

On my hikes, I've shared motels with groups including those in relationships. My choice to share the rooms came down to saving money and the safety and comfort of surrounding myself with people I knew. I never considered it a scenario that would need to make a partner at home uncomfortable. In my mind, the only difference between those nights and the rest of the nights on the trail were the four walls and roof around us. Trust that your hiker wouldn't drag a relationship through a long-distance trail without being fully committed to the relationship.

At the same time, if your hiker is not abiding by set expectations or is neglecting your relationship beyond what is understandable—a conversation dedicated to constructively expressing how this is impacting you may be required. Remember to prepare for a conversation like this and avoid pointing fingers and placing blame. The goal should be to find a solution on which both parties can agree.

"I'M NOT EVEN JEALOUS OF ANOTHER GIRL. I'M JEALOUS OF THE COLORADO TRAIL." - JOANNA, 27, COLORADO

Feeling that your own goals are supported and recognized during your partner's hike will be important. Sharing milestones of your own will keep you accountable and give your hiker ways to praise and encourage you, too. It will be hard to feel support if you're remaining stagnant at home. Your growth will require fostering a life that does not necessitate your partner's presence.

Lewis, Amini, and Lannon write, "The neurally ingrained attractors of one lover warp the emotional virtuality of the other, shifting emotional perceptions... A portion of his neural activity depends on the presence of that other living brain. Without it, the electric interplay that makes up *him* has changed. Lovers hold keys to each other's identities, and they write neurostructural alterations into each other's networks. Their limbic tie allows each to influence who the other is and becomes."[114] If a piece of you feels missing while your partner is away, science shows you aren't alone. In a relationship, the other person becomes a part of who you are. When your partner goes on a long-distance hike, that part of you leaves home and grows in new ways. The rest of you will need to grow too so that your pieces still fit together when they return.

WHEN COMMUNICATION IS LACKING

One of the most challenging aspects of your hiker being away is remaining patient and understanding when communication is lacking. It can be hard to keep your cool when you've waited all week for your partner to check-in and that call arrives later than anticipated or your partner seems distracted on the phone. As someone whose life still remains structured, having your partner not abide to scheduled check-ins can feel disrespectful.

For a hiker, time is fluid. The nature of the trail is to forgo exact schedules and timelines. Hikers can't predict their day-to-day mileage or expected arrival times in towns accurately until days or hours prior, due to variables like weather, energy-level, group morale, and terrain. If I'm unable to accurately guess when I'll get to camp at night or to the next town, how can I possibly predict an exact time to be in an area with cell reception to make a call? It's likely that for your hiker, making the call at all means it was a priority and the exact timing feels somewhat arbitrary.

The problem is that, *"I'll call you when I can,"* is probably not going to go over well with a partner at home. You've accepted that your loved one is going to do the trail, you've encouraged progress during times of self-doubt, you've watched obsessive preparations and worries over gear, mailed resupply boxes, taken care of issues at home, remained supportive and positive—all while maintaining your job, your life, and your goals for yourself. All you want in return is a call that is on time and focused. If you've spent days patiently awaiting communication and it doesn't come when promised, how could you not be upset? Unfortunately, due to the inability to accurately plan on the trail, a lack of communication is sometimes unavoidable. Support through patience, even when frustrated, will mean the world to your hiker. I've observed a habit form in several relationships where the partner at home is so worried that the hiker won't be able to call that it becomes an expectation or demand that the hiker call anytime there is reliable cell reception. Hikers around me have had relationships crumble because the partner at home becomes angry if the hiker has service and isn't on the phone. While regular phone use is increasingly common in the off-trail world, it just isn't feasible on-trail. Daily obligations like filtering water, setting up tents, calculating mileage, and bandaging feet all take precedence over cell phone use. For the hikers whose relationships suffered from this impossible expectation, constant cell communication usually wasn't the pre-set agreement between the partners, but a habit that slowly fell into place.

Not all conversation is healthy or helpful. In 2010, researchers at the University of Arizona found that the happiest students, "spent a third less time engaged in small talk and had about twice as many substantive conversations."[115] Over-communication is neither productive nor beneficial to the relationship, as it prevents the hiker from staying immersed in the trail experience. Pay attention when you set expectations on how often to anticipate communication. Writing down expectations to refer back to could be useful, too. Focus on if your hiker is staying within those parameters rather than if they are a few hours late to check-in. If your agreement is that your partner will call twice a week, frame your expectations around that. For example, it isn't fair to get jealous because you see social-media posts pop up before you've received a phone call if your hiker is adhering to the twice-weekly phone calls as promised. Additionally, hikers want to spend some of their downtime with friends instead of on technology or communicating with those back home. This may seem counter-intuitive since these are the hikers daily companions, but much time on trail is spent accomplishing an arduous task and not relaxing and freely socializing. Certain towns have features or attractions that are not-to-miss, and with limited town-time, they may prioritize those opportunities.

"WE LIVED TOGETHER AND WERE ALWAYS AROUND EACH OTHER, SO BEING SEPARATED WAS REALLY HARD. I KNEW HE WOULDN'T BE ABLE TO COMMUNICATE MUCH, BUT HE JUST WASN'T COMMUNICATING AT ALL, EVEN WHEN HE WAS ABLE TO. THAT CAUSED SOME PROBLEMS, BUT THANKFULLY WE TALKED IT OUT, GOT THROUGH IT, AND HE'S STILL OUT THERE GOING STRONG AND HAVING THE TIME OF HIS LIFE." - ALEX, 21, OHIO

In *We Need to Talk: How to Have Conversations That Matter*, Headlee says, "Sometimes, the best conversation strategy is to not talk at all. If you don't have the energy or motivation to focus on another person, it's best to isolate yourself. That's how you avoid angry outbursts or saying things you don't really mean... It's neither helpful nor productive to involve yourself in a discussion when you're tired or irritated and head-achey. If you force yourself to talk when you don't want to, you won't be satisfied with your end of the conversation and you probably won't retain what was said on either side."[116] As hard as it can be to put down the phone, don't force a conversation through small talk just for the sake of having one, and try to understand if your hiker is too tired or lacks the energy to partake in meaningful conversation. The trail exhausts hikers both physically and mentally in ways they may not have fully anticipated. Keep in mind that the endless responsibilities both on and off trail add to that exhaustion.

If you are having trouble with the amount of communication with your hiker, set a time to talk where you can express why your agreement is not working, and request changes that may help. Chapman says, "When you make a request of your [partner], you are affirming his or her worth and abilities. When, however, you make demands, you have become not a lover but a tyrant. Your [partner] will feel not affirmed, but belittled. A request introduces the element of choice. Your mate may choose to respond to your request or to deny it, because love is always a choice."[117] Your partner may have reasons to counter the new proposal. Listen to their side, try to see where they are coming from, and return to the conversation later if it gets heated.

Fights with your partner will be more difficult on the trail than at home. You may not be able to call each other to apologize or make amends when you're restricted to communicating only when cell reception is available. Even when there is reception, most hikers keep their phones on *Airplane Mode* to preserve battery. If you're trying to call or text an apology or sentiment, it may not be seen right away if notifications are turned off. In *Guardian*, Daniel J. Levitin says, "Unanswered text feels insulting to the sender... You receive a text and that activates your novelty centers. You respond and feel rewarded for having completed a task (even though that task was entirely unknown to you 15 seconds earlier). Each of those delivers shot of dopamine as your limbic system cries out 'More! More! Give me more!'"[118] Texting your hiker sporadically throughout the day may also cause you to feel less connected if your hiker is unable to respond, as our minds are trained to think that unanswered texts mean we're being ignored. Instead, try to write thoughts down and save them for when your hiker's whole attention is focused on you.

TIPS FOR LISTENING

- "DON'T LISTEN TO YOUR [PARTNER] AND DO SOMETHING ELSE AT THE SAME TIME. REMEMBER, QUALITY TIME IS GIVING SOMEONE YOUR UNDIVIDED ATTENTION. IF YOU ARE DOING SOMETHING YOU CANNOT TURN FROM IMMEDIATELY, TELL YOUR [PARTNER] THE TRUTH."
- "LISTEN FOR FEELINGS. ASK YOURSELF, 'WHAT EMOTION IS MY [PARTNER] EXPERIENCING?' WHEN YOU THINK YOU HAVE THE ANSWER, CONFIRM IT... THAT GIVES HIM THE CHANCE TO CLARIFY HIS FEELINGS. IT ALSO COMMUNICATES THAT YOU ARE LISTENING TO WHAT HE IS SAYING."
- "REFUSE TO INTERRUPT. RESEARCH HAS INDICATED THAT THE AVERAGE INDIVIDUAL LISTENS FOR ONLY SEVENTEEN SECONDS BEFORE INTERRUPTING AND INTERJECTING HIS OWN IDEAS."

THE 5 LOVE LANGUAGES: THE SECRET TO LOVE THAT LASTS[119]
BY GARY CHAPMAN

To assume that the hiker is the only half of the relationship that has trouble staying in touch would be incorrect. I have hiked with others who begged their partners at home to show more interest and reach out more. I've seen hikers get to post offices eager to collect a resupply only to become heartbroken that there was no letter from their partner, again. There have been off-trail partners who have canceled calls due to needing to stay late at the office, when the hiker had worked so hard to find cell reception. Learning the right balance isn't easy, which is why setting expectations and following through on them to the best of your ability is crucial.

That being said, if it seems like your hiker is leaning on you and over-communicating to the extent that it may be negatively impacting the trail experience, try to encourage participation in activities in town and spending time with other hikers. Hearing regrets about not having spent time on the trail enjoying and appreciating the experience due to homesickness and missing one's partner is sad because for many hikers this will be their one long-distance hike and they may not get a chance to redo their experience. Keeping yourself busy with your own hobbies and goals will prevent either of you from forming an over-dependency on communication.

"WE MOSTLY FOUGHT ABOUT COMMUNICATION. I HAD A TOUGH TIME THE LAST COUPLE MONTHS AND HAD SOME SETBACKS. IT SENT ME INTO A DARK PLACE. I WASN'T VERY INTERESTING FOR HER TO TALK TO. SHE DIDN'T WANT TO TALK TO ME. I DIDN'T HAVE ANYTHING GOING ON. I WAS SHORT TEMPERED, AND SO WAS SHE. IT WAS TOUGH WHEN WE FOUGHT BECAUSE THERE WERE EXTENDED AMOUNTS OF TIME WHERE I COULDN'T CALL HER UP AND SAY, 'I'M SORRY.' I'D HAVE TO WAIT UNTIL SHE WAS BACK IN RANGE." - RYAN, 30, LOUISIANA

"HE WOULD MAKE VOICE RECORDINGS FOR ME ON HIS PHONE WHEN HE DIDN'T HAVE SERVICE. WHEN HE GOT SERVICE HE'D SEND THEM AND I COULD LISTEN. IT WAS A WAY THAT WE LEANED ON EACH OTHER. IF WE COULDN'T ACTUALLY TALK, THAT WAS THE WAY WE'D COMMUNICATE. HE KNEW THAT I WAS LISTENING TO THE RECORDINGS HE MADE, AND I KNEW THAT HE WAS LISTENING TO THE RECORDINGS I MADE. HE TOLD ME IT WAS A HUGE THING THAT KEPT HIM GOING." - EMILY, 21, KENTUCKY

"BECAUSE THE GUY I HIKED WITH AND I WERE BOTH DATING SOMEONE, I NOTICED THAT WHEN OTHERS WOULD BE HANGING OUT WE WERE MORE RESERVED AND ALWAYS BLOCKING OUT TIME, TO CALL OUR GIRLFRIENDS. WE'D BOUNCE EARLY OR STAY AWAY FROM PEOPLE. WE WERE SPENDING SO MUCH TIME THINKING ABOUT OUR GIRLFRIENDS THAT WE'D JUST WANT TO GO TO BED, GET UP, AND HIKE." - ELLIOT, 25, ARKANSAS

HANDLING ARGUMENTS

Disagreements are inevitable. How you and your partner handle them will determine whether you can learn and move forward, or if they will grow into larger problems. Remaining calm even when frustrated will keep the conversation positive and your partner receptive. Avoid phrases that place blame, like, *you should, you didn't,* or *you never.* Avoid making it personal or bring up faults or flaws. Instead, focus on 'I' statements (I feel, I want, etc.). Share that you want to support your partner's opinions, and then do so. Remain open to re-examining your beliefs once you've heard your partner's side and refrain from letting a disagreement become about winning. Consider if there are things within your control that can be done to manage frustrations.

In addition, try not to become defensive when responding to attacks. When someone is defensive or feels attacked, they are less likely to listen or remain understanding. *Love is Letting Go of Fear,* by Gerald G. Jampolsky, M.D., says, "When we perceive another person as attacking us, we usually feel defensive and find a way, directly or indirectly, to attack back. Attacking always stems from fear and guilt. No one attacks unless he first feels threatened and believes that through attack he can demonstrate his own strength, at the expense of another's vulnerability. Attack is really a defense and, as with all defenses that are designed to keep guilt and fear from our awareness, attack actually preserves the problem."[120] Choosing not to attack will offer a better chance of being heard.

If your partner sees that you want to work to resolve issues rather than place blame and reprimand, it will open the door to constructive conversation. The tone of your voice will matter just as much as the words you use, especially since these conversations don't have the luxury of being in-person.

"SOMETIMES OUR WORDS SAY ONE THING, BUT OUR TONE OF
VOICE SAYS ANOTHER. WE ARE SENDING DOUBLE MESSAGES. OUR
[PARTNER] WILL USUALLY INTERPRET OUR MESSAGE BASED ON OUR
TONE OF VOICE, NOT THE WORDS WE USE... WHEN YOUR [PARTNER]
IS ANGRY AND UPSET AND LASHING OUT WORDS OF HEAT,
IF YOU CHOOSE TO BE LOVING, YOU WILL NOT RECIPROCATE
WITH ADDITIONAL HEAT BUT WITH A SOFT VOICE... YOU WILL
LET HIM TELL YOU OF HIS HURT, ANGER, AND PERCEPTION OF
EVENTS. YOU WILL SEEK TO PUT YOURSELF IN HIS SHOES AND
SEE THE EVENT THROUGH HIS EYES AND THEN EXPRESS SOFTLY
AND KINDLY YOUR UNDERSTANDING OF WHY HE FEELS THAT WAY.
IF YOU HAVE WRONGED HIM, YOU WILL BE WILLING TO CONFESS
THE WRONG AND ASK FORGIVENESS."[122]

THE 5 LOVE LANGUAGES: THE SECRET TO LOVE THAT LASTS
BY GARY CHAPMAN

Self-awareness can prevent arguments triggered by external
frustrations. If you've had a crummy day or are already irritated,
you may be more sensitive with your partner. In *A General Theory
of Love*, Lewis, Amini, and Lannon write, "If a man spills coffee
on himself, his annoyance is relatively short-lived—on the order
of minutes. After the conscious feeling is gone, residual activity in
the anger circuits lingers. He will pass into an irritable mood—a
quickness to anger, the only reflection of the waning activity in those
circuits. If he trips over his son's skateboard on the living room
floor a bit later, his wrath will be faster and greater than the accident
deserves on its own merits. Since the neural activation that creates
a given emotion decreases gradually, provoking it again is easier
within the window of the mood."[121] If you're feeling irritable or close
to snapping, cool off and recharge before having a conversation that
could lead to conflict.

Conversely, don't avoid conversation because you're afraid
of it turning into an argument. Tension increases with time, and
letting issues build will make them more difficult to resolve.
Ignoring problems won't make them go away, but addressing issues
respectfully as they arise can help your relationship survive bumps.

CONVERSATION STARTERS TO BRING UP ISSUES[123]
- YOU AND I SHARE A PROBLEM. WE'VE BOTH LET THIS LINGER. I HOPE WE CAN WORK THROUGH THIS TOGETHER.
- KNOW HOW MUCH I LOVE, TRUST, RESPECT, AND CARE ABOUT YOU AND DON'T WANT US TO ACT AS IF OUR PROBLEM DOESN'T EXIST.
- I'M CONCERNED THAT THERE ARE ISSUES WE HAVEN'T TALKED ABOUT THAT ARE AFFECTING HOW WE SOLVE THIS PROBLEM TOGETHER. I WONDER IF YOU HAVE CONCERNS ABOUT THIS, TOO.
- TALKING ABOUT THIS IS DIFFICULT FOR ME, BUT I'M HOPING WE CAN HELP EACH OTHER SAY WHAT WE NEED TO SAY.

CONVERSATION STARTERS TO LIFT SILENCE[124]
- I FEEL THAT...
- I'VE ASSUMED THAT...
- I THINK I'VE AVOIDED TALKING ABOUT THIS BECAUSE...
- MY CONCERN IS...
- I WOULD LIKE TO...
- GOING FORWARD, I HOPE THAT...

RESPONSES THAT VALIDATE THE OTHER'S FEELINGS + THOUGHTS[125]
- I CAN UNDERSTAND WHY YOU SEE IT THAT WAY.
- YOU MAKE A GOOD POINT. I HEAR YOU.
- I'VE HAD A SIMILAR FEELING, BUT I HAVEN'T KNOWN HOW TO ADDRESS IT.
- I DO LOVE YOU. STILL, I THINK THIS CONVERSATION IS NECESSARY TO KEEP US FROM FURTHER HURT.

SOLICITING YOUR PARTNER'S IDEAS + FEELINGS[126]
- WHAT DO YOU THINK ABOUT THAT?
- DOES THIS COME AS A SURPRISE TO YOU?
- DOES THIS MAKE SENSE TO YOU?
- HOW CAN I SUPPORT YOU IN THIS?
- WHAT IDEAS DO YOU HAVE ABOUT HOW WE CAN MAKE CHANGES THAT WILL BE GOOD FOR BOTH OF US?

WE NEED TO TALK: HOW TO HAVE CONVERSATIONS THAT MATTER
BY CELESTE HEADLEE

FOR THE HIKER

IT CAN BE EASY TO BECOME SO WRAPPED UP IN YOUR HIKE
THAT YOU FORGET TO PRIORITIZE YOUR PARTNER AT HOME AS
MUCH AS YOU SHOULD. TRY TO INCLUDE YOUR PARTNER IN SMALL
MOMENTS IN YOUR DAY TO SHOW YOU ARE THINKING OF THEM.IF
YOU PASS A COOL VIEW AND THERE IS CELL RECEPTION, SEND A
PHOTO AND EXPLAIN YOU WANTED YOUR PARTNER TO SEE IT TOO.
GIVING EXTRA PEEKS INTO YOUR TRIP THAT AREN'T AVAILABLE
TO THE GENERAL PUBLIC ON SOCIAL MEDIA WILL AFFIRM YOUR
PARTNER'S SPECIAL PLACE IN YOUR LIFE. IF SOMETHING FUNNY
OR INTERESTING HAPPENS, SEND A QUICK MESSAGE TELLING
THE STORY AND THAT YOU WISH YOUR PARTNER WAS THERE TO
WITNESS IT.

FOR THE PARTNER AT HOME: UNDERSTAND THAT IF YOU
RECEIVE A PHOTO OR STORY IN THE MIDDLE OF THE DAY,
YOUR HIKER LIKELY NEEDS TO KEEP MOVING AND WON'T
HAVE TIME TO LET IT TURN INTO A FULL CONVERSATION.
TRY TO APPRECIATE THE LITTLE CHECK-INS FOR WHAT
THEY ARE, BUT KNOW THAT IF YOUR HIKER FEELS LIKE
CHECK-INS ALWAYS REQUIRE A FULL CONVERSATION OR
RESULT IN A PHONE CALL, THOSE RANDOM STORIES ARE
LIKELY TO BECOME LESS FREQUENT.

SENDING GIFTS TO YOUR PARTNER AT HOME CAN ALSO
REAFFIRM YOUR COMMITMENT, EVEN IF THE COMMUNICATION
ISN'T AS FREQUENT AS THEY'D LIKE. THESE DON'T NEED TO BE
EXPENSIVE. WHAT IS IMPORTANT IS THAT YOU THOUGHT OF YOUR
PARTNER AND WENT TO THE EFFORT OF SENDING SOMETHING
TO SHOW YOU CARE. POSTCARDS FROM TOWN CAN BE GREAT
KEEPSAKES AND ARE LOW-COST. MANY LONG-DISTANCE TRAILS
WILL ALSO HAVE AT LEAST ONE TOWN THAT IS MORE TOURISTY
THAN THE REST. CONSIDER SENDING HOME A SOUVENIR FROM
ONE OF THESE STOPS TO ADD VARIETY. YOUR PARTNER WILL
BE ABLE TO PHYSICALLY HOLD IT AND WILL APPRECIATE THE
SENTIMENT. A JAR OF HUCKLEBERRY JAM IN WASHINGTON OR
THE SHENANDOAH'S IS A GREAT EXAMPLE OF A SIMPLE BUT
THOUGHTFUL GIFT, BECAUSE WITH EACH USE YOUR PARTNER WILL
THINK OF YOU.

CONCLUSION

At this point you should have a better understanding of what a long-distance trail is like than you had when you first opened this book. You know how hikers eat, drink, sleep, and navigate the trail. You understand the environmental hazards and wildlife your hiker may encounter. You are aware of what to expect in terms of communication and how to support your hiker every step of the way.

Long-distance hiking is a huge undertaking and a life-changing adventure. This will be a journey that your hiker will look back on for the rest of his or her life, and showing that you care and will be there for support throughout the journey will help your hiker through this experience. I hope this book answered questions and gave details on areas that might have been confusing.

Feel free to use the following pages to keep track of important details such as who your hiker is with and when they are reaching towns. Regardless of how far your hiker makes it on trail, they will have attempted something that few people dare to attempt. For that alone, you should be proud.

Wish them luck from me and remind them to bury their poop.

Chaunce

HIKER NAME	PHONE NUMBER	NOTES
_____	_____	_____
_____	_____	_____
_____	_____	_____
_____	_____	_____
_____	_____	_____
_____	_____	_____
_____	_____	_____
_____	_____	_____
_____	_____	_____
_____	_____	_____
_____	_____	_____
_____	_____	_____
_____	_____	_____

LENGTH OF ENTIRE TRAIL: _____

10 %: _____   20 %: _____   30 %: _____   40 %: _____
50 %: _____   60 %: _____   70 %: _____   80 %: _____
90 %: _____   100 %: _____

SHADE THE BOXES AS YOUR HIKER REACHES THESE ACCOMPLISHMENTS

| 10% | 20% | 30% | 40% | 50% | 60% | 70% | 80% | 90% | 100% |

| 100 MILES | 500 MILES | 1000 MILES | 2000 MILES | ACCOMPLISHED GOAL |

DATE OF CHECK-IN LOCATION   NOTES

FOOD LIKES:

_____   _____   _____

_____   _____   _____

_____   _____   _____

_____   _____   _____

_____   _____   _____

_____   _____   _____

FOOD DIS-LIKES:

_____   _____   _____

_____   _____   _____

_____   _____   _____

_____   _____   _____

_____   _____   _____

NOTES:

ACKNOWLEDGMENTS

This book is for my parents, Sarah and Steogn, who have been nothing but supportive in any decisions I make. It is also for all of the friends I made on my hikes, from those I hiked with to those who were kind enough to take us into their homes, offer rides, and provide support that kept us going. Thank you to Courtney for sticking by my side for my first 700 mi of long-distance hiking, to Easy for walking with me from Georgia to Maine, to Gilligan, Ballflap, Buzz, Chocolate Balls, County Dump, Munchies, and Scuba Steve for all the fun on the PCT, and to Jukebox, Fireball, Doc, Ninja, Mr. Perfect, Gandolf, Paris, Deadpool, Ziploc, Boomer, Sheep Dog, Storm Trooper, and General for making my Appalachian Trail thru-hike unforgettable.

A special thank you to Ballflap, Fireball, and Jukebox for all of your support and encouragement during the months I was writing this book. Your willingness to provide feedback, listen to me vent, and offer me advice kept me motivated to continue writing. Ballflap and Fireball, thank you for helping me readjust when I got back to Denver. The transition would not have been as smooth without you both.

Hiking From Home would not have been possible without the hours of informative conversations I had with past and aspiring long-distance hikers, significant others of long-distance hikers, and family members of long-distance hikers. Abigail, Alex, Amy, Andy, Arthur, Brad, Bruce, Carolyn, Chris, Cynthia, Debbie, Don, Elliot, Emilio, Emily, Gary, George, Jackie, Janet, Jennifer, Jim, Joanna, John, Josh, Justin, Katie, Katrina, Keith, Kristen, Lily, Maren, Mun, Nikki, Rob, Ryan, Tabatha, Victoria, and Zach, thank you for answering all of my questions and telling me your stories. You helped me understand how to fill these pages.

I'd also like to thank Dr. Ed Corkran, D.O., Elizabeth Keller, RN, BSN, and Keith Michel, RN, BSN for their assistance with writing the Common Illness & Prevention chapter. Elisabeth Young, PT,

DPT, and Megan Timler, DPT, Heather Pannill, DPT, ATC, LAT, Tom Pannill, and Julie Velasquez, PTA, thank you for all of your valuable input and suggestions in writing the Common Injuries & Prevention chapter. Also, special thanks to Josh Stone, M.Ed., LAPC, not only for his assistance in writing the Post-Trail Depression chapter, but for picking me up from the airport, hosting me, and driving me to the Approach Trail in Amicalola Falls at the start of my Appalachian Trail thru-hike.

In addition, I'd like to thank the beta readers who read this book and provided edits and suggestions that helped shape it into the version it is today. Chris Guynn, Georgia L. Harris, Jen Wooster-McBride, Katie Clements, Ken Bold, Kevin E. Newsome, Kim Nalepinski, Kyle Champine, Lands Fineran, Leah Kunkel, Michelle Pugh, Patti Dinger, and Sarah Chauncey (Mom), the feedback you provided was so helpful in finishing this book. It would not have turned out as well without your suggestions and unique literary strengths.

The beautiful cover of this book was designed by Jack D. Franks and the talented team at Bucket List Prints. Thank you for your patience through each iteration as we found the perfect design. I would like to also thank Joshua Johnson and Melissa Mission for their advice and suggestions on the cover typography.

I would not have learned as much about long-distance hiking without having spent the past two years co-hosting the Backpacker Radio podcast for The Trek. Zach Davis, thank you for always answering my questions, giving great advice, and listening to me vent about the trail and this book. You have been a great mentor in all of this.

Thank you to everyone who took my survey as I researched and prepared to write this book, as well as those who weighed in on questionnaires and polls on social media, and who gave their input and advice when I needed second opinions.

Finally, thank you to Nicole Teresa Miller for providing a cork board for all of my postcards.

ENDNOTES

1 "Why Is Forest-Bathing Necessary?" *Forest Bathing: How Trees Can Help You Find Health and Happiness*, by Qing Li, Viking, 2018, pp. 34.

2 "Why Is Forest-Bathing Necessary?" *Forest Bathing: How Trees Can Help You Find Health and Happiness*, by Qing Li, Viking, 2018, pp. 35.

3 "Why Is Forest-Bathing Necessary?" *Forest Bathing: How Trees Can Help You Find Health and Happiness*, by Qing Li, Viking, 2018, pp. 35.

4 "Is Nature's Appeal Fading?" *The Secret Therapy of Trees: Harness the Healing Energy of Forest Bathing and Natural Landscapes*, by Marco Mencagli, Rodale, 2019, pp. 28–29.

5 Leon Watson, "Humans Have Shorter Attention Span Than Goldfish, Thanks to Smartphones," *Telegraph*, May 15, 2015.

6 "Stress." *Spark: the Revolutionary New Science of Exercise and the Brain*, by John J. Ratey and Eric Hagerman, Little, Brown, 2013, pp. 69.

7 "Nature's Imprint: Is It Truly Forever?" *The Secret Therapy of Trees: Harness the Healing Energy of Forest Bathing and Natural Landscapes*, by Marco Mencagli, Rodale, 2019, pp. 10.

8 "Introduction." *Spark: the Revolutionary New Science of Exercise and the Brain*, by John J. Ratey and Eric Hagerman, Little, Brown, 2013, pp. 3-4.

9 "Nature's Imprint: Is It Truly Forever?" *The Secret Therapy of Trees: Harness the Healing Energy of Forest Bathing and Natural Landscapes*, by Marco Mencagli, Rodale, 2019, pp. 7-16.

10 "Is Nature's Appeal Fading?" *The Secret Therapy of Trees: Harness the Healing Energy of Forest Bathing and Natural Landscapes*, by Marco Mencagli, Rodale, 2019, pp. 29.

11 "Stress." *Spark: the Revolutionary New Science of Exercise and the Brain*, by John J. Ratey and Eric Hagerman, Little, Brown, 2013, pp. 69.

12 University of East Anglia. "It's official -- spending time outside is good for you." ScienceDaily. ScienceDaily, 6 July 2018. <www.sciencedaily.com/releases/2018/07/180706102842.htm>.

13 Dienstman, Allison M. "10 Unexpected Benefits of Spending Time in Nature." *Goodnet*, 27 May 2019, www.goodnet.org/articles/10-unexpected-benefits-spending-time-in-nature.

14 "Learning." *Spark: the Revolutionary New Science of Exercise and the Brain*, by John J. Ratey and Eric Hagerman, Little, Brown, 2013, pp. 53.

15 "Learning." *Spark: the Revolutionary New Science of Exercise and the Brain*, by John J. Ratey and Eric Hagerman, Little, Brown, 2013, pp. 50.

16 "Learning." *Spark: the Revolutionary New Science of Exercise and the Brain*, by John J. Ratey and Eric Hagerman, Little, Brown, 2013, pp. 55.

17 https://www.ncbi.nlm.nih.gov/pubmed/21996763

18 "Stress." *Spark: the Revolutionary New Science of Exercise and the Brain*, by John J. Ratey and Eric Hagerman, Little, Brown, 2013, pp. 74.

19 "Stress." *Spark: the Revolutionary New Science of Exercise and the Brain*, by John J. Ratey and Eric Hagerman, Little, Brown, 2013, pp. 81.

20 "Stress." *Spark: the Revolutionary New Science of Exercise and the Brain*, by John J. Ratey and Eric Hagerman, Little, Brown, 2013, pp. 72.

21 Miyazaki, Yoshifumi, et al. "Preventive Medical Effects of Nature Therapy." *Nihon Eiseigaku Zasshi. Japanese Journal of Hygiene*, U.S. National Library of Medicine, Sept. 2011, www.ncbi.nlm.nih.gov/pubmed/21996763.

22 "Stress." *Spark: the Revolutionary New Science of Exercise and the Brain*, by John J. Ratey and Eric Hagerman, Little, Brown, 2013, pp. 67.

23 Mao, Gen-Xiang, et al. "Therapeutic Effect of Forest Bathing on Human Hypertension in the Elderly." *Journal of Cardiology*, U.S. National Library of Medicine, Dec. 2012, www.ncbi.nlm.nih.gov/pubmed/22948092.

24 Rose, Kathryn A, et al. "Outdoor Activity Reduces the Prevalence of Myopia in Chil-

dren." *Ophthalmology*, U.S. National Library of Medicine, Aug. 2008, www.ncbi.nlm.nih.gov/pubmed/18294691.

25 Li, Q, et al. "Forest Bathing Enhances Human Natural Killer Activity and Expression of Anti-Cancer Proteins." *International Journal of Immunopathology and Pharmacology*, U.S. National Library of Medicine, 2007, www.ncbi.nlm.nih.gov/pubmed/17903349.

26 Li, Qing, et al. "Relationships Between Percentage of Forest Coverage and Standardized Mortality Ratios (SMR) of Cancers in All Prefectures in Japan." *The Open Public Health Journal*, vol. 1, no. 7, 2008, pdfs.semanticscholar.org/0804/696fae7e67588311962157e9b70e597c243a.pdf.

27 "Stress." *Spark: the Revolutionary New Science of Exercise and the Brain*, by John J. Ratey and Eric Hagerman, Little, Brown, 2013, pp. 84.

28 "Immerse Yourself in a Forest for Better Health." *Immerse Yourself in a Forest for Better Health - NYS Dept. of Environmental Conservation*, www.dec.ny.gov/lands/90720.html.

29 Barton, Jo, and Jules Pretty. "What Is the Best Dose of Nature and Green Exercise for Improving Mental Health? A Multi-Study Analysis." *Environmental Science & Technology*, U.S. National Library of Medicine, 15 May 2010, www.ncbi.nlm.nih.gov./pubmed/20337470.

30 "Anxiety." *Spark: the Revolutionary New Science of Exercise and the Brain*, by John J. Ratey and Eric Hagerman, Little, Brown, 2013, pp. 101.

31 "Stress." *Spark: the Revolutionary New Science of Exercise and the Brain*, by John J. Ratey and Eric Hagerman, Little, Brown, 2013, pp. 70.

32 "A Walk in the Shadows." *A General Theory of Love*, by Thomas Lewis et al., Vintage Books, 2001, pp. 209.

33 Finkel, Michael. *The Stranger in the Woods: the Extraordinary Story of the Last True Hermit.* Alfred A. Knopf, 2017.

34 "The 7 Principles - Leave No Trace Center for Outdoor Ethics." *Leave No Trace*, 2019, lnt.org/why/7-principles/.

35 Pasteris, Joe. "How Much Should Your Pack Weigh?" *REI Co-Op Journal*, REI, 12 Apr. 2019, www.rei.com/blog/camp/how-much-should-your-pack-weigh.

36 Dragna, Madison. "Water Treatments for Backpacking and Hiking." *The Trek*, 15 Oct. 2014, thetrek.co/water-purification-trail/.

37 "The Skinny on Soap." *Leave No Trace*, 6 May 2011, lnt.org/the-skinny-on-soap/.

38 "Frequently Asked Questions." *Appalachian Trail Conservancy*, 2019, www.appalachiantrail.org/home/explore-the-trail/thru-hiking/faqs.

39 Krakauer, Jon. Into the Wild. Pan Books, 2011.

40 "Get Off The Soapbox." *We Need To Talk: How to Have Conversations That Matter*, by Celeste Headlee, Harper Wave, 2017, pp. 136.

41 "Aging." *Spark: the Revolutionary New Science of Exercise and the Brain*, by John J. Ratey and Eric Hagerman, Little, Brown, 2013, pp. 225-227.

42 "Hormonal Changes." *Spark: the Revolutionary New Science of Exercise and the Brain*, by John J. Ratey and Eric Hagerman, Little, Brown, 2013, pp. 212.

43 "Aging." *Spark: the Revolutionary New Science of Exercise and the Brain*, by John J. Ratey and Eric Hagerman, Little, Brown, 2013, pp. 228.

44 "Aging." *Spark: the Revolutionary New Science of Exercise and the Brain*, by John J. Ratey and Eric Hagerman, Little, Brown, 2013, pp. 219-220.

45 "Safety and Crime Prevention." Appalachian Trail Conservancy, 2019, www.appalachiantrail.org/home/explore-the-trail/hiking-basics/safety.

46 "Wildlife Viewing Safety." *National Parks Service*, U.S. Department of the Interior, 2017, www.nps.gov/shen/learn/nature/viewing-wildlife-reminders.htm.

47 "Wildlife Safety." *National Parks Service*, U.S. Department of the Interior, 2017, www.nps.gov/romo/planyourvisit/wildlife-safety.htm.

48 "Bears." *Worried?: Science Investigates Some of Life's Common Concerns*, by Lise A. Johnson et al., W. W. Norton & Company, 2019, pp. 245–246.

49 "Bears." *Worried?: Science Investigates Some of Life's Common Concerns*, by Lise A. Johnson et al., W. W. Norton & Company, 2019, pp. 245–246.

50 "Black Bears." *National Parks Service*, U.S. Department of the Interior, 2017, www.nps.gov/grsm/learn/nature/black-bears.htm.

51 "Staying Safe Around Bears." *National Parks Service*, U.S. Department of the Interior, 2019,

www.nps.gov/subjects/bears/safety.htm.

52 "Bear Spray." *National Parks Service*, U.S. Department of the Interior, 2019, www.nps.gov/yell/learn/nature/bearspray.htm.

53 "Mountain Lion Safety." *National Parks Service*, U.S. Department of the Interior, 2015, www.nps.gov/care/learn/nature/cougar.htm.

54 "Wildlife Safety." *National Parks Service*, U.S. Department of the Interior, 2017, www.nps.gov/romo/planyourvisit/wildlife-safety.htm.

55 Bryson, Bill. *A Walk in the Woods: Rediscovering America on the Appalachian Trail*. Broadway Books, 2007.

56 "Moose Safety." *National Parks Service*, U.S. Department of the Interior, 2016, www.nps.gov/wrst/planyourvisit/moose-safety.htm.

57 "Rattlesnakes." *National Parks Service*, U.S. Department of the Interior, 2017, www.nps.gov/yose/learn/nature/rattlesnake.htm.

58 "Snakes." *Worried?: Science Investigates Some of Life's Common Concerns*, by Lise A. Johnson et al., W. W. Norton & Company, 2019, pp. 236–236.

59 "Stream Crossing Safety While Hiking and Backpacking." *Pacific Crest Trail Association*, 2019, www.pcta.org/discover-the-trail/backcountry-basics/water/stream-crossing-safety/.

60 "Stream Crossing Safety While Hiking and Backpacking." *Pacific Crest Trail Association*, 2019, www.pcta.org/discover-the-trail/backcountry-basics/water/stream-crossing-safety/.

61 "What You Need to Know about Wildfires, Campfires and Stoves on the PCT." *Pacific Crest Trail Association*, 2019, www.pcta.org/discover-the-trail/backcountry-basics/fire/.

62 "How to React to Wildfires." *Pacific Crest Trail Association*, 2019, www.pcta.org/discover-the-trail/backcountry-basics/fire/how-to-react-to-wildfires/.

63 "FAQ." *Colorado Trail Foundation*, 2019, coloradotrail.org/traveling-the-ct/faq/.

64 "Lyme Disease." *MedlinePlus*, U.S. National Library of Medicine, 25 Nov. 2019, medlineplus.gov/lymedisease.html.

65 "Treatment." *Centers for Disease Control and Prevention*, Centers for Disease Control and Prevention, 17 Dec. 2019, www.cdc.gov/lyme/treatment/index.html.

66 "Hypothermia." Mayo Clinic, Mayo Foundation for Medical Education and Research, 13 Mar. 2019, www.mayoclinic.org/diseases-conditions/hypothermia/symptoms-causes/syc-20352682.

67 "NOLS Wilderness Medicine." *NOLS Wilderness Medicine*, by Tod Schimelpfenig, 6th ed., Stackpole Books, 2016, pp. 128–129.

68 "Hypothermia." *Mayo Clinic*, Mayo Foundation for Medical Education and Research, 13 Mar. 2019, www.mayoclinic.org/diseases-conditions/hypothermia/diagnosis-treatment/drc-20352688.

69 Khatri, Minesh. "Dehydration - Signs, Symptoms, Causes, and Prevention." *WebMD*, WebMD, 30 May 2019, www.webmd.com/a-to-z-guides/dehydration-adults#1.

70 "NOLS Wilderness Medicine." *NOLS Wilderness Medicine*, by Tod Schimelpfenig, 6th ed., Stackpole Books, 2016, pp. 252-253.

71 "General Information." *Centers for Disease Control and Prevention*, Centers for Disease Control and Prevention, 21 July 2015, www.cdc.gov/parasites/giardia/general-info.html.

72 "NOLS Wilderness Medicine." *NOLS Wilderness Medicine*, by Tod Schimelpfenig, 6th ed., Stackpole Books, 2016, pp. 257.

73 Morris, Jeremy. "Appalachian Trials: 8 Common Hiker Injuries." *The Trek*, 16 Oct. 2015, thetrek.co/injuries/.

74 "Norovirus." *Centers for Disease Control and Prevention*, Centers for Disease Control and Prevention, 5 Apr. 2019, www.cdc.gov/norovirus/index.html.

75 "Heat Exhaustion." *Mayo Clinic*, Mayo Foundation for Medical Education and Research, 14 Dec. 2017, www.mayoclinic.org/diseases-conditions/heat-exhaustion/symptoms-causes/syc-20373250.

76 "NOLS Wilderness Medicine." *NOLS Wilderness Medicine*, by Tod Schimelpfenig, 6th ed., Stackpole Books, 2016, pp. 144.

77 "Malnutrition." *World Health Organization*, World Health Organization, 16 Feb. 2018, www.who.int/news-room/fact-sheets/detail/malnutrition.

78 Henkes, Beth, and Tod Schimelpfenig. "How to Prevent and Care for Blisters: REI Expert Advice." *REI*, 2019, www.rei.com/learn/expert-advice/blister-prevention-care.html.

79 "Plantar Fasciitis." *Mayo Clinic*, Mayo Foundation for Medical Education and Research, 11 Dec.

2019, www.mayoclinic.org/diseases-conditions/plantar-fasciitis/symptoms-causes/syc-20354846.

80 "Plantar Fasciitis." *Mayo Clinic*, Mayo Foundation for Medical Education and Research, 11 Dec. 2019, www.mayoclinic.org/diseases-conditions/plantar-fasciitis/diagnosis-treatment/drc-20354851.

81 "Achilles Tendinitis." *Mayo Clinic*, Mayo Foundation for Medical Education and Research, 17 Sept. 2019, www.mayoclinic.org/diseases-conditions/achilles-tendinitis/symptoms-causes/syc-20369020.

82 "Achilles Tendinitis." *Mayo Clinic*, Mayo Foundation for Medical Education and Research, 17 Sept. 2019, www.mayoclinic.org/diseases-conditions/achilles-tendinitis/diagnosis-treatment/drc-20369025.

83 "Shin Splints." Mayo Clinic, Mayo Foundation for Medical Education and Research, 17 Sept. 2019, www.mayoclinic.org/diseases-conditions/shin-splints/symptoms-causes/syc-20354105?utm_source=Google&utm_medium=abstract&utm_content=Shin-splints&utm_campaign=Knowledge-panel.

84 Cimons, Marlene. "Treating and Preventing Iliotibial Band Syndrome." *Runner's World*, Runner's World, 11 June 2019, www.runnersworld.com/health-injuries/a20797170/treating-and-preventing-iliotibial-band-syndrome/.

85 Wedro, Benjamin. "IT Band Syndrome: Treatment, Exercises, Symptoms, Recovery Time." *MedicineNet*, MedicineNet, 9 Sept. 2019, www.medicinenet.com/iliotibial_band_syndrome/article.htm.

86 French, Matt. "Managing Chafing: REI Expert Advice." *REI*, 2019, www.rei.com/learn/expert-advice/managing-chafing.html.

87 Hodgkins, Kelly, and Chris Cage. "How to Prevent Chafing in 2020: Best Tips and Remedies to Heal Fast." *Greenbelly Meals*, 2017, www.greenbelly.co/pages/how-to-prevent-chafing.

88 "Emergency Beacons, Lost Hikers, Trip Plans, and Search and Rescue." Pacific Crest Trail Association, 2019, www.pcta.org/discover-the-trail/backcountry-basics/safety-tips/emergency-beacon-search-rescue-trip-plan/.

89 "It's Not The Same!" *We Need To Talk: How to Have Conversations That Matter*, by Celeste Headlee, Harper Wave, 2017, pp. 159.

90 "That's A Great Question." *We Need To Talk: How to Have Conversations That Matter*, by Celeste Headlee, Harper Wave, 2017, pp. 161.

91 "Join Our Efforts." *Appalachian Trail Conservancy*, 2019, appalachiantrail.org/home/volunteer.

92 "Conclusion." We Need To Talk: How to Have Conversations That Matter, by Celeste Headlee, Harper Wave, 2017, pp. 233.

93 "You Can't Outsmart A Bad Conversation." *We Need To Talk: How to Have Conversations That Matter*, by Celeste Headlee, Harper Wave, 2017, pp. 37.

94 "Conclusion." *We Need To Talk: How to Have Conversations That Matter*, by Celeste Headlee, Harper Wave, 2017, pp. 231.

95 "Comforting Your Depressed Loved One." *What to Do When Someone You Love Is Depressed: a Practical, Compassionate, and Helpful Guide*, by Mitch Golant and Susan K. Golant, Henry Holt & Co, 2007, pp. 84.

96 "What Is Depression?" *What to Do When Someone You Love Is Depressed: a Practical, Compassionate, and Helpful Guide*, by Mitch Golant and Susan K. Golant, Henry Holt & Co, 2007, pp. 20-22.

97 "What Is Depression?" *What to Do When Someone You Love Is Depressed: a Practical, Compassionate, and Helpful Guide*, by Mitch Golant and Susan K. Golant, Henry Holt & Co, 2007, pp. 23.

98 *Diagnostic and Statistical Manual of Mental Disorders: DSM-5*. American Psychiatric Publishing, 2013.

99 "Drug Therapies." *What to Do When Someone You Love Is Depressed: a Practical, Compassionate, and Helpful Guide*, by Mitch Golant and Susan K. Golant, Henry Holt & Co, 2007, pp. 125.

100 "What Is Depression?" *What to Do When Someone You Love Is Depressed: a Practical, Compassionate, and Helpful Guide*, by Mitch Golant and Susan K. Golant, Henry Holt & Co, 2007, pp. 24.

101 "Depression." *Spark: the Revolutionary New Science of Exercise and the Brain*, by John J. Ratey and Eric Hagerman, Little, Brown, 2013, pp. 139.

102 "Depression." *Spark: the Revolutionary New Science of Exercise and the Brain*, by John J. Ratey and Eric Hagerman, Little, Brown, 2013, pp. 114.

103 "Creative Alternatives." *What to Do When Someone You Love Is Depressed: a Practical, Compassionate, and Helpful Guide*, by Mitch Golant and Susan K. Golant, Henry Holt & Co, 2007, pp. 184.
104 "Depression." *Spark: the Revolutionary New Science of Exercise and the Brain*, by John J. Ratey and Eric Hagerman, Little, Brown, 2013, pp. 122-124.
105 "Creative Alternatives." *What to Do When Someone You Love Is Depressed: a Practical, Compassionate, and Helpful Guide*, by Mitch Golant and Susan K. Golant, Henry Holt & Co, 2007, pp. 184–186.
106 "Conclusion." *We Need To Talk: How to Have Conversations That Matter*, by Celeste Headlee, Harper Wave, 2017, pp. 232.
107 "What Silent Agreements Are and How They Affect Our Relationships." *Silent Agreements: How to Free Your Relationships of Unspoken Expectations*, by Linda D. Anderson et al., Rodale Books, 2019, pp. 10.
108 "What Silent Agreements Are and How They Affect Our Relationships." *Silent Agreements: How to Free Your Relationships of Unspoken Expectations*, by Linda D. Anderson et al., Rodale Books, 2019, pp. 2–3.
109 "Where Do Silent Agreements Come From?" *Silent Agreements: How to Free Your Relationships of Unspoken Expectations*, by Linda D. Anderson et al., Rodale Books, 2019, pp. 22.
110 "What Happens to Love After the Wedding?" *The 5 Love Languages: The Secret to Love That Lasts*, by Gary D. Chapman, Northfield Pub., 2015, pp. 16.
111 "Frequently Asked Questions." *The 5 Love Languages: The Secret to Love That Lasts*, by Gary D. Chapman, Northfield Pub., 2015, pp. 187-188.
112 "Loving the Unlovely." *The 5 Love Languages: The Secret to Love That Lasts*, by Gary D. Chapman, Northfield Pub., 2015, pp. 159.
113 "A Fiercer Sea." *A General Theory of Love*, by Thomas Lewis et al., Vintage Books, 2001, pp. 73.
114 "A Walk in the Shadows." *A General Theory of Love*, by Thomas Lewis et al., Vintage Books, 2001, pp. 208.
115 "Sometimes We Shouldn't Talk." *We Need To Talk: How to Have Conversations That Matter*, by Celeste Headlee, Harper Wave, 2017, pp. 223.
116 "Sometimes We Shouldn't Talk." *We Need To Talk: How to Have Conversations That Matter*, by Celeste Headlee, Harper Wave, 2017, pp. 223.
117 "Love Language #1: Words of Affirmation." *The 5 Love Languages: The Secret to Love That Lasts*, by Gary D. Chapman, Northfield Pub., 2015, pp. 45.
118 Daniel J. Levitin, "Why the Modern World Is Bad for Your Brain," *Guardian*, January 18, 2015.
119 "Love Language #2: Quality Time." *The 5 Love Languages: The Secret to Love That Lasts*, by Gary D. Chapman, Northfield Pub., 2015, pp. 63-64.
120 "Ingredients of Personal Transformation." *Love Is Letting Go of Fear*, by Gerald G. Jampolsky, Celestial Arts, 2011, pp. 38.
121 "Archimedes' Principle." *A General Theory of Love*, by Thomas Lewis et al., Vintage Books, 2001, pp. 45.
122 "Love Language #1: Words of Affirmation." *The 5 Love Languages: The Secret to Love That Lasts*, by Gary D. Chapman, Northfield Pub., 2015, pp. 43-44.
123 "The Four Elements of Change." *Silent Agreements: How to Free Your Relationships of Unspoken Expectations*, by Linda D. Anderson et al., Rodale Books, 2019, pp. 32.
124 "Set The Stage." *We Need To Talk: How to Have Conversations That Matter*, by Celeste Headlee, Harper Wave, 2017, pp. 51.
125 "Set The Stage." *We Need To Talk: How to Have Conversations That Matter*, by Celeste Headlee, Harper Wave, 2017, pp. 51.
126 "Set The Stage." *We Need To Talk: How to Have Conversations That Matter*, by Celeste Headlee, Harper Wave, 2017, pp. 51.